D1382756

EQUALITY

NOMOS
I X

NOMOS

NOMOS IX

Yearbook of the American Society for Political and Legal Philosophy

EQUALITY

Edited by

J. ROLAND PENNOCK   *Swarthmore College*

and

JOHN W. CHAPMAN   *University of Pittsburgh*

ATHERTON PRESS · New York · 1967

OCLC

PREFACE

In this, the ninth yearbook of the American Society for Political and Legal Philosophy, new hands have taken over the editorial task from Carl J. Friedrich, who, in this capacity as in others, has served the Society so well and so faithfully and who fortunately continues to share in its counsels. We shall strive to fulfill the high responsibility with which we have been charged.

As members of the Society know, *Nomos* grows out of the programs of the annual meetings. These are brief, with a minimum of prepared papers, and accordingly it is customary to invite further contributions to deal more fully and adequately with the subject in hand. Meetings are devoted to a single theme or topic; usually, indeed, to a particular concept. Perhaps this year is an appropriate time to remind old and to inform new readers of what has gone before. The titles of the preceding volumes, in order, are: *Authority, Community, Responsibility, Liberty, The Public Interest, Justice, Rational Decision,* and *Revolution.* The next volume is on *Representation,* and it will be followed by *Voluntary Associations.*

Equality: Nomos IX began with the meetings of the Society held in April 1965, in Washington, D.C. On this occasion we joined forces with the American Society of International Law. John T. Noonan, Jr., served as program chairman, and his efforts provided the editors with a direction and a substantial start. Specifically, the first two chapters, by Hugo Adam Bedau and Norman Dorsen, the last two, by Robert W. Gregg and Thomas M. Franck, and also Monroe H. Freedman's contribution, comprise revisions of papers or comments delivered at the sessions. To these writers and to the others who accepted our invitations to contribute, we wish to express our thanks for their illumination of the concept of equality.

J. Roland Pennock
John W. Chapman

INTRODUCTION

Equality is a persistent theme. In political, legal, and philosophical discourse it is always with us; never more so than today. In a measure, to be sure, it is with us because it is a "virtue word." Like justice, of which all seem to agree it is in some sense a part, no one is against it. But of course it does not follow that all men mean the same thing by it. As Aristotle tells us, "equality is of two sorts": "numerical equality" and "equality proportionate to desert."[1] Some favor the one and some the other; and if it is the latter, the questions of what constitutes desert and of how it is measured or "proportioned" provide unending controversy. (Notice how quickly we move from definition to discussion of what is justified; for so quickly do men tend to define commendatory terms in ways that suit their own purposes and value systems.)

Philosophers are widely agreed that there should be some

[1] Aristotle, *Politics*, 1301b. See also 1282b.

form of proportionate equality as the appropriate standard for human affairs. "Radical egalitarianism," as defined by Hugo Bedau, seems hard to defend—and perhaps has few defenders. Yet many would concur with Tocqueville's belief that "the gradual development of the principle of equality is . . . a providential fact," universal, enduring, and eluding all human interference. And Tocqueville was thinking in terms of an absolute equality. "There is," he declared, "greater equality *of condition* in Christian countries at the present day than there has been at any previous time, in any part of the world. . . ."[2] Whether in fact material equality has been increasing as universally as Tocqueville believed is debatable. But perhaps it is true that the pressure to justify inequalities has increased and that purely ascriptive inequalities are almost everywhere on the defensive, where they have not been already eliminated.

In any case, the present volume is more concerned with "right reason," than, as Rousseau would say, with "wrangling over facts." Although Tocqueville spoke of equality of condition, and Rousseau too had this matter much on his mind, in the history of political and legal philosophy, not unnaturally, thinkers have been more concerned with rights and with powers. Also, for the most part, they have been concerned with prescription rather than with description. Thus Locke describes the proper condition of men (which he calls a "state of nature") as "a state . . . of equality, wherein all the power and jurisdiction is reciprocal, no one having more than another: there being nothing more evident than that creatures of the same species and rank promiscuously born to all the same advantages of nature, and the use of the same faculties, should also be equal one amongst another without subordination or subjection. . . ."[3]

Part I of this volume deals largely with the themes mentioned

---

[2] Italics added. All these quotations from Alexis de Tocqueville are from his *Democracy in America*, Phillips Bradley, editor, New York: Knopf, 1945, ch. I, p. 6.

[3] John Locke, *Second Treatise of Civil Government*, § 4. For related modern discussions, see Alan Gewirth, "Political Justice," in Richard B. Brandt, editor, *Social Justice*, Englewood Cliffs, N.J.: Prentice–Hall, 1962, pp. 119–69; Joseph Tussman, *Obligation and the Body Politic*, New York: Oxford University Press, 1960; and Hanna Pitkin, "Obligation and Consent," *The American Political Science Review*, vol. LIX, pp. 990–99 and vol. LX, pp. 39–53.

above. The initial chapter explores the meaning, the justification, and what might be called the dialectics of equality, wherein
some of its manifestations are confronted and limited by others.
Norman Dorsen's contribution immediately follows because it
opens with a criticism of Bedau's essay; the balance of it, the
"lawyer's look," might as appropriately have been placed in Part
III, with other more specifically legal discussions. Richard
Flathman presses the notion of proportionate equality hard, to
what he believes to be its logical conclusion: namely, that it is
a purely formal or logical concept, with no content whatsoever,
except in a derivative sense. Stanley Benn, without having been
exposed to Flathmans' account, proceeds to take issue with that
view, or at least to argue that "egalitarianism" has reference to
human interests, a fact that does give it content. John Plamenatz discusses the issues about which defenders of equality and
of inequality have been most concerned, while George Catlin
ranges widely over some of the fundamental problems that talk
of equality naturally elicits.

Part II deals with some of the sources of beliefs about equality.
Four of the chapters consider respectively the implications for
egalitarianism of Christianity (Sanford Lakoff and Paul Sigmund), of Judaism (Emanuel Rackman), and of Hinduism
(A. H. Somjee). Unfortunately, a scheduled chapter on Mus-
limism did not appear. This part closes with a chapter of a somewhat different order, a discussion by Herbert Spiegelberg that
both examines the treatment of and implications for equalitarianism to be found in the works of existentialist writers and
essays some hints at how the existentialist mode of thought may
contribute to the justification of equalitarian doctrine.

Part III is more concerned with practical applications—political and legal. Inevitably and rightly, several of the authors hark
back to questions of definition and justification, but their
primary concerns are practical. Thus Carl Friedrich suggests
that Tocqueville's "providential fact" might possibly be on the
eve of a reversal; yet at the same time he concludes with his
own justification of political equality. John Schaar launches a
full-fledged attack on the notion of equality of opportunity,
contending that it is not "an authentic expression of the democratic ideal and temper," which requires instead an "affirmation of being and belonging." Monroe Freedman discusses the

highly current problem of equality in the administration of
justice, with particular application to the right to counsel, while
Geoffrey Marshall deals with a series of puzzles and subtle
distinctions involved in application of the idea of the rule of law.
D. D. Raphael, Robert Gregg, and Thomas Franck conclude this
part, and the volume, with treatments of the difficult problem
of equality in the realm of international law and organization.

J. Roland Pennock

CONTENTS

Contents

CONTRIBUTORS

HUGO ADAM BEDAU
Philosophy, Tufts University

STANLEY I. BENN
Philosophy, The Australian National University

GEORGE E. G. CATLIN
Political Science, McGill University (emeritus)

NORMAN DORSEN
Law, New York University

RICHARD E. FLATHMAN
Political Science, The University of Chicago

THOMAS M. FRANCK
International Studies, New York University

MONROE H. FREEDMAN
Law, George Washington University

CARL J. FRIEDRICH
Political Science, Harvard University

ROBERT W. GREGG
Political Science, Syracuse University

SANFORD A. LAKOFF
*Political Science, State University of New York at
Stony Brook*

GEOFFREY MARSHALL
Political Science, The Queen's College, Oxford University

JOHN PLAMENATZ
Political Science, Nuffield College, Oxford University

EMANUEL RACKMAN
Assistant to the President, Yeshiva University

D. D. RAPHAEL
Political Science, The University, Glasgow

JOHN H. SCHAAR
Political Science, University of California, Berkeley

PAUL E. SIGMUND
Political Science, Princeton University

A. H. SOMJEE
*Political Science, Sociology and Anthropology,
Simon Fraser University*

HERBERT SPIEGELBERG
Philosophy, Washington University

CONCEPTS OF EQUALITY

1

EGALITARIANISM AND THE
IDEA OF EQUALITY

HUGO ADAM BEDAU

This chapter undertakes two rather independent tasks. The first section attempts to show how equality is related to *sameness* and how useful it is to distinguish the essentially descriptive considerations in the meaning of "equality" from any question of the desirability, fairness, or justice of equality. The second section offers a review of egalitarian thought, organized around the notion of *radical egalitarianism,* in order to see where the plea for the greatest possible equality among men breaks down. Some with passionate egalitarian sympathies may find my conclusions rather discouraging.

I

Nearly a century ago, Fitzjames Stephen, the conservative utilitarian critic of egalitarianism, complained that "equality is a word so wide and vague as to be by itself almost unmeaning."[1] Even the late R. H. Tawney, one of the warmest friends egalitarianism will ever have, allowed that " 'Equality' possesses more than one meaning."[2] Such charges of vagueness and ambiguity are not without foundation, and they arise from several quarters: the failure to identify the respects in which the (allegedly) equal things are equal; the failure to understand the conceptual network of equality, i.e., the logical relations among such expressions as "equal," "identical," "same," "similar," their cognates and neighbors; the failure to distinguish between whether a certain distribution or policy is in fact an equal one and, if it is, whether the equality is also equitable, justifiable, or just; and the failure to realize that the justifiability of a given distribution is often erroneously argued through alleging its equality, thanks to the conceptual affinity of "just," "equal," and "equitable," quite apart from any demonstration of its actual or factual equality.

It may seem strange that "equality" should sometimes be used to express approval of, or to declare the justifiability or justice of, a distribution the actual equality of which is in some doubt. But this is the only way to interpret John Dewey's statement, for instance, that "Equality denotes the unhampered share which each individual member of the community has in the consequences of associated action."[3] This cannot be literally true; Dewey has not told us what " 'equality' denotes": The fact that our shares are "unhampered" does not imply that they are *equally* unhampered; the fact that each of us has an unhampered share in "the consequences of associated action" does not imply that we have *equal* shares. Yet unless something of this sort were true, what reason could we have for finding equality in such a distribution? Dewey states his position in this language because

[1] J. F. Stephen, *Liberty, Equality and Fraternity* (1873), p. 201.

[2] R. H. Tawney, *Equality* (1952), p. 35.

[3] J. Dewey, *The Public and Its Problems* (1927), p. 150, as quoted in R. P. McKeon, "The Practical Uses of a Philosophy of Equality," in L. Bryson (ed.), *Aspects of Human Equality* (1956), p. 20.

he is defending a social ideal according to which a certain distribution is believed to constitute equality (despite the fact that its equality as such has never been established) on the grounds that it is a desirable and justifiable distribution; as Dewey puts it himself in his next sentence, the sort of distribution he speaks of is "equitable." Thus it is that "equality" comes to be used to endorse a distribution or a policy, in the face of the most flagrant inequalities, simply because the policy is thought to be equitable or fair! No wonder the central concept of egalitarianism is thought to be vague and ambiguous, or "almost unmeaning"!

The concern of this section is fourfold: (1) to try to show how our concept of equality is applied in relatively neutral and uncontroversial contexts, (2) to see how it is applied in cases of interest to the social philosopher, (3) to review some of the conceptual relations among "equality," "identity," "sameness," and "similarity," and (4) to examine three interesting passages in which the argument turns in part on different senses of "equality," such as was illustrated in the passage just cited from Dewey.

1. If a recipe calls for *equal* amounts of sugar and flour, then it calls for the same amounts of sugar and flour; not similar amounts, but equivalent amounts. Different amounts (e.g., a heaping cup of sugar and a level cup of flour) are not equal amounts, though in some cases (e.g., a level cup of sugar and slightly less than a level cup of flour) we could describe them as roughly equal amounts. If several suits are *equally* expensive, then they each cost the same; only if they are not equally expensive can their costs differ. If someone says, "The blue serge, the gabardine, and the tweed are all equally expensive, though you realize the gabardine costs a bit more," he has certainly not said what he meant, for (barring some special explanation) he has contradicted himself. If I am told to *equalize* the tension on a set of springs, I must loosen some and tighten others, in order to put each spring under the same tension. "Equalize the tension, but don't make it the same on all springs" is a self-contradictory order. If you tell me that a peso is *more* nearly *equal* in value to a dime than to a nickel, then I know that the value of a peso and a dime are more nearly the same than are the value of a peso and a nickel. These examples merely illustrate what the dictionary already suggests, that "equality" locutions ("equal,"

"equally," "equality," "equivalent," "equalize," etc.) are typically
used in situations where reference is made to two or more things
that are not identical and that are, or are about to be, or should
be, the same, or the same sort of thing, or the same in some
respect. By "the same" here, I do not mean *exactly* the same,
except of course where "equal" means *exactly* equal. But it
doesn't always; two things, e.g., two equal servings from a pie, can
be equal without being exactly equal. So they can be the same
without being exactly the same.

2. Now, how well, if at all, is this semantic affinity between
equality and sameness borne out in cases of interest to the social
philosopher? Consider first the right to vote. (a) If you and I
have *an equal right to vote,* then neither of us has more or less
right to vote than the other, because we have the same right. The
answer to the question, "With what right do you attempt to
vote?" when addressed to me, must be the same as the answer
when the question is addressed to you. (b) If you and I
have *the right to an equal vote,* then our votes must be counted
at the same rate or value, because my vote is worth no more
and no less than yours. If you vote for White and I vote for
Black, then our votes are equal only if they cancel out. If we
both vote for White, then our votes are equal only if they
yield two votes for White. If you vote for Black and I don't
vote at all, then our votes are equal only if Black gains exactly
what he would have if I had voted for him and you had not
voted at all. Nothing can be different in the rate or value of our
votes without affecting the truth of "We have an equal vote."[4]

Similarly in other cases. "We have an *equal right* to run for
Secretary" means that we have the same right to run for the
office of Secretary. "Everyone over 21 is *equally liable* to the
draft" means that men and women, the halt, lame, and the blind,

---

[4] I accept the valuable point made by R. Wollheim, "Equality," reprinted
in F. A. Olafson (ed.), *Justice and Social Policy* (1961), pp. 111ff., that
"equality of rights" is ambiguous as between the equal right to *x* and the
right to equal *x*. But I disagree, with what I take to be his implication, that
the "liberal tradition" has defended equality of rights only in the former
sense. Where *x* = property (as it is, in his example), it is clear that arguments for the former will fail to justify the latter as well, and that only
a radical egalitarian (see section II, *infra*) would probably want to defend
the latter anyway. But where *x* = votes, as in my example here, "equal
rights" must include "right" in both these senses; and this is as true for
the liberal as it is for the egalitarian.

all have the same draft liability if over 21. "Negroes deserve *equal opportunities* with whites" means that Negroes deserve the same (job, educational, or other) opportunities as whites. "We're all *equal* here" means that we here may all expect to be accorded the same privileges, granted the same rights, and extended the same consideration. Notice that nothing so far said implies that any or all of these equalities are just or justifiable. These analyses merely indicate the meaning, not the merit, of typical claims involving the concept of equality in politics.

3.   Dare we generalize the facts so far by saying that "equal" *means* "same," as though the two words were synonymous? Clearly not; the requisite condition of substitutivity for synonym-pairs fails for this pair. If I gave Mark and Paul equal servings, I did not give them the same serving; what I did was to serve them the same amount, servings of the same size. If I gave you the same answer I gave him, I didn't give you an answer equal to the one I gave him; I gave you the very answer I gave him. To say a man is equal to the task is not to say the man is the same as the task, but that he is up to performing the task. And so on. The relation between equality and sameness is not like that so often claimed for "bachelor" and "unmarried male." Nevertheless, we can co-ordinate the concept of equality and the concept of sameness, as the discussion so far suggests. Barring anything misleading due to excessive abstractness, I think the following proposition holds: *Persons have (received) an equal distribution, equal treatment, or equal rights etc., if and only if they have (received) the same distribution, treatment, rights, etc.*

It is often claimed that (a) things equal to each other are always equal in one or more *respects,* and (b) in these respects the equal things are *similar* to each other. The latter seems to me not so. Things that are equal in a certain respect will normally be quite dissimilar to each other in other respects; whereas in the respect in which they are equal they are not merely similar but the same. A dozen pears and a dozen sheep are equal in number, but they are not therefore similar to each other, least of all is it correct to say they are similar in number. No more can one say that persons who have equal rights are therefore similar to each other; they are not. Being equal in number or in rights is not a respect in which things and persons are similar to each other, rather it is a respect in which they are *the same as* each

other. In light of the Leibnizian principle that things the same
in every respect are the same thing, my position that equality
implies sameness (i.e., the above biconditional) raises the question whether two things could be equal to each other in *every*
respect. If they could, then my position implies that they would
be the same in every respect; and this would imply in turn, given
the Leibnizian principle, that they would be *identical*. But this
is an intolerable consequence. If we know that the man in the
dock is the man who robbed the bank, we know enough not to
say that the men are equal; for we know they are the same man.
Our ordinary concept of equality does not admit of our saying
that Tully is equal to Cicero, or that water is equal to H_2O, or
that any two things are equal to each other unless we are ready
to deny the possibility of their identity. (N.B. Making x and y
more nearly equal does imply making them more nearly identical,
i.e., the same in some respect or in several, but not into the
same thing; think, for example, of making x and y more nearly
equal in shape.) Equality, thus, not only does not imply identity, it
implies non-identity.[5] Does this mean that equality can hold
between individuals or things only in *some* respects and not in
all? Or is there a gross error in my claim that equality implies
sameness? Despite some reservations about the Leibnizian principle itself,[6] I am inclined to the former implication. Generally,
however, we can say that from the fact that equalities are same-
nesses, it no more follows that things equal to one another in
one respect *are* (or cannot be) equal in yet other respects, any
more than it follows that things equal to one another in one
respect *ought* to be equal in that (or some further) respect.

4. The nature of the concept of equality, as it has so far been
outlined, and the importance of distinguishing whether things
are equal or unequal from whether their equality or inequality

---

[5] Thus A. Menne states in "Identity, Equality, Similarity—A Logico-
Philosophical Investigation," *Ratio,* 4 (1962): ". . . 'equal' presupposes two
objects" (p. 51, cf. p. 57). But then it is unclear how equality can also be
reflexive (contra his remarks at pp. 58ff.).

[6] For example, H. Putnam, in the *Journal of Philosophy,* 57 (1960), pp.
39–40, argues that the only "important" version of the Leibnizian principle
is the set theoretic proposition that $x = y \equiv (z)$ $(x \; \epsilon \; z \equiv y \; \epsilon \; z)$, but that
"one can still maintain that there is a *set* (namely $\{x\}$, or the unit-set of x)
which contains x but not y." Therefore, if $x = y$, it is despite the fact that
y is not a member of $\{x\}$ although x is; in which case there is certainly a
sense in which the Leibnizian principle has not been preserved but ignored.

is justified, may be illustrated and perhaps confirmed by examining the following three passages of philosophical argument in which this concept and these distinctions seem to be misunderstood or misapplied.

a. In *Leviathan*, Hobbes writes, "There is not ordinarily a greater sign of the equal distribution of anything than that every man is contented with his share."[7] Suppose you have been given twice as much of the same stuff as I have, although so far as anyone can tell we are equally satisfied with our shares. Perhaps this is because I don't know how large your share is, or if I do know, I think you deserve or need more than I. Is our mutual contentment a "sign" of equal distribution? Suppose, on the facts assumed, a third party thinks so, and says, "The stuff has been equally distributed between the two of them—though, of course, one got twice as much as the other." This remark is too plainly paradoxical as it stands. Either he has incorrectly assessed the distribution—it isn't an equal distribution at all, as is proved by the fact that the one share is double the other, i.e., the shares are not the same—or he expressed himself incorrectly, meaning by "equally distributed" that despite the inequality of the shares, the distribution was *fair*. Had he said, "The stuff has been fairly distributed between the two of them—though, of course, one got twice as much as the other," no one would raise his logical eyebrows, although his moral antennae might bristle pending further clarification. One certainly could not say, "The stuff has been fairly distributed, though of course one got twice as much as the other; and thus the stuff was equally distributed after all." Once we know that the shares were not the same, we know that they were not equal; and even if the distribution was fair, we know too much to countenance the inference. To think otherwise is to rely on some such principle as "Fairness implies equality" (cf. proposition (3) in section II, *infra*). But there is no such principle, at least, none by which we can override a known inequality, declaring that the inequality is an equality merely because it is justified.

b. Consider the following remarks: "Suppose that society is allotting musical instruments to *C* and *D*, and that *C* prefers a banjo and *D* a guitar. If society gives *C* a banjo and *D* a guitar

---

[7] *Leviathan*, I, xiii, ed. M. Oakeshott, p. 80.

it is treating them *differently* yet *equally*."[8] This is curious. The notion of treatment is being made to do double duty, both for the *way* in which C and D were treated and for *what* was allotted to them. The result is that when they are said to have been "equally treated," this cannot mean they were given the *same* treatment, for how could the treatment be both the same and "different"? "Equally treated" here can only mean that the "different" treatment was nonetheless *fair* or *just*. Actually, however, the facts assumed in this example deserve to be stated quite differently. The clearest way in such a case for society to have "treated" C and D "differently" would have been to grant C what he "prefers," to treat him exactly as he wished to be treated, and then to refuse to do this to D (or vice versa). This would have been unequal treatment, not the same treatment, and, presumably, unfair as well. We would understand D's complaint, "We were treated unequally, because C got what he wanted and I didn't." In this statement, "unequally" would be doing double duty, both for *differently* and for *unfairly*, though it is unlikely we would be misled. But in the original case, on the facts assumed, nothing of the sort was done, and so to say that they were "treated differently" makes no sense. Were C to complain, saying "I was treated differently from D, because he got a guitar whereas I got a banjo," we would not know what to make of it. (Consider also the following variant situation: Suppose that C and D had each been allotted what the other preferred. Then neither would have been treated as he—probably—deserved, and thus both could complain of unfair treatment. But they could not complain that they had been treated unequally.) The reason such a complaint would be baseless is not that despite a difference in treatment, C and D were treated "equally," and only unequal treatment would justify C's complaint. The reason is that they were treated in the *same* way and therefore treated equally; there simply was *no difference* at all in their treatment. Saying, in such a case, "They were treated differently but equally" is needlessly confusing, and it does not indicate *what* was different. The difference lies in *what* was allotted, and this constitutes a difference in distribution, not in treatment. Treatment (or consideration) and distribution (or allotment) are different

---

[8] W. K. Frankena, "The Concept of Social Justice," in R. B. Brandt (ed.), *Social Justice* (1962), p. 11; italics in original.

concepts, and therefore equality of treatment and equality of distribution can be independent of each other. But the respect in which each involves equality is the respect in which each raises the question, "Was it (the treatment, the distribution) the same for all involved?" Were there not this relation between sameness and equality, it would be possible for us to understand treating people the same and yet to doubt whether they had been treated equally (by which I do *not* mean "fairly"). This seems to me an impossible possibility.

c. It has lately been argued that the maxim, "To each according to his need," is really a "maxim of equal distribution," for despite the manifest inequality of needs among men, to follow this maxim, we are told, is to practice "the most perfect form of equal distribution."[9] Is this really true? If the question arises in a simple case such as whether I have equally distributed something, for example, some free tickets to our theatre group for a benefit performance, the test is simply whether I have given the same number to each eligible person, according to the rule: One person, one ticket. If I am interested in an equal distribution, then I will see to it that everyone gets the same number of tickets. Now suppose that I don't intend to go to the concert, so I don't need a ticket, whereas you have invited your friend, so you need two tickets. (I do not imply you have a right to a ticket for your friend but only that you have reason to want one and in this sense need one.) If the view we are examining is sound, then "the most perfect form of equal distribution" would seem to require me not to give myself a ticket but to give two to you (one for your friend). Moreover, if in order to make a "perfectly" equal form of distribution, I must hew to the maxim, "To each according to his need," then you have a right to expect a second ticket from me, especially if I really don't need one. Notice, of course, that these remarks have proceeded on the assumption that it is *unfair* for me to keep a ticket and to deny two to you, given that I don't intend to use it and that I know you need two. But if my discussion so far has been correct, there is clearly a prior question, which has not been directly faced, *viz.*, Have I failed to distribute the tickets as equally as I might have? Suppose I keep the ticket. You say, "You'd have distributed the

[9] G. Vlastos, "Justice and Equality," in R. B. Brandt (ed.), *op. cit.*, p. 40, and cf. p. 72.

tickets more equally if you had given me two and had kept none
for yourself." Why? "Because you don't need any ticket, and I need
two." Why would giving you two and me none be *more* equal
than giving us each one? There can be only one answer, "Because the tickets are for those who need them, and you don't have
any right to what you don't need." This may very well be true;
perhaps "under ideal conditions equality of right would coin-
cide with distribution according to personal need."[10] Certainly
one will take differing personal needs into account if it is desired
that the distribution be equitable, i.e., introduce those deviations from strict equality (or any other rigid rule) in order to
be fair. But personal needs have no relevance whatsoever to the
prior question, concerning the equality of the distribution. To
speak of "the most perfect form of equal distribution" as though,
once again, the *justice* of taking variations in need into account
served to make unequal distributions equal, is unnecessary. "To
each according to his need," however much it is a maxim of
egalitarian justice, i.e., of justice defined in terms of *equal rights,*
is not a maxim of equal distribution. It will yield an equal
distribution only in the rare case where needs are the same.

Why are we so slow to admit that equality does, after all, imply
sameness? There are several reasons. We have seen that "equal"
is no mere synonym for "same," nor is any other "equality"
locution. We have also seen that things equal to each other are
never the same as each other, i.e., the very same thing. This
implies that it is consistent with things being equal to each other
that they are different and unlike each other in various ways.
There are other reasons as well to explain our reluctance to
admit this. Egalitarians have had a certain understandable wari-
ness of the uniformity and conformity connoted by "equality."
Because they seldom, if ever, desire such a state of affairs for its
own sake, it has evidently seemed possible to disavow any intention of making things and persons uniformly the same in order
to make them equal.[11] But this rests, as we have seen, on various
confusions. Even though equality does imply sameness, persons
or things equal in one respect need not (usually, must not) be
equal in all others. Finally, there may even be some evidence of

[10] G. Vlastos, *op. cit.,* p. 42.
[11] See for example L. Stephen, "Social Equality," *Ethics,* 1 (1891), p. 278,
and D. Thomson, *Equality* (1949), pp. 3-5.

conceptual confusion, as the three passages previously discussed suggest. Philosophers have assumed, or come close to assuming, that because an inequality may be just or justified, it is really an equality after all, as though the justice or justifiability of certain arrangements could only be expressed by pronouncing the arrangement "equal," as though the most important thing to say on behalf of the morality of an arrangement is that it is "equal." One need not be a defector from the egalitarian tradition to see that this is not true. Moreover, it is dangerous, for it plays into the hands of those who would blur, for their own advantage, the distinction between justifiable and unjustifiable inequalities. Probably, as the argument in the next section implies, egalitarians will have to choose between demanding equality of civil liberties and political rights, of opportunities and consideration, on the one hand, and, on the other, equality in personal goods, economic power, and living conditions. But if this is so, it is not because the latter equalities entail a sameness that the former do not. All involve sameness, in the same sense of "same." This is why they are equalities.

II

To think as an egalitarian is to consider the degree and range of inequalities among men and to explore ways to remove or at least diminish them. The current folk song, "I Shall Be Free No. 10," by Bob Dylan, opens with lyrics expressing how a member of an egalitarian society might see himself:

> I'm just average, common, too,
> I'm just like him, the same as you.
> I'm everybody's brother and son,
> I ain't no different than anyone.
> Ain't no use to talk to me,
> It's just the same as talking to you.*

Sober philosophy can use a formulation of the principle that would make such a society rational. I shall call it *radical egalitarianism,* and state it thus:

(1) All social inequalities are unnecessary, and unjustifiable, and ought to be eliminated.

* © Bob Dylan 1964.

By "social inequality" I mean not only caste, class, or other status differences but also any political, legal, or economic differences among persons, irrespective of whether the inequality results from one's own choice and effort or that of another. Thus, even the differences deliberately planned as rewards or awards, or imposed as punishments, count as social inequalities. Excluded are only such inequalities as those of "wits, bulks, statures, looks,"[12] sex, race, color, or age, which since Rousseau have been thought of as "natural." A social inequality is something which, if others were to treat one differently, could be deliberately produced or removed (e.g., differences in income, wealth, property, employment, education; and in opportunities, rights, duties, privileges). By "unjustified" I mean that the inequalities are morally indefensible not only because they may be unjust or unfair but because any of several other objections can be brought against them (e.g., inutility, incompatibility with self-fulfillment). In particular this means that one finds nothing objectionable in equalities among men despite differences in needs, abilities, or merit. That you should work twice as hard as I at some common task, but in no way earn a greater reward, does not offend. That I should be a grasshopper with my life, while you, antlike, lay up for the morrow, insures only that the radical egalitarian will deny you your excess. If he does not, he has permitted the introduction of differences of wealth, which constitute a social inequality, which in turn will lead to other social inequalities. By "unnecessary" I mean not only that the inequalities can be diminished or eliminated but that they are not in fact a condition of anything worth preserving, and especially that the absence of such inequalities would not result in the dissolution of society or the increase in net unhappiness among men. Finally, by "eliminated" I mean deliberately diminished, through voluntary efforts or coercive action, until they vanish.

Radical egalitarianism, consequently, is not that "state of perfect equality" of which Locke spoke in his *Second Treatise* (§7), for as he later explains (§54), age, virtue, merit, birth, or alliances may properly give one man a "just precedency" over another without in any way interfering in their "perfect equal-

[12] The phrase is from William Dean Howells, "Equality as the Basis of Good Society," *Century Magazine*, 51 (1895), p. 67.

ity." Such social arrangements are clearly prohibited by (1). Karl Popper has said that "the egalitarian principle proper" is "the proposal to eliminate 'natural' privileges."[13] This is implied by (1), but the two statements are hardly equivalent. By the same token, radical egalitarianism approximates only the converse of Ernest Barker's "Principle of Equality" ("Equality is . . . the beginning, not the end").[14] But Friedrich Hayek, when he attacked the principle of "complete and absolute equality of all individuals in all those points which are subject to human control,"[15] in effect had (1) in mind. So did Isaiah Berlin, when he referred to "complete social equality," where "everything and everybody should be as similar as possible to everything and everybody else."[16]

Radical egalitarianism is seldom formulated and rarely, if ever, discussed because its absurdities as a social ideal—not only moral but conceptual and factual absurdities—are too plainly apparent. How closely it approximates the aspirations of earlier utopians, anarchists, socialists and other revolutionaries, how large an influence it exercised over their avowed doctrines and desires, are questions beyond my competence to answer.[17] My interest here in radical egalitarianism is simply that, because it is so extreme, it may best serve the purpose of organizing our thoughts on what is to be said for and against less radical and more attractive egalitarian notions.

We know, of course, that what usually goes under the name

---

[13] K. R. Popper, *The Open Society and Its Enemies* (1950), p. 94.

[14] E. Barker, *Principles of Social and Political Theory* (1951), p. 151.

[15] F. A. Hayek, *The Road to Serfdom* (1958), p. 109.

[16] I. Berlin, "Equality," *Proceedings of the Aristotelian Society*, 56 (1956), reprinted in F. A. Olafson (ed.), *op. cit.*, p. 137.

[17] One writer who seems to declare himself in favor of the principle of radical egalitarianism is Howells (*op. cit.*) when he writes that "the perfection of society" would be a condition of "perfect equality," which would accrue to us in "the absence of any and all man-made distinctions between men" [p. 67]. That Howells devoutly wished for this millennium may be inferred from such flat declarations as these: "Equality is such a beautiful thing that I wonder people can ever have any other ideal. It is the only social joy, the only comfort" [p. 63] and "I do not believe one lovely or amiable thing would be lost if equality were to become the rule and fashion of the whole race" [p. 65]. How extravagant this egalitarian paean looks when, upon closer reading, it turns out that all Howells really desires is for all men to be extended equal "consideration" by their fellows, because inequality of consideration, of opportunity, is not "just" [p. 67].

of egalitarianism is not the uncompromising and categorical demand phrased in (1), but other, humbler ideals. At the root of the desire for economic equality, for instance, lies the conviction that none should have luxuries while some lack necessities.[18] More generally, egalitarianism consists of both a protest and a demand. The protest has been against inequalities based on "arbitrary" or "capricious" distinctions.[19] Consequently, the egalitarian tradition has always maintained that inequalities in class, race, religion, sex, age, wealth, and literacy (to cite only favorite candidates) do not in themselves invariably justify differences in treatment, opportunity, or rights, because these differences never cancel the important similarities among men, nor are they always the source of differences that can justify inequalities (notably and usually, differences in ability, merit, and need).[20] The egalitarian demand (a demand made also by the libertarian) is that all, not merely a favored few, be given the opportunity for the free and unhampered development of their capacities. It is this protest against invidious distinctions and the celebration of individual self-determination that Shelley extolled in *Prometheus Unbound:*

                    . . . . man
    Equal, unclassed, tribeless, and nationless,
    Exempt from awe, worship, degree, the king
    Over himself . . . .

What is the source of this protest and demand, or rather (to please those who think the source is "the ancient vice of envy"[21]) what is its justification? It lies in four fundamental principles which are among what I call the *principles of egalitarianism*. Although they fall well short of radical egalitarianism, they have been generally accepted and I submit they express all that one would wish to say on behalf of that principle.

---

[18] Cf. R. Robinson, *An Atheist's Values* (1964), pp. 180–181.

[19] See for example W. Godwin, *Enquiry Concerning Political Justice* (1795), II. iii, p. 148; L. Stephen, *op cit.*, p. 267; and R. Tawney, *op. cit.*, pp. 119, 264.

[20] Cf. R. P. McKeon, *op. cit.*, p. 7.

[21] R. Robinson, *op. cit.*, p. 179. Also Justice Holmes, in M. De W. Howe (ed.), *Holmes-Laski Letters* (1953), p. 942; cited in R. Lampman, "Recent Thought on Egalitarianism," *Quarterly Journal of Economics*, 71 (1957), p. 262.

The first of these four principles (which has been variously formulated) I shall call the doctrine of *metaphysical egalitarianism,* namely:

> (2) All men are equal—now and forever, in intrinsic value, inherent worth, essential nature.

For generations, it has been recognized that the doctrine of the equality of men vacillates between the apparently straight-forward empirical generalization that (a) all men *are* equal to each other, at least in some respects;[22] the clear though contestable moral demand that (b) all men *ought* to be treated equally, or as equals, at least in certain respects; and the declaration formulated as the principle of metaphysical egalitarianism, (2), the ancient Stoic-Christian doctrine of human equality, a proposition that is neither an empirical claim nor a moral injunction but a different sort of proposition altogether. Consider: (2) neither implies nor is implied by (a) or (b) or their conjunction; hence if (a) is false, its falsity could never be conclusive evidence against (2). On the other hand, if (a) is true, then its truth *suggests* that (2) might also be true, and conversely; if one accepts (2) then one is in a position to *protest* violations of (b). Similarly, (2) neither implies nor is implied by (1), although a radical egalitarian would almost certainly advance some version of (2) in support of (1). But a good deal more will be required to support (1); it is not owing to a lapse in logical acumen that none of the many recent philosophers who profess belief in (2) do not also embrace (1).[23] The exact role of (2) in egal-

[22] In this paper as originally delivered, I dismissed the doctrine of the "natural" equality of men as obviously false; so I discovered later have others, e.g., H. Spiegelberg, "A Defense of Human Equality," *Philosophical Review,* 53 (1944), pp. 106, 111; and Johnson, "The Concept of Human Equality," in L. Bryson (ed.), *op. cit.,* p. 25. I now think I was wrong, at least in supposing that (a) is obviously false—as it would be if it implied that all men are equal to each other in *all* respects. What must be done is first to state exactly what these "respects" are so that (a) is non-trivially true and second to determine whether (a) in such a formulation constitutes a good reason for (b)—which was typically the main point in advancing (a). A recent attempt to satisfy both these requirements is B. A. O. Williams, "The Idea of Equality," in P. Laslett and W. Runciman (eds.), *Philosophy, Politics and Society* (1962), p. 112.

[23] See for example W. K. Frankena, *op. cit.,* p. 14; G. Vlastos, *op. cit.,* p. 45; B. A. O. Williams, *op. cit.,* pp. 110ff.; and R. Robinson, *op. cit.,* p. 181.

itarian thought, apart from its bearing on (1), is not to be underestimated, but I shall not attempt to examine it here.[24]

The second egalitarian principle I shall call the doctrine of *the justice of equality*. Concerning reflections on social justice, Richard Brandt has remarked recently, "The one point of agreement among contemporary thinkers seems to be that equality and justice have a close relation."[25] This close relation is not confined to the concept of *social* justice, and to my knowledge, it has never been seriously denied since Aristotle observed that "All men hold that justice is some kind of equality."[26] Although every recent attempt to analyze the concept of justice shows the acceptance of this principle,[27] it is not easy to state the relation between justice and equality with brevity and accuracy. I shall phrase it this way:

(3) The concept of justice involves that of equality.

This is, of course, exceedingly abstract and vague. It is important to know whether the equality here is an equality of rights (and if so, of which) or of something else; and whether treating persons equally, in the name of justice, involves anything more than treating them with *impartiality,* which is all that Aristotle and many others have thought "equality" meant insofar as they thought (3) was true. I will not attempt to decide these questions here. Unsatisfactory though (3) may be, it nevertheless puts us in mind of what accounts (perhaps entirely) for the attraction the idea of equality has for us: it is the justice of equality. If social equality has to be recommended on any moral grounds other than that of its justice, it has at best a precarious hold on our convictions. The egalitarianism of the classical utilitarians testifies to this. There is always the danger that some "recognized social expediency," in Mill's phrase, will depend upon inequality, and thus will justify overriding the equality normally required

[24] See, however, the essays by Vlastos and Williams, cited previously.

[25] R. B. Brandt, *op. cit.,* p. v, and cf. J. Hospers, *Human Conduct* (1961), p. 147.

[26] *Politics* 1282 b 18, tr. R. Robinson, *Aristotle's Politics, Books III–IV* (1962), p. 41; cf. *Nichomachean Ethics,* 1113 a 13.

[27] See for example C. Perelman, *The Idea of Justice* (1963) and the several essays on justice in C. J. Friedrich and J. W. Chapman (eds.), *NOMOS VI: Justice* (1963); also R. B. Brandt (ed.), *op. cit.,* and F. A. Olafson (ed.), *op. cit.*

for the general happiness.[28] If we turn to altogether nonmoral grounds in order to justify social equality, it is difficult to see how to proceed. Such aesthetic appeal as equality has occasionally had (William Dean Howells thought it "a beautiful thing, . . . the only joy, the only comfort") seems wholly consequent upon a prior recognition of its moral authority. Freed from that sanction, equality has usually been thought to have no claim on us. In Thomas More's *Utopia*, for example, we are presented with a citizenry whose taste is so dulled by egalitarian sympathies that each citizen is content to own but one cloak, and that one identical in cut and color with his neighbor's. It is by the aesthetics, not the morality, of such a society that we are shocked. The flatness and uniformity of an egalitarian society (required at least by the word's etymology) has always repelled all but a few. Were (3) not true, we would gladly yield to the splendors of inequality, whose "fatal beauty," as Henry Alonzo Myers noticed,[29] always exerts a powerful attraction.

The third principle may be called *the presumption of equality*. Again, Aristotle was the first to imply that social inequalities, not equalities, are in need of some justification, and that inequalities for which no adequate reason can be given are unjustified.[30] As Leslie Stephen phrased it more explicitly, "There should always be a sufficient reason for any difference in our treatment of our fellows."[31] If this is so, then we cannot need any "sufficient reason" for treating persons equally. Hence, we may say:

(4) Social equalities need no special justification, whereas social inequalities always do.

If there is a presumption in favor of equality, we may think it is because, *ceteris paribus*, equal treatment is the right treatment for all persons. On this understanding (4) becomes a corollary of (3), since what gives the presumption in favor of equality is the fact that justice requires it. But it is possible, as classical

[28] J. S. Mill, *Utilitarianism*, Part V; and see H. A. Bedau, "Justice and Classical Utilitarianism," in C. J. Friedrich and J. W. Chapman (eds.), *op. cit.*, pp. 293ff.

[29] H. A. Myers, *Are Men Equal?* (1955), p. 20.

[30] *Politics*, 1283 a 2.

[31] L. Stephen, *op. cit.*, p. 267; and similarly I. Berlin, *op. cit.*, *p.* 131, and S. I. Benn and R. S. Peters, *Social Principles of Democratic Thought* (1959), p. 111.

utilitarianism illustrates, to grant the same presumption in favor of equality on the quite different ground that equality is, *ceteris paribus,* in fact a necessary condition of other social and personal goods. Likewise, if in (3), "equality" means only "impartiality," then (4) would not be a corollary of (3), because in (4) "equality" and "inequality" cannot mean "impartiality" and "partiality." I mention these points because there is some danger that (3) and (4) will not be accorded their true logical independence.

The presumption stated in (4), though a powerful theme in egalitarian thought, is clearly rebuttable, and it implies that the egalitarian must limit his aspirations. This need for limitation is evident in *the principle of equality* as it is likely to be formulated nowadays. It is a far cry from radical egalitarianism. In a typical recent formulation, this principle reads:

> (5) All persons are to be treated alike, except where circumstances require different treatment.[32]

There may be nothing deficient about such a view (and we know that it is an exhortation too rarely practiced), but there is also nothing radical about it. It may not be in the direct line of descent from Aristotle's notion of proportionate equality,[33] but it provides ample room to accommodate anti-egalitarian notions.

The limitations to which radical egalitarianism is subject and which issue in a principle of equality such as (5) can all be shown to derive from one or the other of two independent considerations. More than half a century ago, it was alleged that biologists and anthropologists had "proved" that "progress" depends on social inequalities,[34] much as earlier economists had argued that economic progress in any society is contingent on an unequal distribution of income.[35] Today, similar views are defended not only by those who think of themselves as social or economic conservatives. They are an integral feature of every sociological theory of differentiation and stratification. Nor is it only economic or social *progress* that is said to be contingent on

[32] Quoted from M. Beardsley, "Equality and Obedience to Law," in S. Hook (ed.), *Law and Philosophy* (1964), p. 35.

[33] *Nichomachean Ethics,* V. 3. a, and *Politics,* III. 12.

[34] D. G. Ritchie, "Equality," *Contemporary Review* (1892), reprinted in his *Studies in Political and Social Ethics* (1902), p. 31.

[35] R. Lampman, *op. cit.,* p. 247.

inequality. "Social inequality," we are told, "is a *necessary* feature of any social system . . . it is . . . *impossible* to imagine a social system totally lacking in . . . manifestations of inequality."[36] It is not merely that highly industrialized societies are unthinkable except in terms of considerable social inequality. The implication is that every sociological model of human society—in whatever natural environment, at whatever time, and (presumably) of whatever size or duration—involves social inequalities. Even the staunchest critics of this scientific anti-egalitarianism insist only that the social inequalities necessary to social survival are far less than those which now exist or, for that matter, have existed in any known society.[37] Radical egalitarians will draw no comfort from this because it leaves untouched the major point:

(6) Some social inequalities are necessary.

"Necessary" here means that it is in fact not possible to eliminate all inequalities, either because role-differentiation is necessary to the existence of any social system and role-stratification is equally necessary (as the cause or consequence) to role-differentiation, or for other less sophisticated reasons, e.g., because some inequalities can be removed only by introducing others, or because social inequalities are an inescapable consequence of natural (individual) inequalities. As Hume long ago remarked, "Render possessions ever so equal, men's different degrees of art, care, and industry will immediately break that equality."[38] The soundness of this point is not altered if for "possessions" we substitute "social condition." The question that (6) raises for those with egalitarian sentiments is this: What are the minimum inequalities required to maintain a given social system and what is the cost, in terms of existing institutions that would need to be changed and of the frustration of other values, to achieve this minimum? This looks like an empirical question for some be-

[36] W. Moore, "But Some are More Equal than Others," *American Sociological Review*, 28 (1963), pp. 14, 16. Italics added.
[37] See M. M. Tumin, "On Equality," *American Sociological Review*, 28 (1963), pp. 19–26, and further criticism by Buckley, Huaco, and Stinchcombe, *ibid.*, pp. 799–808.
[38] D. Hume, *Enquiry Concerning the Principles of Morals*, ed. L. A. Selby-Bigge, p. 194.

havioral scientist to answer, and it would be interesting to know
the answer for our society.

The necessary inequalities implied in (6) raise no question
of justification. Only that which could be otherwise needs to be
justified. However, if the apparent injustice of these inequalities
is obviated by their social necessity, the apparent injustice of
some other inequalities is negated by their moral necessity, so to
speak. Certain inequalities that are avoidable or eliminable, if
we may believe most philosophers, should nevertheless not only
be tolerated but deliberately introduced or preserved. This is
because:

(7) Some social inequalities are justifiable.

If certain inequalities are justifiable, then they are "required"
in the sense of (5) no less than the inequalities in (6) are "required" because they are necessary. There is a familiar and semi-
popular argument to the effect that equality, whether of rights,
treatment, or condition, (a) is simply incompatible with the
achievement of other moral ideals, such as individual self-develop-
ment and personal freedom, and that (b) there is no rational
ground for a decision (whether by an individual or a government) in favor of equality and against a conflicting ideal, e.g.,
freedom, rather than the reverse.[39] This particular argument depends for its attractiveness in considerable part on a failure of
analysis. First of all, if (b) is true, then it is difficult to see how
any sense attaches to the supposed inference, that certain inequalities are *justified*. Second, before one can conclude that (a)
is true—that equality and, say freedom, are incompatible ideals—
one must show that the competing ideal in question does not
imply its *equal* application to all men. There undoubtedly are
such ideals, but it is difficult to see how they are to survive
criticism. This is most easily seen in the case of freedom itself.
Surely, insofar as freedom is a social ideal, it is the *equal* freedom
of all men that is meant. If this is conceded, then either the

[39] Aside from the support in local ideology and (allegedly) in the Constitution, it is apparent that the twin convictions (a) and (b) in the text
underlie the argument of most of those who oppose equality of civil rights
in America. See for example R. C. Pittman, "The 'Blessings of Liberty' vs.
The 'Blight of Equality'," *North Carolina Law Review*, 42 (1963), pp. 86–105,
and the authorities cited there.

alleged incompatibility disappears (for equality becomes a constituent of the ideal of freedom) or else the conflict is really between (equal) freedom and some other ideal (e.g., unequal power), which may or may not be a defensible ideal. Third, one who believes in the incompatibility between freedom and equality tends to think of the latter in terms of radical egalitarianism. Now, there is no doubt whatever that maximal personal freedom is incompatible with radical egalitarianism, but this hardly seems an interesting deduction; it would be distressing only if no other form or principle of egalitarianism were worth defending—which is surely not so. What holds for the relation between freedom and equality holds also, I think, for the relation between equality and every other genuine social ideal.

To turn to the arguments that philosophers have advanced on behalf of (7), they seem to be mainly of two sorts. Several generations ago David Ritchie argued that "spiritual" but not "material" inequalities among men were justified, on the ground that "spiritual inequalities are advantageous, material inequalities are not."[40] The advantages in this instance, he thought, accrued to the society as a whole. Similarly, Harold Laski argued that "it is consistent with the principle of equality that men be differently treated, so long as the differences are relevant to the common good."[41] These views are echoed by the philosophers who now argue that inequalities that "do more good than harm,"[42] or inequalities that are "required by considerations of weight,"[43] are justified. Most of those who take this view follow the path marked out long ago by Bentham, the Mills, and Sidgwick, *viz.*, that inasmuch as the net social usefulness of any mode of conduct alone justifies it as the rule, the same consideration may justify a breach of the rule; and this applies as much to maxims such as "Treat all persons equally" or "All men ought to be equal in political rights" as it does to any other moral rule. Against this, it has been argued that these purely utilitarian con-

---

[40] D. G. Ritchie, *op. cit.*, p. 40. By "spiritual inequalities" Ritchie meant men's different capacities for and achievement in artistic, intellectual, and moral excellence.

[41] H. Laski, "A Plea for Equality," in his *The Dangers of Obedience* (1930), p. 232.

[42] R. Taylor, "Justice and the Common Good," in S. Hook (ed.), *op. cit.*, p. 95.

[43] R. B. Brandt, *Ethical Theory* (1954), p. 430.

siderations could never demonstrate a given inequality to be a *just* inequality, even if they could demonstrate (for those prepared to accept some version of the principle of utility as their ultimate authority) a given inequality to be *justifiable*.[44]

Other philosophers, however, have argued the more interesting position that certain inequalities are justified because they are just. Such maxims of distributive justice as "To each according to his merit," "To each according to his work," and "To each according to his prior agreements," all appear to be anti-egalitarian maxims.[45] Yet, there seem to be many occasions where conduct is justified by appeal to these maxims in order to override criticism based on egalitarian principles. We do constantly speak of one person deserving one thing and another deserving something else; and in doing so, we often rely on one or another of these maxims and think ourselves justified *and just* in doing so.[46] So these inequalities are presumably thought of as just inequalities. They are inequalities, as William Frankena has put it, which are "required by *just-making* considerations (i.e., by principles of *justice,* not merely *moral* principles) of substantial weight. . . ."[47] And, he adds, the practices that issue from such considerations are "not necessarily very egalitarian." A similar view has been offered by John Rawls, according to whom inequalities are justified as "fair" if they work out to everyone's advantage;[48] such inequalities may be numerous and various, but if they are fair, then they are just and not merely justified.

Some philosophers have even tried to argue that the principle expressed in (3) can accommodate the maxims of distributive

---

[44] This objection is argued in Frankena's valuable essay, *op. cit.,* pp. 15–16.

[45] Vlastos thinks that "To each according to his need" is a "maxim of equal distribution" (*op. cit.,* pp. 40ff., p. 72). So does D. D. Raphael in "Equality and Equity," *Philosophy,* 21 (1946), p. 126. For reasons I have indicated above, in section I, *supra,* I think their description of this matter is misleading.

[46] See for example A. M. Honoré, "Social Justice," *McGill Law Journal* 8 (1962), p. 79, where he speaks simply of a principle of "desert"; D. D. Raphael, *op. cit.,* pp. 123ff.; and W. von Leyden, "On Justifying Inequality," *Political Studies,* 11 (1963), p. 64.

[47] W. K. Frankena, *op. cit.,* p. 10. Italics in the original.

[48] J. Rawls, "Justice as Fairness," reprinted in F. A. Olafson (ed.), *op. cit.,* pp. 81, 83. Rawls also requires that the "positions and offices" (benefits and burdens, privileges and immunities, goods and evils) in which these inequalities are manifest or from which they derive "are open to all." Without this proviso, the inequalities are not fair.

justice without inconsistency, that is, they have offered an egalitarian defense of just inequalities. Wolfgang von Leyden has argued that treating persons unequally is justifiable only if "we must do so in order to treat them equally in another and more 'important' or more 'fundamental' respect."[49] Gregory Vlastos has gone further, insisting that inequalities (e.g., an unequal distribution of some good) can be justified only if the reasons justifying them are the very reasons normally justifying equality.[50] On such views, a correct understanding of the principle of equal distribution, of recognizing persons' equal right to whatever good may be in question (freedom, security, welfare, property), in fact not only permits but requires introducing inequalities. Hence, inequalities may not only be just, they can even be justified by the principles of egalitarian justice!

The result is a conception of egalitarianism that not only is immeasurably distant from radical egalitarianism but that has also gone a long way to accommodate meritarian considerations. It has become enormously complex in theory as well. To treat people equally now involves always considering (and often trying to effect) deviations from strict equality in at least three dimensions simultaneously (to accommodate variations in persons' merit, work, and prior agreements). Surely the ironic consequence of such attempts to justify inequalities in the name of egalitarianism is that by all odds the strongest practical argument for egalitarianism has always been recognition of the fact that "human justice has, in many cases, to be the justice of mere equality, simply because of the difficulties of assigning proportionate equalities fairly."[51] This is not to say that giving way to "mere equality" on grounds of simplicity is to fall back upon utilitarian considerations, as is sometimes alleged.[52] The reason that justifies distribution according to mere equality when the complexities of proportionate equality get out of hand is presumably that this is the *fairest* way to make a distribution; in effect, one has in mind (3) and (5), and *ex hypothesi* the circumstances make the "except" clause of (5) inapplicable. In

---

[49] W. von Leyden, *op. cit.*, p. 68.

[50] G. Vlastos, *op. cit.*, pp. 39ff.

[51] D. G. Ritchie, *op. cit.*, p. 34; cf. L. Stephen, *op. cit.*, note 11, *supra*, p. 265.

[52] D. G. Ritchie, *ibid.*, and also D. D. Raphael, *op. cit.*, p. 125.

such situations, it remains an open question whether the simplest pattern of distribution is the most useful; the strict egalitarian need not worry if it is the most useful *because* it is the fairest! But it is not an open question whether it is the fairest, for one is unable to carry out a properly weighted or proportionately equal distribution, i.e., to identify and carry out any distribution that is *fairer*. There is not space to argue for one rather than another of these ways to defend (7). But I see no way to reject (7), whatever its proper defense may entail. The upshot for radical egalitarianism is the same in any case.

Once we isolate the principles of egalitarian thought, (2) through (5), and the limitations they must face, (6) and (7), there is not much left of (1). (6) and (7) show that (1) is false, although, of course, they do not likewise refute any or all of (2) through (5). These principles remain as the quadrants of social justice, equalitarian instruments for social criticism and reform. And instead of the extreme and somewhat frightening notion of radical egalitarianism, what we have left is the injunction that *all social inequalities not necessary or justifiable should be eliminated*. This is rather tepid by comparison with (1), and taken by itself, it may not be very interesting or novel, though it is hardly a platitude. Even so it will be too radical for some, although they can take some comfort in its ample ambiguities and in the theoretically endless factual arguments it invites.

What this review of egalitarian thinking shows is that egalitarianism is incapable of resisting considerations of social necessity and of morality (including, perhaps, considerations of "egalitarian justice" itself) that have the effect of justifying, or at least of removing from condemnation, an enormous number and variety of social inequalities. "We have as yet no direct experience," one sociologist has recently reminded us, "of the way of life of an egalitarian society."[53] Nor are we likely to. At any given time, some inequalities are bound to be socially necessary, others morally justified, and still others naturally necessary. We are and will remain surrounded both in fact and in theory by inequalities of every sort. This may help us to understand how it is possible for so many persons to question the wisdom (and impugn the motives) of those who would condemn and under-

[53] T. B. Bottomore, *Elites and Society* (1964), p. 140.

take to eliminate a particular social inequality. For the truth of the matter is that almost every actual difference among men can be a source or basis of some justifiable inequality, if not in public life then in private, if not in large matters then in small. The permanent task for the egalitarian remains one of scrutinizing existing inequalities among men in order to assure us that they are based on justifiable (or at least unavoidable) differences, and to eliminate those which are not.

2

A LAWYER'S LOOK AT EGALITARIANISM AND EQUALITY

NORMAN DORSEN

In these pages I shall attempt two tasks. Part I will contain comments on Professor Bedau's article, "Egalitarianism and the Idea of Equality." Professor Bedau is a philosopher, and I am a lawyer, and I suspect that from what I shall say it will be obvious that interdisciplinary learning has not yet bridged all gaps. Part II considers "equality" independently of Professor Bedau's analysis. These remarks, too, may suggest major differences in the way in which philosophers and members of the legal profession view the problem of equality.

I

Let it be clear at the outset that the following criticisms are not intended to detract from the worth of Professor Bedau's paper, every page of which reflects the scholarship and care lavished on it. Instead, these remarks should convey the desire of a foreigner to the discipline of philosophy to grapple with one of its hard problems.

One of my difficulties in following the paper comes from the frequent failure of Professor Bedau to deliver what he promises. At the beginning he says that some with "passionate egalitarian sympathies" may find his conclusions rather discouraging. Why this should be so is never explained; as one who harbors egalitarian sympathies, sometimes passionately, I was not in the least discouraged. If the source of discouragement was thought to be that meritarian considerations or those of fairness must be accommodated in any theory of equality, this seems to me desirable, inevitable, and in no event disheartening.

A second interesting suggestion that is never brought home occurs at the end of Part I: "Probably, as the argument in the next section implies, egalitarians will have to choose between demanding equality of civil liberties and political rights, of opportunities and consideration, on the one hand, and, on the other, equality in personal goods, economic power, and living conditions." Apart from the fact that there seems abundant empirical evidence of the doubtfulness of the statement—the Negro revolution, for example, suggests that the two sets of goals can and perhaps must be achieved in tandem—the second part of the paper nowhere "implies" the contrary, at least to me.

A third and important deficiency of this sort is the failure to make good, at least in part, on what appears to be a central concern of the paper. On page 15 it is stated, "My interest here in radical egalitarianism is simply that, because it is so extreme, it may best serve the purpose of organizing our thoughts on what is to be said for and against less radical and more attractive egalitarian notions." Although the pages that follow explore with considerable imagination the nature of radical egalitarianism as well as its deficiencies as a realistic standard, the promised task of analyzing the "less radical and more attractive egalitarian notions" is not attempted.

A related and perhaps more basic problem of Bedau's analysis is that the central conclusions, particularly of Part II, do not follow from argument but instead seem merely the inevitable consequence of the author's premises.

As I understand it, Professor Bedau ultimately endorses "a

conception of egalitarianism which not only is immeasurably
distant from radical egalitarianism, but which has also gone a
long way to accommodate meritarian considerations." This ac-
commodation must be made because "egalitarianism is incapable
of resisting considerations of social necessity and of morality." Although radical egalitarianism is deemed "false," principles of
egalitarianism "remain as the quadrants of social justice, egalitarian instruments for social criticism and reform." Finally, "all
social inequalities not necessary or justifiable should be eliminated."

If these precepts reflect the core of Bedau's thinking, my
criticism of it is not that the precepts are incorrect, but that they
are not proved; certainly they do not emerge as a result of weighing arguments "for and against less radical and more attractive
egalitarian notions." As I have said, they reflect the author's
premises; all else flows from the presumption established by propositions (1) to (3) and confirmed in propositions (4) and (5).

These numbered propositions and the arguments supporting
them are flawed by the author's failure to deal with some of the
hard questions they raise. For example, in the course of establishing the "presumption of equality," Bedau does not really justify
the proposition that "the concept of justice involves that of equality." He apparently assumes this is self-evident, but in certain
circumstances, some of which are explored in Part II, there may
be difficult problems in establishing the truth of the proposition.
And although at another point he states that a critical question
is the determination of "minimum equalities required to maintain a given social system" and of the "costs" of achieving this
minimum, he assigns the problem to "some behavioral scientist."
(Incidentally, my quarrel here is not that Bedau did not answer
the questions himself, but that he did not discover by an attempt
to do so that they are essentially unanswerable, at least according
to behavioral scientists of my acquaintance.)

These deficiencies come to a head at the end of the paper,
where it is stated, "The permanent task for the egalitarian remains one of scrutinizing existing inequalities among men in
order to assure us that they are based on justifiable (or at least
unavoidable) differences, and to eliminate those which are not."
Is not the critical problem, and the one that invites ground-
breaking, how to determine the specific criteria by which to

ascertain whether existing inequalities are based on justifiable or unavoidable differences? Similarly, although Bedau recognizes that "to treat people equally now involves always considering . . . deviations from strict equality in at least three dimensions simultaneously (. . . work, merit and prior agreements)," there is a failure to pursue this theme by exploring these matters concretely. To be sure the difficulties in dealing with these problems are enormous (and this is not the path Professor Bedau has chosen to follow), but any other course tends to lead to general comments that may have only limited value.

II

This section discusses equality as it appears from the vantage point of a lawyer or at least a teacher of law and, incidentally, will provide some contrast with the approach employed by Professor Bedau.

The subject can be approached in different ways. I have selected as my theme the proposition that at least two related aspects of legal problems involve "equality"—drawing lines of distinction between matters that are at least arguably similar and the propriety of these lines as judged by an official institution. In other words, legal entities must draw fine distinctions, with the risk that they may be found invalid.

I shall shortly elaborate my double-barrelled proposition by exploring three simple legal situations. It will be helpful, however, initially to state two important premises about the legal system. First, the issues of line-drawing and validity cannot be understood without an appreciation of the relevant reasons and purposes underlying a particular legal act.

Second, line-drawing and validity cannot be understood without an awareness of the differences in characteristics and role among legal institutions, in particular between courts and legislatures:

Legislatures are responsible politically to the electorate; they have committees and staffs equipped to make long studies and garner elusive facts as a basis for comprehensive treatment of broad subjects, whether labor relations, securities regulations or civil rights; they act prospectively; and they must be concerned with the impact of legislation, with few exceptions, on an entire constituency.

Courts ordinarily are not politically responsible; they lack machinery for establishing facts other than those applicable to a particular controversy; they exist primarily to "do justice" to the parties before them; and the law they make is tied to a concrete situation and frequently must await future judicial action or administrative follow-up before it can be generalized and applied.

The three legal situations that I hope will give substance to all these abstractions follow.

The first concerns state statutes, similar to the federal Fair Labor Standards Act of 1938, that fix minimum wages and maximum hours for certain workers.

The second concerns the famous case of *Gideon* v. *Wainwright* (1963), in which the United States Supreme Court, overruling an earlier decision, held that the fourteenth amendment to the Constitution requires states to provide free lawyers for criminal defendants who cannot afford them.

The third concerns the legal implications of a storekeeper's refusal to serve Negroes who enter his restaurant.

Let us examine, in light of these three cases, the basic two-part proposition that legal problems involve drawing hard distinctions that run the risk of being declared invalid.

Take the first situation of the state fair labor standards act. As a legislature frames the statute, it must decide as a matter of policy whether it covers all that ought to be included and exempts all that ought to be excluded. More specifically, should all workers be covered or should there be exemptions for employees in small enterprises, agricultural workers, domestics, or professionals such as lawyers and economists? Similarly, should the minimum wage be $.25 an hour, as it was in the early years under the federal law, $1.25, or $1.50 now that conditions have changed? Similar questions arise with respect to maximum hours of work and other issues under the statute.

Issues of validity are also involved. If the legislation exempts certain employees or occupations, is it vulnerable under the federal Constitution, in particular the provision of the fourteenth amendment prohibiting a state from denying to any person the "equal protection of the laws"? Is it vulnerable under similar equal protection clauses contained in most state constitutions? That is, are the lines drawn by the legislature permissible under governing constitutional canons that attempt to assure equal treatment? There is of course a long history to the meaning of equal protection clauses, but the following summary of the governing rules, taken from a Supreme Court ruling, will suffice:

1. The equal protection clause of the Fourteenth Amendment does not take from the State the power to classify in the adoption of police laws, but admits of the exercise of a wide scope of discretion in that regard, and voids what is done only when it is without any reasonable basis and therefore is purely arbitrary.

2. A classification having some reasonable basis does not offend against that clause merely because it is not made with mathematical nicety or because in practice it results in some inequality.

3. When the classification in such a law is called in question, if any state of facts reasonably can be conceived that would sustain it, the existence of that state of facts at the time the law was enacted must be assumed.

4. One who assails the classification in such a law must carry the burden of showing that it does not rest upon any reasonable basis, but is essentially arbitrary.

As these criteria suggest, it is now established that the prohibition of the Equal Protection Clause goes no further than the "arbitrary" discrimination. As the Supreme Court has recently said, "a statute is not invalid under the Constitution because it might have gone farther than it did, or because it may not succeed in bringing about the result that it tends to produce." Under this criterion the distinctions drawn in a fair labor standards act would certainly be sustained judicially, as have similar discriminations contained in numerous other laws dealing with social or economic matters. Indeed, over recent decades in only one maverick case has the Supreme Court found a violation of the Equal Protection Clause.

The second legal situation presented—the *Gideon* case—also involves questions of degree. Does the decision, for example, require assignment of counsel in all criminal cases or only in felonies? If in more than felonies, was it meant to include such petty offenses as traffic violations? Another range of questions concerns whether *Gideon* means that counsel must be provided during appellate review to the state supreme court, in the preparation of papers seeking discretionary review by the United States Supreme Court, or on petitions for habeas corpus by persons already incarcerated. At the other end of the criminal law spectrum, does *Gideon* mean that individuals arrested or even merely under investigation by the police are entitled to free counsel if unable to afford a lawyer? And finally, does the principle underlying the case require, at least in some circumstances, the provision of free counsel in civil suits?

What is an "indigent," anyway? How poor must a person be before he is entitled to assigned counsel? Must he be bereft of his last cent? If not, when does his bank account dwindle to the point that he becomes eligible for a lawyer at the expense of the state?

These questions (based on real cases) are addressed in the first instance to the state courts that must interpret the *Gideon* decision. The state courts must decide where to draw the lines, but in so doing the issue of validity is very much in the background because if their decisions are erroneous, the Supreme Court will exercise its reviewing power and overturn convictions in which the defendant did not have a lawyer. In other words, the state courts must draw lines (as did the state legislature in drafting its fair labor standards act), with the essential difference that the state court will probably be rebuffed if a mistake is made.

Why will the Supreme Court use its power of nullity in overseeing the appointment of counsel to indigent defendants by state (and federal) courts and not in overseeing the determination of what is a fair minimum wage by a state legislature? There is the sixth amendment, which provides specifically that in criminal prosecutions the accused shall have the "assistance of counsel for his defense." The other two reasons closely relate to the different institutional tasks and capacities of legislatures and courts. That is, the Supreme Court is able to decide whether a lawyer is needed just as well as a state court, whereas it lacks the fact-finding mechanism for extensive investigation into economic conditions and cost-of-living indices, as required in considering the validity of minimum wage laws. Moreover, although rules of criminal procedure as well as of economic legislation carry important and uncertain consequences, a court seems more justified in aggressive action in the sphere where it has special institutional experience—that is, in judging fairness of criminal trials.

But nowhere does the opinion of the Supreme Court in the *Gideon* case suggest how broadly the ruling should be interpreted. The net effect is that state courts must apply its principle "equally," that is, with the full scope "intended" by the Supreme Court, even though the intent is not immediately discernible. Lest one recoil at this procedure, it should be understood that it is the time-tried lawyer's way of establishing the meaning of any precedent—through case by case development of the underlying principle. Thus, a similar process is involved in determining whether or not a prisoner's confession was "coerced" at the stationhouse (and therefore "invalid," i.e., inadmissible at trial) or whether certain evidence was "illegally" obtained by the police (also inadmissible). The police must draw distinctions based on factual nuances, that is, they must decide whether two situations are to be treated "equally," with the sanction of invalidity as the check in the background.

Returning to our specific questions concerning the scope of *Gideon,* it is important to isolate the reasons underlying the decision. On the one hand, if it was rendered solely to protect criminal defendants from the bewildering complexities of a criminal trial, the ruling would not logically be extended, for example, to an appeal that lacked similar complexities. On the other hand, if the premise of *Gideon* is that the criminal process, with its vital consequences for each embroiled individual, must in a free society provide the poor with the same caliber of justice as the well-to-do can afford, the ruling should be applicable to proceedings before and after trial as well as during it.

The third hypothetical situation presents a set of questions no less pertinent to the theme of equality. Here there is line-drawing of a different character, conducted on the basis of race and by a private individual rather than by an institution of government. The restaurant owner decides who is a "Negro" and whether he wants to serve Negroes.

At least two issues of validity are involved in this decision. First, is there anything in the common law that forbids a shopkeeper from discriminating against Negroes? In those states where the answer has been determined to be negative, we turn to the equal protection clause of the fourteenth amendment. One must initially ask whether discrimination on account of race is "arbitrary" within the meaning of the governing standard. The federal courts have now answered this question in the affirmative, although the "separate but equal" doctrine long delayed the consummation of this rule.

The more difficult question relating to validity under the equal protection clause derives from the fact that it is a private individual who is discriminating, and the terms of the fourteenth amendment apply only to "States." The Supreme Court has never resolved this problem, although some Justices have opined that it *is* the State that discriminates, albeit indirectly, when it licenses the shopkeeper, and other Justices have claimed that it was the intention of the fourteenth amendment to eliminate discrimination because of race in all "public accommodations," such as privately owned restaurants open to the public.

Assuming, however, that neither of these theories is accepted and that the Constitution does not forbid private discrimination, the storekeeper may find that he is prohibited from refusing to serve Negroes by a state antidiscrimination law or the federal Civil Rights Act of 1964.

If we focus on the legislative enactment, we discover considerations of "equality" similar to those discussed in relation to the state fair labor standards act. There is first the issue of line-drawing. For example, should the new law be drafted to exempt private membership clubs and restaurants operated by religious and educational institutions on the ground that in these instances the value of free association outweighs the policy against racial discrimination? Second, is the statute valid; will it be upheld under the equal protection clause if it "arbitrarily" exempts such clubs and church restaurants? Conversely, if it does *not* provide exemptions, could the statute be invalidated by the courts on the ground that it interferes with freedom of association or religion?

It will be clear by now that the purpose of this paper has not been to answer questions but to pose them and particularly through concrete instances to suggest the problems of "equality" that constantly face lawyers and courts. General theories may be useful, but far more valuable to the lawyer is the ability to isolate precise legal issues and to perceive the considerations governing the wise and valid drawing of factual distinctions. Such is the ever-present and practical character of the problem of "equality" in the law.

3

EQUALITY AND GENERALIZATION,
A FORMAL ANALYSIS

RICHARD E. FLATHMAN

To treat people equally is to treat them in the same way. To treat people in the same way is to treat them according to a rule. "Equally" is defined in the *Oxford English Dictionary* to mean "According to one and the same rule." Philosophers, aware of this relationship, have attempted to explicate and refine the notion of equality through the notion of general rule or generalization. Historically, the salient names in this connection are Rousseau and Kant. Many contemporary philosophers have concerned themselves with generalization, but few have applied their conclusions to "equality." The purpose of the present paper is to analyze the concept of equality in the light of recent discussions of generalization. I will argue that the concept of equality can be explicated in terms of generalization, and that to do so shows that as normative concepts both equality and generalization are of derivative significance. These conclusions will lead to suggestions concerning the importance of utilitarian considerations in morals.

I

Recent work in ethics or meta-ethics has been concerned to identify and provide formalized statements of the principles and rules that operate, if only in a concealed manner, in moral discourse. The concept of generalization has been the object of substantial attention in these respects, and we now have several analyses of what has been called the Generalization or Universalizability Principle (hereafter GP). Professor Marcus Singer, who has made the most detailed study of the topic, states GP in the form we will adopt for the purposes of this paper: "What is right (or wrong) for one person must be right (or wrong) for every relevantly similar person in relevantly similar circumstances."[1] According to this formulation, if X is right for A, it must be right for B, C, D, . . . N unless A or his circumstances is different from B, C, D, . . . N or their circumstances in a manner justifying making an exception of A. There is, it would appear, a presumption in favor of equal treatment of all persons and any departure from that rule must be justified.

One feature of GP, its "formal" or "neutral" character, requires immediate attention. Before the universal principle that GP expresses can be applied to a problem, two particular premises must be established. The first is of the form: "This X is right for this A"; the second: "This B is, vis-à-vis this A, a relevantly similar person in relevantly similar circumstances." GP states a relationship between these premises; it does not tell us how to establish them in any instance. Until they have been established, GP, although valid as an abstract principle, has no

---

[1] Marcus Singer, *Generalization in Ethics*, New York: Alfred A. Knopf, 1961, pp. 19–20; alternative formulations are presented on pp. 5 and 31. There is a very extensive critical literature concerning Singer's book, and I have profited substantially from it. It would be impracticable to cite that literature here, but mention should be made of Alan Gewirth's "The Generalization Principle," *Philosophical Review*, Vol. 73 (April, 1964), p. 229, in which the reader will find arguments similar in important respects to some of those presented here.

application. GP does one thing: When it has been established that X is right for A and that A and B are relevantly similar, the principle requires that it be wrong for A to act or be treated differently from B. Hence GP is formal or neutral in the sense that, taken alone, it does not prescribe the proper content of any decision. Clearly, then, the crucial problems are those involved in establishing the particular premises in specific cases. Those problems, and the question of GP's utility once those problems have been resolved, will be our primary concern. We will also give attention to an argument that a substantive doctrine of equality is concealed by the ostensibly formal or neutral character of GP.

II

It will facilitate the analysis to use a real controversy concerning equality as a source of examples and illustrations. The recent United States Supreme Court decisions concerning apportionment in state legislatures, the "one-man, one-vote" decisions, are well suited to this purpose.[2] In the Court's view, the question before it in the Reynolds Case was whether the Equal Protection clause[3] permits a state to employ a system of apportionment in which the representatives of some districts represent substantially fewer citizens than the representatives of other districts. Although insisting that "mathematical exactitude" is neither desirable nor practicable as a standard for determining the adequacy of a plan, the majority nevertheless found that Equal Protection ". . . requires that a state make an honest and

[2] The leading case is *Reynolds* v. *Sims,* 377 U.S. 533 (1964). A series of companion cases follows immediately in the same volume. I would like to emphasize that it is not the purpose of this paper to present an evaluation of the Court's decisions in these cases. The arguments of the paper would be relevant to such an evaluation, and in it critical statements will be made concerning Chief Justice Warren's argument in the Reynolds case. But the purpose of these remarks will be to question the logic of the argument by which the conclusion is reached, not the conclusion itself. A competent evaluation of the latter would require a much wider investigation than I have undertaken. Also, because I am using the cases purely for illustrative purposes, I have not scrupled to ignore complexities in the Court's reasoning, which would lead beyond present purposes. It is my belief that the following interpretation of Warren's argument can be defended in terms of the text of his opinion, but I have not attempted to defend it here.

[3] Article 14, Section 1.

good faith effort to construct districts in both houses of its legislature as nearly of equal population as practicable."

In terms of **GP**, the issue can be restated as follows: "Is it constitutional for A (the citizens of legislative district A' in state Q') to have X (number of citizens per representative) if B, C, D, . . . N (the citizens of legislative districts B', C', D', . . . N' in state Q') do not have X (have Y, a larger or smaller number of citizens per representative)? Under GP the answer could be, for example, "Yes, if X is right for A and if vis-à-vis B, C, D, . . . N, A is (the class of A consists of) relevantly different persons in relevantly different circumstances. The decision, in other words, would seem to turn on establishing the two premises we have identified. We will try to show, however, that what appears to be two tasks is in fact one—establishing the rightness of X.

Many of the arguments of Warren's opinion, by contrast, suggest that in matters of apportionment "right" and the kind of equality demanded by the equal population rule are equivalent; they collapse the first premise of **GP** into the second. Much of his opinion is designed to show that various differences among citizens such as class, economic status, place of residence, and other characteristics, although alleged to justify differences in treatment, are irrelevant to apportionment. The assumption seems to be that "equal" in the Constitution establishes a presumption that the equal population rule is right (constitutional), and the task is less to defend that presumption than to show that the conditions required for its application (relevant similarity of all citizens) are satisfied. If challenges to the relevant similarity of all citizens can be met, the question of "right" (constitutionality) will be answered. In common with many egalitarian arguments, in other words, Warren treats equality as a sufficient normative principle. To clarify the logic of this argument we will examine some of the key contentions that Warren offers to support his conclusion.[4]

---

[4] Inasmuch as Warren is interpreting a Constitution to which he must be faithful, it might be thought misleading or worse to say that *he* "treats equality" as a sufficient principle. The Constitution, it might be alleged, established the principle and Warren is required to accept it in his role as judge. If the content of "equal" in "equal protection" were entirely clear, this argument would be persuasive. We will try to adduce logical considerations to show that it is not, and hence that the language used above is appropriate.

Warren's aim is to support the conclusion that all citizens should be treated according to the rule, "Equal representatives for equal population." To do so he asserts: "With respect to the allocation of legislative representation, all voters as citizens of the State stand in the same relation. . . . "[5] Presumably this means that there are no differences among citizens or their situations that would significantly affect their opportunity to participate effectively in or the manner in which they are affected by the system of representation. But the empirical proposition crucial to Warren's argument is highly doubtful. A citizen's relation to the system of representation, his opportunity to participate in and benefit from that process, can be affected by such factors as the predominant interest pattern in his district, whether his party affiliation is that of a majority or a minority party, difficulties of communication with political and governmental centers, informal political tradition, size (in area) of districts, and perhaps others. By adopting the equal population rule Warren *makes it* true that all citizens "stand in the same relation" to the system in the respect required by that rule. But they may stand in very different relations to the system in other respects.

It is of course possible that Warren could justify rejecting these other differences. Indeed it is certain that some of the above-mentioned factors would have to be ignored, especially in establishing constitutional requirements concerning the conditions of participation. It would be difficult and perhaps undesirable to refine those requirements to take account of all of the differences that have been alleged to be relevant.[6] But this possibility, al-

---

[5] *Reynolds* v. *Sims*, 565. The sentence ends ". . . regardless of where they live." But in the course of the opinion Warren makes the same contention for all differences alleged to be relevant (there is something of an exception for existing political subdivisions) and hence it is not a distortion to broaden the passage by omitting the restriction.

[6] To assume difficulty or undesirability too readily, however, is to risk assuming away the issues concerning proper apportionment. It is instructive in this connection to consider the British practice, a practice that has gone to great lengths in adapting to some of the differences mentioned above. The British have evidently found this practicable, and they have rejected the conclusion that the numerical equality for which Warren opts will provide a base from which the citizen can overcome all other inequalities. For a general account of British practices see Vincent E. Starzinger, "The British Pattern of Apportionment," *The Virginia Quarterly Review*, Vol. 41 (Summer 1965), pp. 321ff.

though relevant to whether Warren's conclusion could be defended, does not support the logic of the argument by which the conclusion is reached.

More particularly, it does not support the assumption that "right" (constitutionality) and "equal" can be equivalent, that establishing the second premise of GP will establish the first premise as well. If the premise that all citizens "stand in the same relation" with regard to representation is not literally true in all respects that affect representation, then treating them according to a rule based on that premise will mean that there will be respects in which they will be treated differently (unequally). In opting for the equal population rule, Warren treats all citizens equally in the respect required by that rule. But in doing so he accepts inequalities with regard, for example, to size (in area) of electoral districts, distance from governmental centers, and perhaps others. Once again, he might be entirely justified in so doing. But his justification cannot be in terms of equality. For he has, if only tacitly, chosen between equalities. He has preferred the equality of the equal population rule to the equality of, say, size of electoral districts.[7] Inasmuch as he is choosing between competing equalities, he has, again if only tacitly, turned to some principle other than equality to make that choice, that is, to decide what is right. "Right" and "equality" are not equivalent; equality is not an independent or a sufficient normative principle.

These considerations can be generalized. They suggest that "right" and "equality" could be equivalent, that establishing the second premise of GP would also establish the first, only if the decision-maker was not faced with the kind of choice Warren had to make. This choice, however, can be avoided only if all those involved in or affected by a decision are similar persons in similar

[7] Here again (cf. note 4 above) it might be argued that Warren did not "choose" between equalities but read the Constitution as *requiring* the equal population rule. Leaving aside general issues concerning the difficulty of interpreting the Constitution, the foregoing argument is intended to show that it is logically impossible for the words of the document, taken alone, to require this finding. Perhaps the usual materials of constitutional interpretation, previous court decisions, intent of the Framers, etc., support Warren's finding. Inasmuch as our concern is not constitutional law but the logic of "equality," this fact, if it is a fact, is of little relevance here and does not affect the above argument.

situations in *all* respects that might affect the results of the decision. Given the diversity of men and their situations, it is difficult to believe that such decisions are a regular occurrence—especially in politics where we are typically concerned with very large numbers. Hence questions arise about the significance of the principle of equality.

It might be useful to restate the foregoing argument in terms closer to those used in our preliminary discussion of GP. When GP is applied to a concrete issue, it serves to raise a comparative question—whether X is right for A *and* for B, C, D, . . . N. The foregoing argument supports our earlier contention that this comparative question cannot be answered until we have determined whether X is right for A. Warren's argument, and all arguments that treat equality as a sufficient standard of right, suggests that X can sometimes be right for A *because* A and B, C, D, . . . N are treated in a like manner. But this argument either begs the question of the first premise of GP—"Is X right for A?"—or simply restates it for B, C, D, . . . N and A. The question whether X is right for A must be independent of GP. It is not a comparative question (that is, not in the sense of GP or equality; it may be comparative in the sense of comparing the merits of alternative policies or actions) and it cannot be answered by a comparative formula or rule. If we treat A wrongly, it will not help to say that we have treated him the same as B, C, D, . . . N.

The same is true of B, C, D, . . . N. The rightness or wrongness of giving X to B, C, D, . . . N could turn on a relationship of equality or inequality between B, C, D, . . . N and A only in the circumstances specified above. (Even in those circumstances questions of ethical naturalism might arise.) Treating them equally in one respect will usually involve treating them unequally in another, possibly more important, respect. If we treat B, C, D, . . . N badly, it will not help that we have treated B, C, D, . . . N and A alike. To decide the rightness or wrongness of X for B, C, D, . . . N, we must repeat for the latter those steps taken to determine whether X was right or wrong for A.

Our reason for contending that establishing the first premise of GP is the main task should now be clear. For the procedure just described establishes the second as well as the first premise. It tells us whether B, C, D, . . . N are, vis-à-vis A, relevantly similar persons in relevantly similar circumstances. Our purpose is to discover whether X is right or wrong for both A and B, C, D, . . . N; and, by hypothesis, we have now done so. What could be more relevant than that the same policy is right or wrong for both? Indeed, what other proper answer could there be to the question of whether they are relevantly similar? The second premise of GP, in short, is properly established through the same procedures as the first, by determining the rightness or wrongness of applying X to B, C, D, . . . N. If that determination accords with the result obtained in making the same decision with regard to applying X to A, then A and B, C, D, . . . N are relevantly similar persons in relevantly similar circumstances and what is right or wrong for B, C, D, . . . N must (logically) be right or wrong for A. If the results of the two determinations differ, A and B, C, D, . . . N are not relevantly similar—and what is right for A is not right for B, C, D, . . . N.

GP demands a certain relationship between A and B, C, D, . . . N; but that relationship is a logically necessary relationship between the results obtained by the application of tests that are independent of GP. The moment we lose sight of this fact we are in danger of mistreating a person, or class of persons, on the irrelevant grounds that he, or it, is receiving the same treatment as others.

III

It might be contended that the foregoing analysis fails to consider certain dimensions and characteristics peculiar to equality questions. We have dissolved equality questions into a series of right-wrong questions connected in a *post hoc,* formal manner. At the least, it might be alleged, this analysis ignores prominent aspects of moral and political thought and practice.

The objection is justified in that one aspect of equality questions is partially masked by the foregoing discussion. The difficulty in the above account is its apparent suggestion that judgments about the rightness or wrongness of X for A are *entirely* independent of, and cannot be upset by, concern with B, C, D, . . . N. There are cases in which this is obviously not true. If A and B, C, D, . . . N are part of the same moral or legal system, giving X to A might have consequences for B, C, D, . . . N, consequences that must be considered in deciding whether it is right to give X to A. In the cases discussed thus far, we have assumed we had accounted for the impact of X on both (all) parties or classes; but there are other types of cases to be considered. Hence the foregoing discussion is incomplete; it needs to be supplemented by an enumeration and further analysis of the combinations that logically can arise under GP. Although this will involve some repetition of earlier arguments, it should summarize the results of those arguments and show what must be added to them in order to handle the objection before us.

We will continue to assume that X is right for A taken alone (that is, without considering the impact on B, C, D, . . . N, of giving X to A). Holding this constant, there are two basic types of situations (A and B) and six types of cases (A. 1-3 and B. 1-3) that can arise under GP.

Situation A.: If X is not right for B, C, D, . . . N, A and B, C, D, . . . N are not relevantly similar, and what is right for A is, by hypothesis, not right for B, C, D, . . . N.

Hence: A.1. To treat A and B, C, D, . . . N alike would be to treat unlike cases alike and would violate GP.

This is the standard type of case in which GP is violated. The Reynolds decision illustrates the point nicely. The Court holds that the equal population rule is the "controlling criterion" under the Equal Protection Clause. All citizens must be treated equally in the respect indicated by that rule. A.1. shows that this rule can be a requirement only if it would not be wrong to treat B, C, D, . . . N in this way. Critics of the decision hold that this condition is not satisfied in some states, that use of the equal population rule will lead to results of the A.1. type. To insist that all citizens be treated equally in this respect might involve treating them unequally in respects more important to the citizens in question and to the system.

To apply the equal population rule to Colorado, for example, might require that citizens of area D', an isolated mountain district with unique interests, be placed in a legislative district (D) which is uniquely large in terms of area, which poses very difficult transportation and communication problems, in which the overwhelming majority of the population have interests and political affiliations (for example, party) markedly at variance

with those of the citizenry in D', and in which the citizens of
D' share no mechanisms and channels of informal political activity with the other citizens of D. If these conditions do not obtain
in other districts of the state, or, as posited, for other citizens in
D, the citizenry of D', although treated equally in terms of the
equal population rule, are treated unequally in other respects.
Hence to impose the equal population rule upon them would be
to treat unlike cases alike. More important, it might be to treat
unlike cases alike in a manner that results in treating some
groups well and other groups badly.

To treat A and B, C, D, . . . N differently in situation A, for
example to give X to A but not to B, C, D, . . . N, might appear
to be acceptable under GP. But this is one of the situations
prompting the objection that the present analysis ignores distinctive aspects of equality questions. Before we can decide
whether it is right to give X to A but not to B, C, D, . . . N, we
must decide whether it would be right not to give X to B, C, D,
. . . N when one of the conditions is that we are giving X to A.
Although we have posited that it would be wrong to give X to
B, C, D, . . . N, we do not yet know whether it would be wrong
to treat B, C, D, . . . N in the proposed manner, that is, subject-
ing them to whatever effects would result from giving X to A.

This case (A.2.) is not covered by A.1.; it is an entirely different
case and an entirely different problem. But the principle employed to decide A.1. must be used to decide A.2. (and A.3.) as
well. We can decide A.2. only by asking whether it is wrong to
treat B, C, D, . . . N in this manner.

Hence: A.2. If the policy of giving X to A but not to B, C,
D, . . . N is not wrong for B, C, D, . . . N, a permissible classification has been made and it is right to give X to A.

A.2. is the paradigm case of the permissible classification, and
a great deal of governmental action falls under it.

A.3. If giving X to A but not to B, C, D, . . . N wrongs B, C,
D, . . . N, the classification is not permissible and the policy
must be abandoned. Note that it is not the mere fact that A
and B, C, D, . . . N are treated differently (unequally) that
renders X obnoxious. Or rather, there is only one sense of "unequal" in which this is true, namely that one is treated well and
the other badly. They are also treated unequally in many re-

spects under A.2., which is unobjectionable. Again, we can decide only by looking at the effects of the policy for B, C, D, . . . N.

A.2. and A.3. are common in government. A.2. allows a degree of flexibility that is essential if government is to act widely but with discrimination. And the search for A.2.'s sometimes leads to A.3.'s instead. It would be undesirable to tax those with incomes under five thousand dollars at 90 per cent, but it would also be undesirable if we were thereby prevented from taxing multimillionaires at that rate. It would be wrong to conscript men over sixty years of age, but it might be disastrous if we were thereby prevented from drafting men under twenty-six. For another illustration, consider the problem in Reynolds. Strict adherence to the equal population rule renders it impossible for cases of type A.2. to arise in the area of apportionment. Because the rule is satisfied only if everyone in the system is treated equally in this particular respect, the rule must be right for everyone or for no one.

Situation B.: If X is right for B, C, D, . . . N, A and B, C, D, . . . N are relevantly similar persons in relevantly similar circumstances, and what is right for A must be right for B, C, D, . . . N.

Hence: B.1. If X is applied to A and to B, C, D, . . . N, it does not violate GP. If Warren's argument is tenable, the equal population rule falls under this heading. Notice that this is the one and only case in which that rule is consistent with GP as it has been interpreted here.

B.2. If the policy of giving X to A but not to B, C, D, . . . N does not wrong B, C, D, . . . N, a permissible classification has been made and GP is not violated.

This is another situation that prompts an objection to the analysis. But the fact that B.2. is not fully covered by B.1. does not upset the above analysis or indicate that it cannot take account of the distinctive features of equality questions. B.2. is a different policy from B.1., and it must be evaluated independently. But nothing in the analysis prevents us from noticing and evaluating the fact that giving X to A has consequences for B, C, D, . . . N despite the fact that B, C, D, . . . N are not given X.

B.2. is perhaps the most interesting result with regard to equality. The argument is that the fact that X is right for both A and B, C, D, . . . N does not require that it be wrong to give X to A but not to B, C, D, . . . N. To prove that giving X is right is not to prove that withholding it is wrong. To show that it would be wrong to withhold X from B, C, D, . . . N while giving it to A would require a demonstration that the results of withholding X from B, C, D, . . . N, under these circumstances, would be wrong.

Consider the following hypothetical case. School districts A and B would both benefit from receiving X dollars of state aid. State resources are sufficiently great to give X to A and B without hampering other programs, but A has a large population of educationally deprived children and B does not. It would be right to give X to both A and B and to give X to A and not to B would be to treat them unequally in one important respect. But if we are right about B.2., to do the latter would not be wrong. The inequality would not lead to bad results for B and hence it would be based upon a permissible classification.

This point is at the heart of the present argument. "Equally" means "according to one and the same rule." Whenever we treat according to a rule, we will be treating equally in respect to that rule. Clearly then, the crucial question will be "according to what rule should we treat people in this case?" The principle of equality will rarely answer this question because ordinarily we must choose between equalities. If we choose to treat A and B equally in respect to educational achievement, we will treat them unequally in respect to the size of the grant awarded. This must be defended in terms of the relative importance of equal educational achievement as against equal grants of money. To dramatize the example, let us consider whether we could justify giving a larger grant to B despite the fact that B is already ahead of A in terms of educational achievement. To justify such a policy we would have to find another rule that we regard as more important than either size of grant or educational achievement. Let us say that the national defense would be served by concentrating the bulk of our resources in B. If our rule was "maximize contributions to the national defense," we could properly say that A and B had been treated equally if B received a larger grant, unequally if A and B received an identical grant. Hence one could not object to the rule on the ground that it violated the principle of equality. One could only object that the kind of equality served by the rule was less important than other kinds of equality that might have been served in the same situation. Such an objection would involve an appeal from equality to some other principle.[8]

B.3. If to refuse to give X to B, C, D, . . . N while giving it to A wrongs B, C, D, . . N, GP is violated and the policy must be abandoned.

The problem in Reynolds is instructive concerning B.2. and B.3. If B.2. would be unobjectionable under GP, the equal population rule would not be a requirement in situations of this type. It would be acceptable to follow the rule in such cases, but it would not be wrong to depart from it. If Colorado employed the equal population rule in most of its legislative districts, there would be no *prima facie* bar to departure from that rule in dealing with cases such as our hypothetical D'. Special treatment for D', regardless of how great the departure from the equal population rule, would be condemned only if it could be shown that it wronged non-D's. If, say, all non-D's, by every measure other than the equal population rule, were receiving effective representation, special treatment of D' would no more be a problem than the special treatment we accord to some people virtually every time government acts. For the rule to be a requirement, all departures from it must fall under B.3. This is the position that defenders of a strict "one-man, one-vote" rule, or any comparable egalitarian rule, must defend.

These cases, allowing for recombination among the situations and types, exhaust the logical possibilities under GP. Although they complicate the earlier analysis, none of them upsets that analysis. If correct, the analysis shows that GP, or equality, is not

[8] It has been suggested that this example strains ordinary usage; that "equally" would be used in connection with the effects of the policy on A and B, not its effects on the country at large. One response to this objection would be that the argument considers the effects of the policy on A and B in what Rousseau would call their corporate capacities. Both are members of the system; the system is affected in a particular manner; and hence both, as members, are affected in the same way. It is my view that much public policy is justified, and can only be justified, in this way. But this response concedes more than is necessary to the objection. "According to one and the same rule" is a standard meaning of "equally" and the above argument is in conformity with it. The objection that the argument strains usage could be sustained only if another interpretation of "equally" could be sustained. My suspicion is that an exchange on this point would show not that the argument strains ordinary usage of "equally" but that it departs from widespread conceptions as to which kinds of equality are most important.

a sufficient criterion of a justifiable decision. We must decide whether policies are right or wrong, good or bad; since we will rarely, if ever, be able to treat equally in one respect without treating unequally in others, to equate "right" with "equal" and "wrong" with "unequal" produces the logically absurd result that our decisions must be both right and wrong. This absurdity is avoided by using a criterion other than equality to choose between competing equalities. GP states a logical relationship between the results obtained through use of such a criterion. Hence the analysis indicates that equality is a significant normative criterion only in a *derivative* sense.

IV

The force of the foregoing analysis is primarily negative. It seeks to demonstrate that equality or equal treatment is a derivative criterion inadequate for determining rightness or wrongness. Attempts to elevate it to the status of a sufficient standard involve logical errors that could readily lead to unsatisfactory decisions. The question of how rightness and wrongness are *properly* determined, of how we decide whether X is right for A, is too large for adequate discussion here; but the previous analysis has implications for that question, which we will explore briefly.

We emphasized the difficulties stemming from the fact that equality, as ordinarily understood, is concerned with comparative questions. Such questions are derivative in status and significance. But the argument that led to this conclusion included a more fundamental point, one that has application beyond equality questions. In arguing that substantive (as opposed to formal or neutral as above) egalitarian rules deal with derivative considerations, we suggested that such rules cover only one of many relationships relevant to or created by policies implementing those rules. Our immediate attack was upon the concern with a certain kind of relationship, which, it was suggested, should be replaced by concern with the consequences of treating a person or class of persons in a certain manner. But relationships with which egalitarian rules are concerned are sometimes a consequence of and are almost always affected by the adoption of a policy implementing such a rule. The argument, then, that the rightness of X for A can be determined only by examination of consequences is, in a more basic sense, an argument that egalitarian rules are concerned with an overly narrow range of the consequences of X for A. The equal population rule, for example, establishes, in advance of the application of the policy, not only the criterion of rightness that districting policy must meet but also the aspects of the policy that will be relevant to determining its rightness. A considerable range of the consequences of the policy are classed as irrelevant for purposes of evaluation.[9]

Against the narrowing effect of concern with equality, we suggest the need for a broader, indeed an—in principle—unrestricted, definition of the range of consequences potentially relevant to the evaluation. In morals and in law our primary purpose is to discover whether those affected by our actions and policies are treated well or badly by them. Because our actions and policies have a great variety of effects, any one or all of which might be morally or legally significant, it is dangerous to rule out the possibility that any one of those effects might be crucial for our evaluation.

These considerations suggest that the most general and perhaps the primary principle of moral and legal evaluation would be along the lines, "consider the consequences." Conveniently, Singer has developed a more sophisticated formulation of such a utilitarian principle. He calls it the Principle of Consequences (hereafter, PC).[10] The principle has both a negative and a positive formulation. The negative version reads, "If the consequences of A's doing X are undesirable, A ought not to do X." The positive formulation reads, "If the consequences of A's not doing X are undesirable, then A ought to do X." These two versions result in moral imperatives. There is also a non-imperative version (which Singer rejects as invalid). "If the consequences of A's doing X are desirable, then it would be good if A did X." Since the fact that an action would be morally desirable or good is not in and of itself sufficient to generate an imperative to do that action (other actions might be as good or better) the last formulation would be invalid if it concluded

---

[9] Once again, this might be a defensible *conclusion* in the Reynolds case or in related types of moral and political decisions. But it is not defensible as an assumption used in the making of such decisions.

[10] Singer, *op. cit.*, pp. 63–67.

that "A ought to do X." But if PC in general is valid, there are no difficulties with the non-imperative version, and it is of considerable importance to public policy.

The strength of PC in the present context, and the only defense that will be offered for it here,[11] is that it provides a standardized statement of some of the findings of the foregoing analysis. As with GP, it is a formal principle. It has no force in any concrete case until the particular premise of the form, "the consequences of this X for this A are desirable," has been established, and the principle itself does not aid us in establishing that premise. But the principle does direct our attention to the most fundamental considerations in any moral decision (including legal decisions with moral dimensions). Before we adopt the equal population rule, or any substantive moral or legal rule, we must test the results of the use of that rule against the requirements of PC. If they fail that test, we search for a more satisfactory rule. The equal population rule, or any other substantive moral or legal rule, will be viewed as a secondary rule useful as a guide in establishing the particular premise of PC. But if a rule fails to satisfy the requirements of PC, if it leads to undesirable consequences in a specific case, it will be abandoned or modified as a rule for that case. If a rule regularly leads to undesirable consequences, it will be abandoned entirely.[12]

With PC available, we can state earlier arguments concerning equality in a more standardized manner. GP states a logical relationship between the conclusions reached through two or more applications of PC. We determine whether X is right for A under PC, and whether it is right for B, C, D, . . . N under PC. If it is right for each, the particular premises of GP are estab-

---

[11] Singer discusses a number of the issues that arise in connection with PC. See *ibid.*, per Index. I have examined the principle in detail in my recent work, *The Public Interest*, New York: John Wiley, 1966, Chapter 8.

[12] Cf. H. L. A. Hart's notion of "defeasibility." See his "The Ascription of Responsibility and Rights," in Antony Flew (Ed.), *Logic and Language*, First Series, Oxford: Basil Blackwell, 1963. In minimizing equality and other formalist or deontological rules and considerations, the foregoing argument involves a condensed version of act-utilitarianism. There are a number of standard objections to this position, the most relevant here being that the logic of the position eliminates all moral and legal rules and requires that decisions be made exclusively on their individual merits. Hart's discussion of defeasibility rebuts important aspects of this objection, and I have discussed the objection at length in *The Public Interest, op. cit.*

lished and what is right for A is right for B, C, D, . . . N. If not, the second premise is not established. From a moral or legal standpoint, then, GP reduces to "Don't treat people in a manner that violates PC."

If this argument is correct, the formal principle of GP is not subject to the limitations noted in connection with substantive egalitarian rules such as the equal population rule. But the argument might also suggest that GP is trivial. GP has no moral force until PC has been applied, and hence it might appear that it can teach us nothing that we cannot better learn under PC. This inference is unwarranted. If I say that X is red, I do so in virtue of certain properties of X. When I do so, I commit myself to saying that any other object that has the same properties is red. If Y has all the properties that led me to say that X is red, I must say that Y is red as well (or retract my statement concerning X). To deny that Y is red is to contradict myself. There is a logical relationship between the statements "X is red" and "Y is red."

GP states the same logical relationship between two (or more) moral judgments as obtains between "X is red" and "Y is red." The first particular premise of GP is of the form: "This X is right for this A." We establish this premise by applying PC. We say "X is right (or wrong) for A by virtue of the desirability (undesirability) of the consequences of X for A." The second particular premise is established in the same manner. We determine the relevant similarity of A and B by examining the consequences of X for B. Having applied PC, we say "X is right (or wrong) for B by virtue of the desirability (undesirability) of the consequences of X for B." Between the two particular premises of GP stands "must be." "Must be" has the same status as the logical rule that requires us to say "Y is red" if Y has the same properties that led us to say "X is red." GP states a logical relationship between the conclusions reached through two (or more) applications of PC. A logical relationship between two conclusions is not the same thing as the two conclusions themselves, and GP is not the same as two (or more) applications of PC.

Hence GP does not inform us concerning the moral status of any action. But it does not follow that GP lacks utility in discourse concerning morals and politics. If X has properties (P) such that we call it red, and if Y has P, we do not need a rule of logic to tell us that Y is red. When we see that Y has properties P we say that Y is red simply because it has the properties by virtue of which we apply the word "red." But in morals and politics matters are more complicated. To say that X is right for A by virtue of its having desirable consequences is not merely to describe X. It is also to evaluate or commend X. We commend in order to guide conduct, to convince people, including ourselves, to act in a manner that might be contrary to our inclinations. To say "X is right for A because P" is not simply to describe X; it is to say that A ought to do X. And hence, under the logical rule of GP, it is to say that every A ought to do X. If I say "Jones ought to give $1000 to charity because P" and if my giving $1000 to charity produces P, then I must give $1000 (or retract my statement concerning Jones). But giving $1000 to charity is apt to conflict with my inclinations in a manner that saying "Y is red" is not likely to do. I am apt to want to say that giving $1000 to charity is not right for me. But GP provides a logical principle, neutral to the moral question, that can discipline my thinking in a salutary manner. "Didn't you say Jones ought to give $1000 to charity?" "Yes." "How does his case differ from yours?" If I am unable to show a relevant difference, if I am unable to show that for A to do X produces P, whereas for me to do X produces Q, then it will be inconsistent for me to refuse to do X. Hence although I do not share Hare's lofty estimate of the significance of GP (he calls it the universalizability principle) for moral discourse, I do not see how it can be regarded as trivial.[13] Because GP is a formalized statement of the principle of equality, the same conclusion applies to that principle.

V

Our conclusion concerning equality runs counter to a pervasive and influential strand in Western thought. The primary justifications for the conclusion are those presented in

[13] R. M. Hare has developed these points in great detail in his two books on ethics: *Language of Morals*, Oxford: Oxford University Press, 1952; *Freedom and Reason*, Oxford: Oxford University Press, 1963. But Hare makes no explicit use of PC or any equivalent principle, and this leads to serious difficulties. See especially his discussion of "fanatics" in *Freedom and Reason*.

the course of the analysis, but it will be useful to deal more explicitly with some of the basic contentions with which the present conclusions conflict.[14] Conveniently, some of these have been restated in recent papers by William Frankena and Gregory Vlastos.[15] Consideration of these arguments will lead to the question mentioned earlier: whether, despite the foregoing analysis, a substantive moral principle lurks beneath the logical rule to which we have reduced GP and equality.

Both Frankena and Vlastos contend that an aspect of treating men well is to treat them equally in a non-derivative sense. In Frankena's words, "all men are to be treated as equals, not because they are equal in any respect, but simply because they are human."[16] Equal treatment in this fundamental sense is regarded as an irreducible value that depends in no way upon utilitarian considerations. Both writers concede that very dissimilar treatment is often consistent with, indeed demanded by, recognition of equal worth, and that in most cases relevant equalities are to be identified by reference to good treatment. But they insist that there are actions or policies that would be unjustified solely because they are inconsistent with "recognition of the equality or equal intrinsic value of every human person-

[14] It should be noted that the "egalitarian tradition" is anything but well defined. For recent attempts to sort out some of the important strands in the tradition, see the papers by Richard Wollheim and Sir Isaiah Berlin in Frederick Olafson (Ed.), *Justice and Social Policy*, Englewood Cliffs, N.J.: Prentice-Hall, 1961. See also S. I. Benn and R. S. Peters, *Social Principles and the Democratic State*, Chapter 5, London: George Allen and Unwin, 1959. For a general historical survey, see Sanford A. Lakoff, *Equality in Political Philosophy*, Cambridge: Harvard University Press, 1964. Berlin and Benn and Peters make a number of arguments closely akin to those presented above.

[15] See Richard Brandt (Ed.), *Social Justice*, Englewood Cliffs, N.J.: Prentice-Hall, 1962. These papers are concerned with questions of justice and rights, and there is some suggestion in them that these questions are regarded as distinct from those of rightness and wrongness, goodness and badness, which are discussed here. (This suggestion has been made more strongly by H. L. A. Hart in another symposium related to present concerns. See the papers of Hart, Frankena, and Stuart M. Brown, Jr. in *Philosophical Review*, Vol. 64, No. 2 [April, 1955], pp. 1ff.) The present writer is not convinced that there is a radical distinction between the logics of these different concepts. It is impossible to enter into the question here, but it may be that some of the disagreements between the aforementioned papers and the present one are to be explained in this way.

[16] Brandt, *op. cit.*, p. 19.

ality."[17] One of Vlastos' examples is that cruel treatment, even of a cruel man, is always unjustified because it singles the man out for treatment contrary to a moral rule based not on any merits distinctive of the man but on recognition of human equality, on the man's "birthright as a human being." In such cases, if their analysis is correct, good treatment would be derivative of equal treatment rather than the reverse.[18] If I understand them correctly, it is only in respect to such cases that their position is at odds with that argued here.

As suggested by the phrase "equal intrinsic value of every human personality," Frankena and Vlastos are arguing against meritarian justifications for certain kinds of unequal treatment. Now if "intrinsic value" is to provide a meaningful ground for moral judgments, it must be identified sufficiently to allow us to know what it will support and when it has been disregarded or violated.[19] The task of identifying it has proved to be a difficult one, productive of considerable controversy.[20] However defined, respect for intrinsic value might require, in particular situations,

---

[17] *Ibid.*, p. 14.

[18] The non-derivative, irreducible status of "all men are to be treated as equals" suggests that this imperative is unanalyzable. In this respect the argument is deontological or formalistic in character and it raises the problems associated with deontological positions generally, particularly the problem of how one could defend or justify the imperative or action taken in accord with it.

[19] Cf. Benn and Peters, *op. cit.*, especially p. 109. See also R. M. Hare, *Freedom and Reason,* especially pp. 211–213.

[20] Frankena identifies it as follows: "I accepted as part of my own view the principle that all men are to be treated as equals, not because they are equal in any respect but simply because they are human. They are human because they have emotions and desires, and are able to think, and hence are capable of enjoying a good life in a sense in which other animals are not. They are human because their lives may be 'significant' in the manner which William James made so graphic . . . : 'Wherever a process of life communicates an eagerness to him who lives it, there the life becomes genuinely significant. Sometimes the eagerness is more knit up with the motor activities, sometimes with the perceptions, sometimes with the imagination, sometimes with reflective thought. But wherever it is found . . . there *is* importance in the only real and positive sense in which importance anywhere can be.' By the good life is meant not so much the morally good life as the happy or satisfactory life. As I see it, it is the fact that all men are similarly capable of enjoying a good life in this sense that justifies the *prima facie* requirement that they be treated as equals." Brandt, *op. cit.*, p. 19. For Vlastos' statement see *ibid.*, pp. 47–52. See also the related arguments of H. L. A. Hart, *loc. cit.*

that one person's intrinsic value be served, another's not served at all or disserved. If (a) the intrinsic value of one man differs in its manifestations from that of others, its manifestation as a specific need, interest, or demand might conflict with the needs, interests, and demands of others. Even if (b) the intrinsic worth of all men is the same in nature and manifestation, scarcity of resources, administrative difficulties, human shortcomings, and the like might make it impossible to serve all men equally. In the case of either (a) or (b), if a decision must be made, the decision-maker will require a principle that will allow him to justify serving the intrinsic value of one person or set of persons over the intrinsic value of others. By hypothesis, equality of intrinsic value cannot provide that principle. This is the main reason that equal rights for which equal worth provides the ground[21] are *prima facie* rights, the claim to which can be defeated in particular circumstances.[22]

The doctrine of equal intrinsic value, then, can provide a basis for moral and political decisions and policy only if the various manifestations of value are self-regarding in significance or if there is a harmony between them such that all can be served equally well. I am not prepared to deny the possibility of such cases. But moral and political questions arise primarily where other-regarding behavior and conflicts of needs, interests, and demands are present. In such cases the doctrine of equal intrinsic value cannot provide a basis for decision. To assert that particular decisions of this kind are justified because they serve equality is to assert that one kind of equality is preferable to other kinds of equality that might have been served in the same situation. If the foregoing analysis is correct, the more fundamental principle is: "Treat people well as demanded by PC."

This conclusion leads to a final problem. Assuming that the present argument is correct and that equal treatment (GP) must be interpreted through good or right treatment (PC), it nevertheless appears that GP commits us to treating everyone equally in the sense of equally well. Hence it might appear that a sub-

---

[21] See Vlastos, *op. cit.*, pp. 50–52.

[22] See especially Frankena's paper in the symposium cited above, pp. 227–232 and *passim*. See also the very important note 44 on p. 52 of Vlastos' paper.

stantive moral principle underlies GP even as it has been interpreted here.

We want to treat people equally in the sense of equally well. To determine whether we are treating people well, we examine the consequences of policies and actions and evaluate them in terms of moral standards. Satisfaction of the standard or standards selected in any case will often require treating people dissimilarly in respect to standards that have been rejected in the case in question. If we institute selective conscription, we might draft all healthy, unmarried men between the ages of eighteen and twenty-six on the grounds that such a classification best serves the standard, "Maintain national security." If we draft all those who fall into the class, and none who do not, we will be treating the citizenry equally in terms of that standard. But our policy might produce inequalities in terms of other standards. Draftee A is in the throes of a passionate love affair, the interruption of which causes him enormous psychic distress; Draftee B, on the other hand, is bored with his life and finds military service a welcome relief. Drafting them both creates inequality in terms of the standard "minimize psychic distress." We justify this inequality by arguing that the national security requires it and that in the circumstances the rule "maintain national security" is more important than the rule "minimize psychic distress." But if the national security is our standard, we cannot justify treating A differently from B in terms of that standard. If the consequences of drafting A and B were the same with regard to service of the national security, we could not exempt A on grounds of his love affair. We must treat everyone equally in the sense that we must apply our standards *impartially* to all. To defer A but draft B under the posited conditions would be to give preference to A in a manner that could not be justified in terms of the standard.

The last phrase, together with a notion of impartiality, is the key to the significance of the notion that we must treat people equally well. We attempt to decide how to treat people by looking at the consequences of different policies for them and evaluating those policies in the light of standards that we can defend. Because men are extraordinarily diverse in person and circumstance, adhering to our standards often requires that men be treated very differently. But we treat men differently because we have good reasons for doing so, namely that treating well according to the best standards that we can construct requires that we do so. Where no such reason can be offered, it would be impossible to defend or justify unequal treatment. In such cases we describe differences in treatment as based on partiality or bias. The question then becomes: "Why are we opposed to partiality and bias?"

Vlastos and Frankena contend that our opposition stems from a sense of the equal intrinsic value of all men. Granting that we have or should have such a "sense," for the reasons noted this position will rarely if ever help us to reach and defend a decision. A second position is suggested by Hare, who argues that the requirement of generalization (universalization) is a purely logical requirement and that departure from it is a logical mistake.[23] On this view we are against partiality and bias because they lead to violations of the logical rule that it is inconsistent to treat unlike cases alike and like cases unalike. We are against violations of the rules of logic. But in the moral realm violation of these rules coincides with violation of the moral rule PC. And we are against violations of PC because we are in favor of treating people well and against treating them badly. Treating them unequally in the sense identified by violations of GP will be to treat them badly, and hence we are against it for moral as well as logical reasons. It is because partiality and bias are productive of such results that we are right in objecting to them. Hence there is a respect in which unequal treatment is morally wrong, but it is derivative in the sense argued throughout the paper.

[23] See R. M. Hare, *op. cit.*, especially pp. 10–13 and 30–35.

4

EGALITARIANISM AND THE EQUAL CONSIDERATION OF INTERESTS

STANLEY I. BENN

Egalitarians persist in speaking of human equality, as a principle significant for action, in the face of all the evident human inequalities of stature, physique, intellect, virtue, merit, and desert. Claims pressed so tenaciously, in the face of seemingly manifest and overwhelming objections, can hardly be summarily dismissed as naive absurdities. The task for the philosopher is to look for ways of construing such claims, consistent with the evident inequalities, compatible with commonly accepted conceptions of justice, yet still with bite enough to make a difference to behavior worth contending for. I shall argue that in many contexts the claim to human equality is no more than a negative egalitarianism, a denial, a limited criticism of some specific

61

existing arrangements. If one were to interpret such claims as implying a universal positive assertion about human rights and social organization, one would be going beyond what was necessary to make good sense of them. But because such a negative interpretation does not seem to exhaust the possibilities of egalitarianism, I shall formulate a principle that, while satisfying the aforementioned criteria, can still be applied quite generally, and can be properly expressed in the formula "all men are equal." This is the *principle of equal consideration of human interests*. I shall further maintain that this principle is required by current conceptions of social justice. It can be effective in public policy-making, however, only to the extent that agreement can be reached on the proper order of priority of human interests.

I

Things or persons can be equal in several different ways. In one sense equality presupposes an ordering of objects according to some common natural property or attribute that can be possessed in varying degrees. So, although objects said to be equal occupy interchangeable places in such an ordering, their equality in this respect is necessarily implied neither by their possessing this property in common nor by their common membership of a larger class of which all members possess the property. Although two cabbages happen, for instance, to be of equal weight, their equality is not a necessary feature of their both being cabbages, even though every cabbage has weight. In this sense at least, not all cabbages are equal. Things can be equal in a second sense according to some standard of value or merit. Two students' essays may be equally good, though their properties may differ, one being detailed and painstaking, the other original and imaginative. Here, differences in their properties are weighed against one another in assessing their relative merit; however, in a final ordering of all essays, in which some stand high and others low, these two occupy interchangeable places. Here, again, their equality is not a necessary feature of their both being essays. A third kind of equality is that of need, entitlement, or desert; the remuneration to which a man is entitled for his

work or the dose of medicine he needs for his cough may be
equal to another's, though it could conceivably have been different without prejudice to their common status as workers or
sick men.

These three ways of ascribing equality—descriptive, evaluative,
and distributive—are not of course independent of one another.
There may be a logical connection: two knives, equally sharp,
equally well-tempered, possessing indeed all relevant properties
in the same degree, are equally good knives, sharpness, temper,
and the like, being the criteria of a good knife.[1] However, the
equal merit of the students' essays does not follow necessarily
from a list of their properties but depends on a complex
appraisal in the light of multiple standards. Different again is
the case of two men entitled to equal pay for doing equal
amounts of work. In this case, their equality depends on a
particular convention; according to a different practice, if one
man worked longer than the other, their deserts would be different, even though the results might be the same. In all these
instances, however, though the possibility of comparison depends
on the subjects being members of the same class, it is not a
necessary condition of their membership that they possess the
property by virtue of which they are equals in the precise degree
that they do. Mere membership of the same class does not entail,
therefore, that the subjects are equals in any of the three senses
discussed. Consequently, although two members of a class happen
to qualify for equal treatment, this is not a necessary result of
their common membership.

To say, then, that two things are in some respect equal is to
say that they are, in that and perhaps related respects, interchangeable—that no rational ground exists for treating them in
those respects differently from each other. Egalitarians would
maintain, however, that the reason for considering them equal
need not always be that they satisfy some qualifying condition
to the same degree; it may be because, with regard to some
manner of treating them, the qualifying condition does not admit
of degrees; it may be enough simply to possess the properties
necessary to make them members of that class. There may then

---

[1] The phrase "possessing all relevant properties to the same degree"
guarantees the tautology, of course, by exhausting all the possible criteria.

be something to which all members of a class have an equal claim, in the sense that none has a better claim than another, nor could have, given their common membership. If, for instance, all sane adults have the right to vote, and there are no other qualifying (or disqualifying) conditions, no qualified member of the class of sane adults has any better right than another, nor has any member a right to any more votes than another, by virtue of some further property that they possess in varying degrees. All qualified voters, qua voters, are equal.

II

Those who demand social equality do not necessarily take universal adult equal suffrage as a paradigm for all social institutions and practices. There may be egalitarians for whom a society without differences is both a possibility and an ideal; most, however, have more limited aims. When egalitarianism is translated into concrete political programs, it usually amounts to a proposal to abandon existing inequalities, rather than to adopt some positive principle of social justice. The egalitarian in politics usually has quite specific objectives and is critical of quite specific kinds of differentiation rather than of every kind of social discrimination. Indeed, differences are rarely called "inequalities" unless, in the first place, they affect the things which men value and for which they compete, like power, wealth, or esteem. One complains of inequality if one has to pay more tax than another man but not if, for some administrative reason, the demands arrive in differently colored envelopes. Egalitarians protest when, in the second place, they see no rational justification for differentiating a particular class for the purpose of allocating certain specific privileges or burdens. The campaign for equal pay for women is a case in point. To treat people according to their skill or productivity would not be to discriminate between the sexes, even though some women might in fact receive less than some men (or, conceivably, all women less than all men), for skill and productivity are generally recognized as relevant and legitimate criteria. Sex differentiation as such is intolerable because, it is argued, no one has yet shown good enough reasons for thinking a person's sex relevant to the income he should earn—and the burden of proof rests on the discriminator. On the other hand, discrimination according to sex for military service has been generally accepted without much question and is usually considered well-grounded; so it is rarely called an inequality.

A race, sex, religious, or class egalitarianism denies the justice, then, of some existing modes of discrimination, possibly in a relatively limited range of social practices; it does not press for the removal of all forms of differentiation. Or it may endorse existing grounds of discrimination but question whether they ought to make as much difference as they do. Of course, the conditions under attack, and the related forms of differentiation not under attack, may be contextually supplied and not explicitly stated; nevertheless, they may be perfectly well understood by all parties to the debate.[2]

III

Although most movements for equality can be interpreted in terms of protests against specific inequalities, a strong disposition nonetheless exists, among philosophers and others, to argue that whatever men's actual differences and whatever their genuine relevance for certain kinds of differentiation, there yet remain important values in respect of which all men's claims are equal. Whatever these may be—and catalogs of natural and human rights are attempts to formulate them—they are such that no difference in properties between one man and another could affect them; all men qualify simply by virtue of belonging to the class *man*, which admits of no degrees (just as, in my earlier example, all voters are equally qualified provided they are sane adults). This certainly looks like a positive and quite general claim to equality rather than a denial of specific irrelevant inequalities.

In a recent article, "Against Equality,"[3] J. R. Lucas contends that egalitarianism rests on a confusion of two principles, each

[2] A favorite way of discrediting the egalitarian, however, is to make it appear that he seeks to remove forms of discrimination that neither he, nor anyone else, would for a moment question. Though the Levellers were concerned only for equal political rights, for removing monopolistic privileges in trade, and for legal reforms, they were frequently accused, despite vigorous disclaimers, of wanting to level property.

[3] *Philosophy,* Vol. XL (1965), pp. 296–307.

sound in itself but which, if pressed, together lead to incompatible conclusions. One, the principle of formal equality, is the familiar principle underlying all forms of what I have called negative egalitarianism: if two people are to be treated differently there should be some relevant difference between them. Lucas does not regard this as really an egalitarian principle at all, because in itself it prescribes neither equality nor inequality, but, taking it for granted that there might be good reasons for treating men differently in some respects, it lays down the form that a justificatory argument must take. The other principle, that Lucas calls the principle of universal humanity, makes this assertion:

> men, because they are men, ought not to be killed, tortured, imprisoned, exploited, frustrated, humiliated; . . . they should never be treated merely as means but always as ends in themselves. . . . We should treat human beings, because they are human beings, humanely.

But this, he says, has little to do with equality:

> To say that all men, because they are men, are equally men, or that to treat any two persons as ends in themselves is to treat them as equally ends in themselves is to import a spurious note of egalitarianism into a perfectly sound and serious argument. We may call it, if we like, the argument for Equality of Respect, but in this phrase it is the word "Respect"—respect for each man's humanity, respect for him as a human being—which is doing the logical work, while the word "Equality" adds nothing to the argument and is altogether otiose.[4]

I suspect that Lucas has dealt too shortly with positive egalitarianism, in representing it simply as rules about how we ought to behave in relation to objects or persons of a given class. He is perfectly right in saying, for instance, that the duty not to inflict torture has nothing to do with equality, but then, it is not a duty in respect of human beings alone but also of animals. This is not a duty we *owe* to men as men, for it is doubtful whether, properly speaking, we *owe* it to the object at all. In-

---

[4] *Ibid.*, p. 298.

flicting needless pain is simply wrong; it would not be a case of unequal treatment, but simply of cruelty. It would be a case lacking altogether the characteristic feature that makes inequality objectionable—namely, unfairness or injustice.

But some of Lucas' examples of inhumanity do seem to have more to do with equality than that. In particular, the injunction to respect all men, simply as men or as ends in themselves, unlike the injunction not to torture them, involves recognizing them as subjects of claims, and not merely as objects, albeit objects that ought to be handled in one way rather than another. To treat a man not as an end but simply as a means is to give no consideration to his interests, but to consider him only insofar as he can promote or frustrate the interests of someone else—to treat him, in short, like Aristotle's "natural slave," with no end not derived from that of a master. Now to adopt such an attitude can be said to be not merely wrong (as is cruelty), but wrong in the special way that it disregards a fundamental equality of *claim*—the claim to have one's interests considered alongside those of everyone else likely to be affected by the decision.

Now this *principle of equal consideration of interests* seems to me to involve an assertion of equality that is neither purely formal nor otiose. It *resembles,* it is true, another principle, which is deducible from the principle of formal equality—therefore itself formal—and which is often called the principle of equal consideration. The principle of formal equality states that where there is no relevant difference between two cases, no rational ground exists for not treating them alike; but, conversely, where there is a relevant difference, there is a reasonable ground for treating them differently. This involves, as a corollary, that equal consideration must be given to the relevant features of each, for to have good reasons for favoring one person or course of action rather than another surely implies that there are no conclusively better reasons on the other side; and how could one know that, without having given them equal consideration?[5]

[5] See S. I. Benn and R. S. Peters, *Social Principles and the Democratic State,* London, 1959 (reissued as *Principles of Political Thought,* New York, 1964 and 1965), Chapter V, for a fuller discussion of the formal principle of equal consideration.

This is certainly, then, a purely formal or procedural principle, for it offers no criterion for good reasons nor makes any substantive recommendation for action. The principle of equal consideration of interests, on the other hand, is specific at least to the extent that it directs consideration to the *interests* of those affected, and so lays down, as the other principle does not, a criterion of relevance. After all, if I preferred A to B because A could be of more use to me, I should still be acting consistently with the formal principle of equal consideration, provided I had first considered how useful to me B could be. But this would not be consistent with the equal consideration of interests, for I would have given thought to the interests of neither A nor B, but only to my own.

If the principle is not purely formal, neither is it otiose. For it would be perfectly possible to consider the interests of everyone affected by a decision without giving them *equal* consideration. Elitist moralities are precisely of this kind. Although the elitist would allow that ordinary men have interests deserving some consideration, the interests of the super-man, super-class, or super-race would always be preferred. Some men, it might be said, are simply worth more than others, in the sense that any claim of theirs, whatever it might be and whatever its specific ground, would always take precedence. Such a morality would maintain that there was some criterion, some qualifying condition, of race, sex, intellect, or personality, such that a person once recognized as satisfying it would automatically have prior claim in every field over others.

The egalitarian would deny that there is any such criterion. Whatever priority special circumstances or properties confer on a man in particular fields, no one of them, neither a white skin, male sex, Aryan ancestry, noble birth, nor any other whatsoever, would entitle a man to move to the head of *every* queue. That is not to imply that any man can always claim the same treatment as any other, nor, indeed, that one man's interest could never have priority over another's, as, for instance, when we tax the rich to assist the poor. But every claim must be grounded on criteria specifically appropriate to it, and every demand for privilege must be argued afresh, since arguments valid in one field have no necessary consequential validity in others. This, I think, is the claim fundamental to the idea of social equality or equality of esteem. It is related to the claim to self-respect, which J. C. Davies has put in these words: "I am as good as anybody else; I may not be as clever or hard-working as you are, but I am as good as you are."[6] It bears also on the concept of equality of respect. No one could respect all men equally; nor does it seem likely, leaving aside the differences in respect we have for men on account of their different virtues and merits, that there is still a residual respect we owe to each merely as a man. What is there to respect in what alone is common to all men—membership of this particular biological species? It makes perfectly good sense, however, to say that, whereas we respect different men for different things, there is no property, such as a white skin, which is a necessary condition of a man's being worthy, whatever his other merits, of any respect at all. So every man is entitled to be taken on his own merits; there is no generally disqualifying condition.

That this is not mere empty formalism is clear when we contrast the case of men with that of animals. For not to possess human shape *is* a disqualifying condition. However faithful or intelligent a dog may be, it would be a monstrous sentimentality to attribute to him interests that could be weighed in an equal balance with those of human beings. The duties we have in respect to dogs would generally be discounted when they conflict with our duties to human beings—discounted, not set aside, for we might well decide to waive a minor obligation to a human being rather than cause intense suffering to an animal. But if the duties were at all commensurate, if, for instance, one had to decide between feeding a hungry baby or a hungry dog, anyone who chose the dog would generally be reckoned morally defective, unable to recognize a fundamental inequality of claims.

This is what distinguishes our attitude to animals from our attitude to imbeciles. It would be odd to say that we ought to respect equally the dignity or personality of the imbecile and of the rational man; it is questionable indeed whether one can treat with respect someone for whom one's principal feeling is pity. But there is nothing odd about saying that we should respect

[6] *Human Nature in Politics*, New York, 1963, p. 45.

their interests equally, that is, that we should give to the interests of each the same serious consideration as claims to conditions necessary for some standard of well-being that we can recognize and endorse.[7]

The imbecile has been something of an embarrassment to moral philosophers.[8] There is a traditional view, going back to the Stoics, that makes rationality the qualifying condition on which human freedom and equality depend. But if equal consideration of interests depended on rationality, imbeciles would belong to an inferior species, whose interests (if they could properly be allowed to have interests) would always have to be discounted when they competed with those of rational men. What reason could then be offered against using them like dogs or guinea pigs for, say, medical research? But, of course, we do distinguish imbeciles from animals in this regard, and although it would be quite proper to discriminate between imbeciles and rational men for very many purposes, most rationalist philosophers would concede that it would be grossly indecent to subordinate the interests of an imbecile to those of normal persons for *all* purposes, simply on the ground of his imbecility.

Nevertheless, the link between rationality and our moral concern for human interests cannot be disregarded. If the human species is more important to us than other species, with interests worthy of special consideration, each man's for his own sake, this is possibly because each of us sees in other men the image of himself. So he recognizes in them what he knows in his own experience, the potentialities for moral freedom, for making responsible choices among ways of life open to him, for striving, no matter how mistakenly and unsuccessfully, to make of himself something worthy of his own respect. It is because this is the characteristically human enterprise, requiring a capacity for self-

---

[7] I do not argue for this conception of interests in this paper, except by implication. I have done so explicitly, however, in " 'Interests' in Politics," *Aristotelian Society Proceedings,* Vol. LX (1959–1960), pp. 123–140.

[8] For example, Bernard Williams, "I omit here, as throughout the discussion, the clinical cases of people who are mad or mentally defective, who always constitute special exceptions to what is in general true of men." "The Idea of Equality," in P. Laslett and W. G. Runciman, Eds., *Philosophy, Politics and Society,* Oxford, 1962, p. 118.

appraisal and criticism normal to men but not to dogs, that it seems reasonable to treat men as more important than dogs.[9]

Still, we respect the interests of men and give them priority over dogs not *insofar* as they are rational, but because rationality is the human norm. We say it is *unfair* to exploit the deficiencies of the imbecile, who falls short of the norm, just as it would be unfair, and not just ordinarily dishonest, to steal from a blind man. If we do not think in this way about dogs, it is because we do not see the irrationality of a dog as a deficiency or a handicap but as normal for the species. The characteristics, therefore, that distinguish the normal man from the normal dog make it intelligible for us to talk of other men as having interests and capacities, and therefore claims, of precisely the same kind as we make on our own behalf. But although these characteristics may provide the point of the distinction between men and other species, they are not in fact the qualifying conditions for membership, or the distinguishing criteria of the class of morally considerable persons; and this is precisely because a man does not become a member of a different species, with its own standards of normality, by reason of not possessing these characteristics. On the other hand, the deficiency is more than an accidental fact, for it has a bearing on his moral status. For if someone is deficient in this way, he is falling short of what, in some sense, he *ought* to have been, given the species to which by nature he belongs; it is, indeed, to be deprived of the possibility of fully realizing his nature. So where the mental limitations of the dog can be amusing, without lapse of taste, those of an imbecile are tragic and appalling. Moreover, so far from being a reason for disregarding his interests, they may be grounds for special compensatory consideration, to meet a special need.

IV

I said earlier that an egalitarian would deny that any property could confer an automatic general priority of claim on

[9] If we were able to establish communication with another species— dolphins, for instance—and found that they too were engaged in this "characteristically human enterprise," I think we should find ourselves thinking of them as a fishy variety of human being, making much the same claim on our consideration.

anyone possessing it, but that this need not preclude one man's interests having priority over others' in certain respects. I want to enlarge on this point and in doing so to compare the principle of equal consideration of interests with John Rawls' account of justice as fairness.[10]

Rawls asserts that "inequalities are arbitrary unless it is reasonable to expect that they will work out for everyone's advantage, and provided the positions and offices to which they attach . . . are open to all." He then seeks to show that only a practice that satisfied these conditions could be accepted by free, equal, rational, and prudent participants in it, given that they knew their own interests and that each ran the risk of filling the least favored roles. Rawls' model appears to derive justice from consent. However, what really counts is not what a man would actually accept but what, understanding his interests, he could reasonably accept. Thus objections to a practice based purely on envy of a privileged position would not be admissible, because avoiding the pangs of envy would not be an interest of a rational, prudent man. Rawls' model looks like a way of saying that a practice is just if it sacrifices no one's interest to anyone else's and makes only such distinctions as would promote the interests of everyone, given that the interests are not simply desires but conditions of well-being that rational men could endorse as such. This in turn looks rather like the egalitarian principle of equal consideration of interests. There are, however, difficulties in trying to equate the two accounts.

Rawls' model suggests an adequate schema for justifying discrimination in terms of desert or merit (the traditional problems of justice) ; it can be fitted, however, to modern conceptions of social justice, only at the cost of so abstracting from reality that the model loses most of its suggestiveness.[11] These conceptions are characteristically compensatory and distributive; they are implicit in the institutions and policies of welfare states, which

[10] John Rawls, "Justice as Fairness," in P. Laslett and W. G. Runciman, op. cit., pp. 132–157; and "Constitutional Liberty and the Concept of Justice," in Carl J. Friedrich and John W. Chapman, Eds., Justice, Nomos VI, New York, 1963, pp. 98–125.

[11] Cf. John Chapman's point that, admitting the justice of Rawls' strictures on utilitarianism, the latter has this merit, as against the contractualist theories of justice, that it can take account of need. "Justice and Fairness" in Justice, op. cit., pp. 147–169.

provide for the needs of the handicapped by taxing the more fortunate. At first glance, at least, Rawls' principles of justice would give wealthy but sterile people who are taxed to help educate the children of poor but fertile people legitimate grounds for complaint, as victims of a discriminatory practice that imposes sacrifices without corresponding advantages.

It could be argued, perhaps, that Rawls meets the case by presupposing in his model that all participants start equal, and that all roles are interchangeable. The restrictions that the community's practices would put on individual interests, or the sacrifices that would be accepted by some for the benefit of others, would then be such as "a person would keep in mind if he were designing a practice in which his enemy were to assign him his place." Rawls may argue that it is always prudent for the fortunate to insure against misfortune; it would be reasonable, in that case, for a man to consent to a tax for someone else's advantage, if there were a risk of his finding himself in that person's place. But which of all the features of a man's situation, character, talents, and incapacities, by which he could be at a disadvantage, are to be taken as intrinsic and irremediable, and which conjecturally subject to reallocation, as part of the "place" to which his enemy might assign him? Need the normal, healthy person really reckon with the risk of being called upon to fill the role of the congenitally handicapped? Similar questions can be asked of some socially conferred disadvantages. While the rich must, perhaps, take account of the risk of poverty, need a white man take seriously the risk of having to fill the role of a colored man in a racially prejudiced society? To meet these arguments, Rawls would need to postulate as one of the conditions of his model, not that the participants are equal but that they are completely ignorant of all their inequalities.[12]

When pressed, then, the model becomes increasingly remote from reality. Rawls' account of justice seems to rely, at first glance, on the conception of principles to which self-interested individuals would agree; it soon becomes evident, however, that these are principles to which such individuals *could reasonably* agree. Moreover, if the primary motivation of self-interest is to be

---

[12] Or, as John Chapman has put it to me, "Rawls assumes you don't know who you are."

preserved, we must suppose these individuals ignorant of their identities and thus unaware of any circumstances that would distinguish their own interest from anyone else's. What they are really called upon to do, then, is to safeguard a paradigmatic set of interests from a number of typical hazards. We need not now suppose a collection of egotists, so much as creatures with standards of human well-being and with both a concern for and a knowledge of the conditions necessary for achieving or maintaining it. Now the lack of some of these conditions, food and shelter for instance, would frustrate the attainment of such standards more completely than the lack of others, such as holidays or books. One must arrange human interests, then, in an order of priority, distinguishing basic from other less urgent needs. So a participant in one of Rawls' practices would be well advised to reckon with the possibility of being deprived of basic needs, as well as of being subject to a range of natural and social handicaps that would impair his capacity to supply them. Consequently, he would be rash to concur in any practice that (subject to certain provisos considered below) does not guarantee the satisfaction of basic needs and compensate for handicaps before conceding less urgent advantages to others, even if that means giving the handicapped special treatment at the expense of the normal and healthy.

Developed in this way, Rawls' model would take account of the fact that questions of social justice arise just because people are unequal in ways they can do very little to change and that only by attending to these inequalities can one be said to be giving their interests equal consideration. For their interests are not equal in the sense that every interest actually competing in a given situation is of equal weight, irrespective of how far each claimant's interests have already been attended to; they are equal, instead, in the sense that two men lacking similar conditions necessary to their well-being would, *prima facie,* have equally good claims to them.

This analysis throws some light on the paradoxical problems of compensatory welfare legislation on behalf of Negroes. A recent collection of essays[13] has drawn attention to the ambiguous im-

---

[13] R. L. Carter, D. Kenyon, Peter Marcuse, Loren Miller (with a foreword by Charles Abrams), *Equality,* New York, 1965.

plications of the notion of equality and, in particular, of the "equal protection" clause of the Fourteenth Amendment, for the desegregation and social integration of Negroes. Even liberal friends of the Negro have been known to argue, it seems, that the law should be color-blind, and that compensatory legislation on the Negro's behalf is discrimination in reverse. If (it is said) color is irrelevant to eligibility for jobs, housing, education, and social esteem, to make special provisions for the Negro as such would be to reinstate an irrelevant criterion, and so to treat equals unequally, or alternatively, to deny the human equality that it is so important to affirm. This argument disregards, however, a vital ambiguity. Negroes and whites are equal in the sense that their interests deserve equal consideration; they are painfully unequal in the sense that society imposes on the Negro special disabilities. So although black and white may equally need housing or education, the obstacles placed by society in the black man's way add extra weight to his claim to public assistance to meet these needs. Where society imposes handicaps, it can hardly be unjust for the state to compensate for them. Nor is it far-fetched to call this a way of providing equal protection for the interests of black and white. Where the interests of a group are subject to discriminatory social handicaps on the irrational ground of color, it is not irrational for the state to apply the same criterion in giving them protection on an appropriately more generous scale. Equal protection ought not to mean an equal allocation of the means of protection—for the protection must be commensurate with the threat or impediment.[14]

V

Finally, it is necessary to qualify the principle of equal consideration of interests in two respects, the first theoretical, the second practical.

The first corresponds to Rawls' qualification that "an inequality is allowed only if there is reason to believe that the practice with the inequality, or resulting in it, will work for the

---

[14] G. Vlastos makes a similar point in connection with the right to security, "Justice and Equality," *Social Justice,* R. B. Brandt, Ed., Englewood Cliffs, N.J., 1962, p. 41.

advantage of every party engaging in it."[15] The principle of equal consideration of interests provides for the satisfaction of interests in order of urgency, every individual's claim being otherwise equal. A departure from this principle could be defended by showing that it would increase the capacity to satisfy interests in general and that it would not weaken the claims of someone who, without the adoption of the variant practice, could reasonably claim satisfaction under the main principle. It may be expedient, but not just, that one man should starve that others might grow fat; but there is no injustice if, in allowing some to grow fat, we can reduce the number that would otherwise starve. In this way we take account of incentive arguments for distribution by desert, as well as of claims to special treatment to meet functional needs.

The second qualification applies to the practical application of the principle. I have argued that it prescribes that interests be satisfied in order of their urgency, men without food and clothes falling further short of some presupposed conception of well-being than men who have these things but lack guitars. But clearly, this principle works as a practical guide for social policy only so long as there is a very wide measure of agreement on priorities. And there is such agreement in that range of interests we most commonly call "needs," those, in fact, from which most of my examples have been drawn. But it is not easy to see how a society that had solved the problem of providing for everyone's generally agreed needs could go much further in applying equal consideration of needs as a direct distributive principle.

Throughout this paper I have been relying on a conception of interests as conditions necessary to a way of life or to forms of activity that are endorsed as worthwhile, or (what probably amounts to the same thing) as conditions necessary to the process of making of oneself something worthy of respect.[16] Now, hermits

---

[15] "Justice as Fairness," *op. cit.*, p. 135.

[16] It is not necessary for my present purpose to discuss what could be good reasons for approving some ways of life, or forms of activity, or kinds of personality, and rejecting others. I ask the reader's assent only to the following propositions: that we do in fact make judgments of this kind, and that the notion of what is in a man's interest must ultimately be related to such

and ascetics apart, we shall probably agree on the basic conditions necessary for any good life at all. Once given those preliminary conditions, however, we shall encounter very diverse opinions on the absolute eligibility of certain ways of life, on their relative worth, on the conditions necessary for them, and on the relative urgency of such conditions, as claims to our attention. This would make it very difficult indeed to put a schedule of interests into a socially acceptable order of priority. Furthermore, it is difficult to see how an authoritative and general allocation of resources according to interests could avoid laying down an official ruling on what ways of life were most eligible. Yet, as Charles Fried has argued,[17] the freedom to judge, even mistakenly, what is in one's own interests is itself an important human interest.

This may, however, point the way out of the dilemma. My main criticism of Rawls has been that, unless amended along the lines I have indicated, his postulate of equality is either unrealistic or restrictive, removing some of the most insistent problems of social justice from the scope of his principles, by presupposing a condition that it is in the interests of justice to bring about. But in the conditions of affluence I am now considering, where basic interests are already being satisfied, and there is no further common ground on priorities, the postulate of equality would come much closer to reality. If there are equal opportunities to pursue one's interests, and freedom to determine what they are is recognized as itself an important interest, even at the risk of error, Rawls' principles of justice come into their own. Rawls lays it down that a practice is just if everyone is treated alike, unless a discrimination in favor of some is of advantage to everyone. We can now translate this into the language of equal interests: If all basic interests are already being satisfied and if there is no universally acknowledged order of priority as between further interests competing for satisfaction, then, given that the individual has a fundamental interest in determining what are

---

a judgment, at any rate at the stage at which it is said that he is mistaking where his real interest lies. There may be sufficient consensus in a society for "interests" to function descriptively; but this is only because, at that level, the normative element is not in dispute and not therefore obtrusive.

[17] "Justice and Liberty," in *Justice, op. cit.*, pp. 126–146. See also my " 'Interests' in Politics," *loc. cit.*

his own interests, a practice would be just that gave all interests actually competing in a situation equal satisfaction, save insofar as an inequality made possible a greater degree of satisfaction without weakening claims that would be satisfied without it. On this interpretation, Rawls' original account of the criteria of a just practice turns out to be a special application, in conditions where all handicaps have already been remedied, of the principle of the equal consideration of interests.

5

DIVERSITY OF RIGHTS AND KINDS OF EQUALITY

JOHN PLAMENATZ

I

If equality meant everyone having the same abilities, the same rights, and the same obligations, no society could be a society of equals. For in every society, no matter how simple, there is diversity of functions; and every function calls for some abilities rather than others and carries its proper duties, and also its rights. The idea of a complete identity of rights, though not self-contradictory, is unrealistic to the point of absurdity. This identity could exist only where there was no division of labor, even between the sexes. In his ideal society Foigny wanted only hermaphrodites.

In every society everyone, no matter how humble, has some rights. Not even the slave is literally at the mercy of his master, for there are always customs, if not also laws, to restrain the master. Every social relation, even that of master and slave, is part of a moral order, of a system of rights and obligations. Only the helpless and insane have rights and no duties, and we do not envy them their privilege. To be without obligations is a mark of social incompetence. Whatever social superiority may be, it clearly does not consist in a man's having a greater balance of rights over duties than his inferiors have.

Most identities or differences of ability are not called equalities or inequalities. Bakers are usually better at baking bread than gardeners are, and gardeners better at tending plants; but we do not speak of bakers as being either more or less able than gardeners, though we speak readily enough of one man being a better baker or gardener than another. Yet we do speak, for example, of poets or physicists, even of politicians (at least when they are good of their kind), as being abler than bakers and gardeners. Their superior ability consists, presumably, in their possessing skills which are rarer, or more useful, or more admired, or required in some occupation or social role carrying exceptional prestige. We also speak of one man being abler than another, without reference to any particular occupation or social role, when he possesses in higher degree skills required in a wide range of occupations or roles.

So, too, we do not say of a bishop and a judge that they are unequal merely because they have different rights. Nor do we say of a bishop and his chaplain that they are equals because, on account of the cloth, they have many rights in common. We would not say it, even if we discovered that they had more rights in common than have the bishop and the judge. When we contemplate the bishop doing his pastoral duty and the judge presiding in his court, it does not occur to us to call them equal or unequal. It is only when we find them engaged in the same or similar business (for example, trying to exert influence at an election) that we notice that one of them, owing to his office, and thus by virtue of his rights, has opportunities the other lacks, and therefore has more influence. But this kind of inequality scarcely touches us; we call it inequality, and therefore something more than a mere difference of right and opportunity, only when we notice people ordinarily engaged in separate and dissimilar activities pursuing similar ends or momentarily competing for something. It is an inequality which hardly matters.

But the difference of right between bishop and chaplain is an inequality that matters greatly because they are engaged together in activities which it is the bishop's office, and not the chaplain's, to direct. The bishop is superior to the chaplain because he has authority over him, and also because he has greater prestige, so that, even outside the sphere of their official duties, the bishop is much better placed to influence the chaplain than the chaplain to influence him. The inequality between them is important not only because it is necessary to their doing their work properly but also because it is liable to abuse. The bishop may use his authority over the chaplain in ways that impede the proper exercise of both their duties, or he may use his greater prestige to frustrate or humiliate the chaplain.

Scarcely anyone condemns every kind of subordination. If we disapprove of churches, we may wish to do away with bishops and their underlings. If we disapprove of the way a particular church does its work, we may want greatly to diminish the authority of its bishops over its lesser priests. But that is quite different from wanting to abolish subordination as such. Even anarchists are rarely abolitionists in a wholesale manner, though they sometimes speak as if they were. Most of them condemn only some kinds of subordination, or certain attitudes liable to accompany it in all its kinds, though in some more than others. Anarchists believe that there is much more subordination than there need be if men are to provide for their wants and aspirations adequately. Also, they heartily dislike what so often goes along with it—the arrogance which disregards the needs and sensitivities of inferiors and the servility which seeks to propitiate superiors.

A difference in right or ability between two persons is an inequality if it gives one of them authority over the other, or enables him to influence the other much more than the other can influence him, or attracts more deference generally, or puts him in a better position to realize the aspirations he already has or to acquire others he should have and realize if he is to live well.

For example, a master may be said to be superior to his servant because he has authority over him, or can greatly influence him even outside the sphere of his service, or is held in greater honor, or is better able to get what he wants, or is (or has been) better placed to acquire and to realize aspirations deemed admirable or whose realization gives a deeper and more lasting satisfaction. Certainly, when we say that one man is superior to another in rights, we take into account more than his authority, influence, prestige, and ambitions; we also take into account aspirations he may or may not have but which we think he ought to have if he is to live happily or well. So, too, when we say that one man is abler than another, we take into account his capacity to acquire and realize aspirations of this kind. Quite often, when reformers speak for the "unprivileged," asking that they be given rights and opportunities they now lack, they ask for what the unprivileged do not want until the reformers have persuaded them to want it.

There are three kinds of identities and differences of ability or right: the kind that engages our attention so little that we never call them equalities or inequalities; the kind that we sometimes attend to and call by these names, although we do not feel strongly about them; and the kind that excite us. The excitement I have in mind relates not to the abilities and rights considered in themselves but to their being identical or different. We may think it enormously important, for example, that nursing mothers should have certain skills and rights and yet not be in the least excited by their being different from the skills and rights of coal miners.

For an identity of right or ability to be an exciting equality, or for a difference to be an exciting inequality, it must relate to something we care deeply about. If it seems to us to stand in the way of that thing, we condemn it; if it seems to promote it, we commend it. But we care deeply about many things; and, unless we make up our minds what it is that we care for most, we are apt to be in a muddle when we discuss equality or the lack of it. We can also get into a muddle if the persons we talk to care deeply about things which mean little to us, or are indifferent to what to us is important; especially when, as so often happens, neither we nor they have troubled to discover just how we differ. No doubt, this lack of concern sometimes matters very little; as, for example, when we speak to persons whose social status and education is much like ours, for they often care deeply about the same things as we do. With them we need to take few precautions to ensure that we do not talk at cross purposes. But, at a time when all societies are changing fast and are exposed to many external influences, the need to take these precautions is greater than ever it was.

II

In the West, in modern times, champions of equality have been concerned above all to preserve or to enlarge the following things: personal security, symmetry or due proportion, freedom, decency, and dignity; while defenders of inequality have been concerned chiefly to preserve social stability and to encourage efficiency and excellence. I speak, not of their real motives, but of the arguments they have used. And I am aware that I oversimplify, for sometimes the same or very similar arguments are used on both sides, since each side likes to turn the weapons of the other against it. The friends of inequality have, for example, often argued that it is a means to freedom, just as its enemies have argued the opposite. But those who argue for inequality for the sake of freedom have nearly always been on the defensive; they have mostly tried to show that to diminish inequality in some particular respect would also diminish freedom. They have rarely argued that inequality needs to be increased if freedom is to be enlarged. At times, they have regretted inequalities that have recently disappeared, but they have almost never ventured to argue that forms or degrees of inequality hitherto unknown should be deliberately introduced so that men should be more free.

Though differences of right—and also of ability, to the extent that ability depends on training and not just on natural gifts—are more apt to be challenged than identities, nobody need speak up for them unless they are challenged. There are always countless such differences, most of them accepted by almost everyone. Only when they are attacked, does anyone feel the need to find arguments for them.

With the emergence of new occupations and new social roles, there emerge new claims and also new ideas about how men should live. Old claims are seen as obstacles in the way of the new ones, and are therefore challenged; and it is only then that attempts are made to justify them. The conservative who argues his faith is more than a lover of the established order; he is a defender of the old faith. He is a Burke among the radicals.

Everyone, even Burke, believes in equality in at least one sense. Burke, at his most conservative, wanted everyone to keep the rights he already had, no more and no less. He wanted authority to see to it that everyone enjoyed the rights recognized as his; he wanted an equal protection of all rights, no matter whose.

This is the simple demand for personal security, for the impartial protection of rights, for equality before the law. This demand, this sort of equality, is everywhere admitted in principle; for merely to say that the law ought to be observed is to admit this demand, to uphold equality in this sense. But what is admitted in principle can be denied in practice. There are practices without which this equality cannot be realized; there are others which subvert it—as, for example, "people's courts," secret tribunals, certain kinds of police methods, and high fees for judicial services. These subversive practices are defended on all sorts of grounds by writers who do not admit that they are subversive, that they undermine this sort of equality.

We could perhaps distinguish between practices which are merely insufficient to secure this equality or are incompatible with it and practices which are subversive of it. If rights are to be impartially protected, it is important that men should be able to establish what their rights are and should not be responsible for injuries not done by them. But in some communities (especially primitive ones) methods of establishing rights and responsibilities may be insufficient or unsuited to their purpose, though the people who use them are unaware that they are so. In such communities effective methods have never been discovered, so that it would be misleading to say that the methods actually used are subversive. But in communities where effective methods have been used and then later discarded from political or other motives, there is usually a pretense made that the methods actually in use ensure that rights are impartially protected and that men are held responsible for injuries they have done. Of these communities we can say properly that the methods they use are practices subversive of this sort of equality.

Symmetry or due proportion is what we aim at when we insist that rewards "correspond" to achievements and services, or that rights "correspond" to abilities and obligations. Rewards do not stand to achievements and services quite as rights do to abilities and obligations. Though hope of reward may be a motive for doing something, the reward is not involved in the actual doing—not even when the reward is a right. For example, schoolboys who get high marks may be given the right to go out of bounds at certain times when other boys are confined within bounds. They do not need to go out of bounds to get these marks, and the right to do so is merely a reward. But to acquire or exercise an ability or to carry out an obligation usually involves having certain rights; it involves the making of two kinds of claims against others: that they should not interfere with some of our activities and that they should render us services. Unless these claims are met, we cannot acquire the ability or exercise it successfully, or we cannot do our duty. These claims need not be made by the persons whose abilities and obligations are in question. For example, the right of a child to a "proper" education does not involve the child's claiming it: It is claimed for the child by others largely on the ground that, unless the child gets this education, it will lack certain abilities and, therefore, fail to carry out certain obligations when it grows up.

If most people who perform certain services or achieve something get a reward, then, if we find someone who has performed them or has achieved it not getting the reward, we say that he is entitled to get it. Or, if certain rights are justified on the ground that persons having certain skills or certain obligations must have them in order to use their skills or carry out their obligations effectively, then, if we find someone who has the skills or obligations but lacks these rights, we say that he ought to have them.

The claim to equality as due proportion is in itself neither conservative nor radical. Even the requirement that rewards be "commensurate" with services is not always radical. For men can differ both about what is to be considered a service and about the proper reward for it. Activities unknown or condemned as useless in some communities are in others held to matter greatly and earn large rewards.

I have spoken of services earning rewards, and of rights involved in the exercise of abilities and the carrying out of obligations. But to do service is to exercise some abilities and to carry out some obligations: The shoemaker exercises skills and carries out obligations in performing the services expected of him. Again, I have spoken of rewards and of rights, but we can say of men who earn their rewards that they have the right to them. We can therefore say that services carry rights in either of two senses: in the sense that they cannot be done at all, or not properly, except by persons who have certain rights, or in the sense that rights are attached to them as rewards by law or custom. To mark the distinction between these two kinds of rights, I shall call the first kind "inherent rights" and the second kind "privileges." Disputes about privileges are more frequent and more bitter than disputes about inherent rights.

These disputes arise whenever there is a sharp increase in the number of persons who aspire to perform services carrying attractive privileges, or when the services cease and the privileges continue, or when the utility of the services comes to be widely questioned by groups strong enough to make trouble for the privileged. As social conditions change, so too does the relative importance attached to different activities and privileges. What was once considered a service comes to be denounced as a form of exploitation; or else a right that nobody cared much about begins to look precious. The rules of symmetry differ from society to society, from age to age, and from group to group within the same society, but there are always many such rules, and the requirement that they be respected is a powerful demand for equality.

The principle that privileges should correspond to services is recognized in all societies. So too is the principle that persons required to exercise certain skills or to carry out certain obligations should enjoy the rights "inherent" in those skills or obligations, that is to say, the rights needed for their proper exercise. But, in modern times, at least since the French Revolution, there has been added to these two principles another which, though closely connected with them, needs to be distinguished from them. This principle is equality of opportunity.

So far, I have spoken of abilities without distinguishing skills from the capacity to acquire them; but now I must take notice of this distinction. Of two children lacking a skill, one will often have a markedly greater capacity to acquire it than the other. This difference in capacity may be natural, or it may be an effect of different training or of different environment. One kind of training may increase a child's (or an adult's) capacity to benefit from another kind. Similarly, one kind of environment may increase a child's capacity to acquire some skills and reduce its capacity to acquire others.

In very primitive societies, most men acquire much the same range of rudimentary skills. There is little or no division of labor, except that women's work is different from men's so that the skills they acquire are also different. In societies economically more advanced, there is a much greater division of labor and acquisition of specialized skills. But, until quite recent times, even in economically more advanced societies, sons usually followed the occupations of their fathers and acquired much the same skills. This kind of division of labor, though it enables men to acquire delicate and intricate skills, does not ensure that they acquire the skills they are best fitted by nature to acquire. At most, it provides them with the kind of social environment that increases their capacity to benefit from the training they receive. This is division of labor without equality of opportunity.

But where equality of opportunity is recognized as a principle, it is thought desirable that men should be able to acquire the skills they are by nature best fitted to acquire, no matter what the occupation and the social status of their fathers. This principle can be defended on utilitarian grounds by people who care nothing for freedom. They can argue that services are too dear when only a privileged few, regardless of their natural aptitudes, are allowed to perform them, and that therefore all services should be open to anyone who can prove his ability to perform them adequately. The standard of adequacy must be determined, at least in part, by the need to ensure that the demand for the service is met. If the demand increases sharply, the standard may have to be lowered, but still only those whose performance is adequate by that standard are to be allowed to serve. The just price of a service is what would be paid for it in a free market, and if more is paid, society is exploited. In its own interest society must ensure, as far as it can (for in practice there are always many obstacles to success), that anyone who wishes to render a service for which there is a demand is not prevented from doing so except by his being less able than others to render it—though his opportunity to get the required training is as great as theirs. This, I take it, is what is meant by the rule, *to every talent its opportunity of service.*

Equality of opportunity, thus conceived, does not entail either democracy or freedom. It can be as easily achieved in an authoritarian as in a liberal country. The rulers may control the economy and other kinds of social activity without being responsible to their subjects for how they do it; they may fashion society to a model not in keeping with the aims and principles of most people before the fashioning began. They may decide, in a general way, what services will be in demand and what opportunities available, and yet they may think it important that there should be for everyone equal opportunity of service, limited only by differences in natural aptitudes.

In the West we mean by equality of opportunity not only this equal opportunity of service but also something else, which we do not always distinguish clearly from it. We also think it important that everyone should have as good a chance as anyone else of living as he wants to live. We believe that there should be for everyone, not just equal opportunity of service, but also equal opportunity of freedom. Since this second equality presupposes the first, and the first is more easily defined than the second (and perhaps also easier to get close to), it is not surprising that the first should so often be mistaken for the second. In practice, even in the best run authoritarian society aspiring to equality, the ideal of equal opportunity of service is very far from attained, because to devise tests of aptitude for this or that service and to determine what kinds of training are most effective is easier than to decide what conditions must hold if everyone is to have as good a chance as anyone else of living as he wants to live.

Even in the freest of societies imaginable in the kinds of natural environment known to us, a man's freedom would have to be limited by much more than the duty not to harm others. It would have to be limited, for example, by the need to get a living, which a man can do only if his work is useful, if there is a demand for its products. If he works to produce only what he himself consumes, he gets the barest of livings and lives precariously, and if he works to produce mostly what others consume, if he benefits from a division of labor, he lives more abundantly and securely but also in greater dependence on others. To live he must serve, and the kinds of service open to him are determined by the needs and demands of others. How, then, does equal opportunity of freedom differ from equal opportunity of service?

Does it differ because, unlike equal opportunity of service, it forbids an authoritarian and rigorous direction of labor? Certainly, it does forbid it, but then equal opportunity of service, though it does not forbid it, also does not require it. Logically, no doubt, the rigorous direction of labor is compatible with equal opportunity of service. Those in authority could, in theory, devise tests of aptitude, could apply them to children and to adults, and could then decide what training everyone was to get and what work he was to do without taking his wishes into account. But this, though possible in theory, would be disastrous in practice. The rulers of an authoritarian society would be well advised to take large account of individual preferences, for quite often a man's strong preference for one kind of work over another is better evidence that he can acquire quickly the skills needed to do it efficiently than an aptitude test would be. If the rulers want both efficient work and contented workers (and the two tend to go together), they are well advised to take account both of individual preferences and of aptitude tests. They are well advised to allow considerable freedom of choice, not only to adults, but also to children old enough to understand how one kind of training differs from another and what skills are acquired by means of it. The authoritarian character of their rule does not consist so much in their limiting freedom of choice of occupation or of training as in their attempt to induce in everyone certain attitudes to authority and to service. Everyone is to believe, or to act as if he believed, that the rulers are the best judges of what is good for the community, and everyone is to look upon his work primarily as a service to the community rather than an activity satisfying to himself.

Where equal opportunity for freedom is recognized as an ideal, it is thought important that children should be so educated as to be able to discriminate between the kinds of training and the occupations open to them, that they should be taught that work should satisfy the doer of it as well as be useful, that they should be given (as far as possible) the chance to rectify mistaken choices of training and occupation, that they should spend their leisure hours more or less as they please provided they do no harm, that they should be encouraged to experiment, inquire, and criticize, that they should be taught to be tolerant and considerate and to put a high value on privacy. Also, where this ideal is recognized, it is held that no irresponsible elite have the right to decide how society shall be organized and what kinds of work shall be done. Those who govern no doubt always have their principles and their policies, which may require them to take far-reaching decisions deeply affecting the lives of the people, but they get the chance to take these decisions only after they have won elections during which their principles and policies are severely criticized. And the criticism continues through the period of their government. Those who govern, especially nowadays when so much is required of them by their subjects, necessarily, in explaining, justifying, and carrying out their policies, create demand and influence opinion. An important difference between a free country and one not free is that, in the first, the demands governments create come of what they do to meet demands which arise out of activities and discussions they cannot control, because they have to compete for influence with many other people.

Again, the more this ideal is recognized, the less it matters that people should be successful in competition with others, that they should rise above them and prove their superiority to them, and the more it matters that they should discover for themselves, among the occupations and roles which society offers them, those that suit them best. The more, too, it matters that they should combine independence of judgment and purpose with a willingness to meet their social obligations. Just as the best lover is the one who can love deeply without needing either to dominate or to idolize the object of his love, so the best citizen is the one who can be loyal to his neighbors and his community without accepting their standards uncritically and without seeking to impose his standards on them.

Men's standards and preferences do not drop down upon them out of the sky; they are acquired in social intercourse, through action with and against others and through reflection on that action. In a free country, as much as in any other, men are creatures of society. Indeed, it is good that they are so; for otherwise they would be hard put to choose occupations and other activities congenial to themselves and at the same time useful and tolerable to others. It is because men are creatures of society that there is usually an effective demand, and also some kind of reward, for the work they want to do. Men are free when the useful occupations and tolerable activities they can choose to engage in do not depend primarily on the schemes and the social philosophy of an organized and irresponsible minority or on traditions beyond the reach of criticism but on the needs and aspirations of all and sundry, who are not answerable to authority for what they make of their lives and are free to criticize received standards, and when they have as good a chance as others to understand the alternatives open to them and to fit themselves for the occupations and activities of their choice. They are free also when they can compete with others in influencing opinion and taste so as to create a demand for the kind of services they want to render or to see rendered, or to foster the tolerance and good will they need to be able to live as seems good to them.

Decency and dignity are closely connected ideas. Men, we say, ought not to live like dogs; they are worthy of something better merely because they are men. They are self-conscious beings. If they are to be happy, it is important that they should retain their self-respect, which they will not do unless they enjoy the respect of others. There are in every society—or at least in all materially and culturally more advanced societies—widely accepted ideas about how men should live if they are to live decently; there are minimal standards of decent living, though they differ considerably from society to society. Anyone who falls short of these standards is apt to be despised by those more fortunate than himself; no doubt, not by all the more fortunate, not by the more compassionate and imaginative among them, but by the great majority.

In many societies, though it is thought desirable that everyone should live decently, it is not held to be the duty of the government or even of neighbors to provide for those who lack the means to do so. But where this duty is acknowledged, there is a belief in equality for the sake of decency; it is admitted that everyone has the right to be provided with a decent living, no matter how small the contribution he makes, no matter how meager his abilities. Everyone is held to have a right to certain services from his neighbors or from the government merely because he is a man. The more strongly people feel about decent living, the more likely they are to acknowledge society's duty to provide everyone with the means to it. Belief in this kind of equality is often found along with belief in equality for the sake of freedom, but it can also exist without it. It can flourish in an authoritarian as well as in a liberal society.

The last kind of equality I mention relates to dignity alone and not to decent living. No doubt, when we are concerned for decent living we are concerned, at least to some extent, for dignity as well; we want people to live decently so that they can have self-respect and the respect of others. But we can be concerned for dignity without needing to be concerned also for decent living. Social superiors can behave arrogantly to social inferiors who live relatively well by the standards of their society, and we are often quick to resent this arrogance as an outrage to human dignity, as a failure to treat a man with the respect owing to him merely as a man, the respect he can forfeit only by his own bad behavior.

Concern for dignity is by no means more common among civilized than among primitive peoples; indeed, among many civilized peoples it has been much less common than among most primitive peoples, for it is among the civilized that the "well-born" or the "upper classes" have treated their "inferiors" with the greatest contempt or indifference. Of course, in no society, not even the most primitive, are the same attentions due to everyone, to men and to women, to the old and the young, to those having authority and to those without it. Also, there are different forms for different occasions. But, in spite of these differences, there may be equality at another level: there may be quick sympathy and a kind of ease of intercourse which comes of not taking social distinctions too seriously. There may be, beneath the external forms putting some men socially higher than others, a sort of courtesy extended to all. There may be, even in the absence of all explicit doctrine, a feeling widely shared that men should deal considerately with one another merely because they are men.

We might expect this feeling to be strongest in countries where the people are most attached to democracy and freedom. But I doubt whether it is so; it is as strong, I suspect, among primitive peoples as among any. In the West, in countries whose economies are intricate and quickly changing, it may be stronger among the more democratic and liberal peoples than among the others. But there are, I think, in all highly industrial and socially mobile societies, democratic and authoritarian, causes serving to weaken it. In these societies so many human contacts are brief and shallow that, though standards of formal politeness are often high, there is little of the deeper courtesy which brings men close to one another in spite of all the distances that social hierarchy puts between them. In the West those who think it their duty to bring the blessings of the welfare state to the less fortunate sometimes conspicuously lack this courtesy. They treat as inferiors (though perhaps without being aware that they do so) the very people whose equality with themselves they loudly proclaim. This kind of discourtesy often goes with respect for rules and with high standards of efficiency; and is then perhaps the more apt to give offense because it looks so much like hypocrisy. It makes as many and as bitter enemies as all but the worst forms of oppression. This business of doing good to others is hazardous and delicate; it is difficult to do it without behaving as if you thought yourself superior to the persons you do good to.

The last three kinds of equality I have discussed—the equal right to choose a congenial way of life, the equal right to a decent living, and the equal right to courtesy—are usually justified by reference to certain capacities and needs peculiar to man. Man is rational and purposeful, as other animals are not: He knows himself as a man only in society with other men. He needs, as other animals do not, self-respect and the respect of others; he needs to be treated by others as if his needs and purposes mattered to them. He is capable of foresight, deliberation, and choice; he makes plans for his future, and it matters to him that he should be able to carry them out. Having certain capacities peculiar to his kind, which are developed by social intercourse, he has these needs for self-respect and for freedom in all societies. Which is not to say that they are equally strong or take the same forms in all societies. For example, in tradition-bound and slowly changing societies, man makes do with as much freedom as he can get within the occupations and roles to which he is born. In industrial and quickly changing societies, he aspires to a larger freedom.

III

The kinds of equality I have been discussing are not always compatible with one another. I do not mean that they are logically incompatible but rather that in practice it is often difficult to get more of one kind except at the cost of getting less of another. Let me give examples.

I distinguished earlier between equal opportunity of service and equal opportunity of freedom, and I tried to show that, though the first is a condition of the second, it can exist without the second. There can be equal opportunity of service in an authoritarian society as much as in a liberal one. Indeed, an authoritarian society, if it is industrial and sets great store by efficiency, can sometimes go further than a liberal society towards achieving this equality, if only because the government's control over the people is more complete.

But, even in a democratic and liberal society, the pursuit of equal opportunity of service can be such as to put obstacles in the way of achieving equal opportunity of freedom. If ability is to be measured, there must be tests, and where there are tests, the competitive spirit is easily aroused. Emulation is a spur to effort, and effort is needed if abilities are to be developed. Yet it is easy for children to be diverted from the kind of effort which develops their peculiar abilities to the kind which ensures that they pass tests better than other children do. It is also easy for them to be diverted from preparing for the adult occupations and roles which they would find congenial and absorbing to preparing for the kinds carrying the greatest prestige. Their elders who guide them know beforehand what carries prestige but not what would prove congenial and absorbing to the children for whose welfare they are responsible. Children cannot make reasonable choices when they are very young; they have to be taught some skills, whether they like it or not, if they are to become discriminating and adventurous. The desire to please their elders and the desire to excel are powerful motives with them, which their elders cannot but appeal to if children are to be taught what they must learn before they can be expected to make reasonable choices. But to continue to appeal to these motives in controlling and guiding children, even when they are older, is easier than to encourage them to think independently and to come gradually to an understanding of their own abilities and their own more enduring inclinations and tastes. The pursuit of success, though in the end too often frustrating and painful, is simpler than the pursuit of happiness, if by happiness is understood not a Utilitarian sum of pleasures but the congenial and absorbing occupations which make a man feel that life is well worth living despite all its difficulties. We come to understand ourselves largely by comparing ourselves with others, and yet the very comparison stimulates in us ambitions whose service requires that we should have illusions about ourselves.

Where the pursuit of success is fierce, though there may be a wider range of choices for the able and the ambitious, a choice once made is apt to be irrevocable, if only because time and money have been spent in training the young to pass the tests that bring success. Both the successful and those who have helped them to succeed are reluctant to waste the "investment" made in their success. But the more young people are irrevocably committed to a career by early decisions and successes, the less they are free. There are more roads to success, and more travellers on the roads, but there is also less passing from road to road and more travellers on the wrong road. Society stiffens as it grows more elaborate and confines each of its members to a smaller part of itself.

It has been said that in an ideally free society there would be parity of esteem between all occupations; it would be no better, no more honorable, to be a farmer than a baker, an artist than a judge. What would then matter would be that every man should be so placed socially and so educated as to be able to make the important choices of his life in such a way that he would not later come to regret them.

But this is an impossible ideal. In every society there is a division of labor and some kind of hierarchy; there are some men with much greater power than others. They enjoy far greater prestige, and there are more people coveting what they have than coveting what others have. Further, wherever there are recognized virtues and skills, those whose virtue or skill is greatest are the most admired. Even the most sophisticated and independent person, who quite genuinely cares almost nothing for what to most people are marks of success, has his own standards of excellence; and by those standards not only will some men be superior to others but also some occupations to others. It is impossible that all men should be equals in the sight of man, except in the sense that some rights, some services, some marks of respect and sympathy are acknowledged to be due to them all merely because they are men.

Still, it is possible to distinguish the pursuit of happiness from the pursuit of success, both in ourselves and in others for whom we are responsible; and it is possible to take thought how to use the desire to excel to draw people to the occupations and activities likely to bring them happiness. For the pursuit of mere success can be a terrible burden and source of misery, both to those who succeed and those who fail. Children and young persons more than usually intelligent are encouraged, often regardless of temperament and peculiar gifts, to try for success where success brings the greatest social rewards. Or worse still, they are encouraged to pass tests which are not even good tests of the abilities required for doing a certain kind of work well; the tests select not the ablest candidates but the candidates most congenial to the selectors or to those who "set the tone" in a profession. In that case, we have equal opportunity not of useful service but only of success, for the skills and qualities needed to bring success are useful rather to the successful than to the people supposed to benefit from their services.

The keener the pursuit of success and the greater the number of persons allowed to compete, the more fierce the competition. The fiercer the competition, the greater the sense of failure among those who fail. The people who have to make do with the jobs carrying the least prestige and the smallest rewards, the people who are "at the bottom," are there because they lack the ability to rise. The social ladder is offered to them on the same terms as to the fortunate; they too are given a chance to climb it. But the chance is more apparent than real; the ladder is there for them to climb, provided they have the ability to climb it. The ladder, as they see it, is there less for them to climb than to advertise to all and sundry their lack of ability to climb it. Living in a society where there is an immense variety of occupations, the work left for them to do is the dullest and the least rewarding. Their wages may be considerable, and they may have leisure in plenty, for the welfare state by no means neglects them. But where success is prized above all things, they carry with them, as the humble never used to do, the marks of an inferiority as much personal as it is social.

A country, when it becomes socialist, may be not less but more competitive than it was before; it may confine and depress spiritually both the successful and the unsuccessful, even though it provides everyone with a decent minimum of comfort and goes a long way toward achieving equal opportunity of service. It may become classless and yet leave its people divided into groups more cut off from one another than the old classes were. The men and women getting the most attractive jobs may come, more often than ever before, from the poorer and less educated families, but once they get these jobs, they may be cut off if not altogether from their families then at least from the social groups to which their families belong. As they rise socially, they are lost to some groups and absorbed into others, while the groups remain as much separate and as much higher and lower as before. Making it easier for the young and gifted to pass from groups of lower to groups of higher status need not ensure that there is greater intercourse and better understanding between groups. Indeed, it may do the opposite. For it is in urbanized and industrial societies, where social mobility is greatest, that men and women, no matter how diverse their social origins, once they are launched on their careers, keep close company only with people who do the same kind of work as they do. Like turns to like. Though the diversity of occupations and ways of living within the great society continually increases, men and women inside it keep more and more to their own kind. The compact local community, which brings men together in spite of great differences of education, ability, income, taste, and social status, can be as much weakened in an industrial society when it is socialist as when it is capitalist. It is in simple, static, and uncompetitive societies, that men are brought easily together in spite of the differences between them; in highly competitive and socially mobile industrial societies, even when they are socialist, differences tend to keep men apart. The tendency can, no doubt, be combatted, but it must first be recognized as an effect not of capitalism but of industrialism. It will not disappear with capitalism nor with the class-structure which is typically capitalist.

It is not equal opportunities but at least some tastes and pleas-

ures in common that put men at their ease with one another so
that they can enjoy each other's company in comfort and courtesy.
To have a common culture, they need not have the same formal
education, for there can be, within a country, both a common
culture and a wide diversity of cultures. Indeed, it can happen
that a country partly illiterate comes closer to having a common
culture than a country where everyone goes to school. For the
illiterate may have a folk culture which some at least of the
formally educated (and often the most gifted) understand and
admire as Pushkin did in Russia or Goethe in Germany. In
countries where everyone goes to school, the folk culture of the
illiterate gives way to a culture of the half-literate, which is quite
unlike what it replaces; it is much more a parasite on the culture
of the sophisticated than a source of inspiration to it. When this
happens, the more highly educated despise it, try to shut it out
of their lives, and are perhaps themselves the poorer for having
nothing strong and pungent to feed on. The revulsion of the
fastidious from the vulgar, no less than the contempt of the
powerful for the weak, diminishes spiritual energy, deadens
sympathy, and restricts the imagination. It also divides society.

I have not wanted in this paper to deny that equality is a
means to freedom and serves to bring people closer together. It
can be a means to freedom and to fraternity as well, but the
pursuit of it, in some of its forms, can also diminish freedom and
put a distance between people. I have tried to distinguish between different kinds of equality, to consider how far, in industrial societies, they are compatible with one another and with
the enlargement of freedom and fraternity. I have raised a few
questions and have gone only a little way toward answering
them.

6

EQUALITY AND WHAT WE MEAN BY IT

GEORGE E. G. CATLIN

Along with "love," among the much abused words of language are "freedom," "liberty," "equality." They are loud in emotional resonance and men will fight for them, but (as one citizen said of the Monroe Doctrine), although prepared to die for these words, men remain uncertain as to what precisely they mean. Lincoln lamented that no good definition of "liberty" existed.[1] We may say precisely the same of "equality"; and largely for the same reasons. Despite the contributions of the great Greeks, men (it may be suspected) do not really *want* to define these words too closely, lest they lose emotional steam.

The curse of political theory (and especially of political science) has been rhetoric, superstition, and unanalyzed words—

[1] *Vide* George Catlin, *Systematic Politics* (2nd ed.), Toronto, 1965, Chs. IV and VI.

even poetic words, best set to music. However one may judge the verbalism of much current philosophy, perhaps too reminiscent of the late Scholastic Age of Duns Scotus (alias Dunce) , so hostile to the wider vision of the New Learning (a philosophy which indeed no longer discusses how many angels can dance, as immaterial beings, on the point of a needle, because it is busier discussing the meaning of the word "needle") , one must nevertheless be aware that a great opportunity and even duty arises for logical analytical philosophers to probe into the exact meanings of these hot and cloudy verbal nebulae of politics. "Equality" is such a nebula.

Certain of the more usual routes of evasion must promptly be shut off. It is customary to comment that we must not confuse "equality" with "identity." Surely we must not. We have only to study our fingers and thumbs to discover that the imprints of no two human beings, even twins, are strictly identical.

So this question scarcely arises. Indeed, at this level and in this context, we may state the maxim that "no human beings whatsoever are born equal," any more than (despite Jefferson's original draft) they are "born independent"—whatever subsequent culture may do for them.[2] But this gives no logical particle of ground for saying that races or nations are thus "unequal." With Plato, we have to ask what is to be our level of discourse. As to equality, "equality for what and as to what?" Plato, that great pioneer of modernity, was able to anticipate feminism by two millennia by asserting that men and women should be equal as touching the functions of the vote. He had a less high opinion about its educational requirements (except for the "political producers") than some people today.

Another route of evasion (used, I recall, by the late Dr. Delisle Burns) is to allege that nobody ever seriously contended that men were generally equal for all significant purposes. This is unhistorical. Many eighteenth-century writers propounded just this. The substantial sentiment is perhaps best expressed by a namesake, the poet Robert Burns: "The rank is but the guinea's stamp; the man's the gowd for a' that." Paine, Godwin, and the

---

[2] Cf. W. G. Runciman, *Relative Deprivation and Social Justice*, London, 1966. This valuable book begins with the words, "All societies are inegalitarian."

Gironde followed in his wake. The French sensationalist philosophers and their utilitarian successors relied upon feeling: "If you prick a man, he bleeds." The pains of all men were (are they?) the same, and so, it was more dubiously suggested, are their pleasures in the pursuit of happiness. In the somewhat modernistic phrase of a British Member of Parliament, Mr. Robert Maxwell, publisher, "all men alike use sanitary paper"; though anthropologically untrue, this statement underlines the fundamental argument (and makes pungent its limitations). For Rousseau there was an aboriginal equality, corrupted by private property and society. It was indeed patent, even to simpletons, that two men are not always equal in physical strength. But, a century earlier, the shrewd Hobbes replied that this difference would be obviated by a quick Iago dagger-thrust on a dark night. It is not for nothing that, in pioneer Texas, the Colt revolver was called "the equalizer." Once the fervor of the French Revolution, parading (in France only) the banners of Egalité, was over with Thermidor, the weary Barras could comment that all, at the end, that was left of equality was "equality before the law," equality *ad hoc*.

What, then, just do we mean? *Omnes homines, iure naturali, aequales sunt,* following the Stoics said the Roman lawyers and Justinian. *Doctrina inaequalitatis surget ex fonte superbiae,* said Pope St. Gregory the Great. In discussing these dicta let us first consider the matter on the basis of experience and the empirical studies of natural science.

The field of empirical research into human inequality, although of patent political and social importance, has still been quite inadequately tilled. Recent and still very speculative research into the behavior of earthworms (a favored subject with Darwin) indicates that if a flat worm, "taught" certain elementary Pavlovian responses (environmental), is then swallowed by another worm, this latter can, owing to chemical absorption of memory, acquire these responses more rapidly than a non-cannibal earthworm. This is in line indeed with the old cannibal belief that if one ate the heart of a brave enemy one would become more courageous. In logic it would lead to the preposterous conclusion that if an ardent student ate a Harvard or Balliol man, he would later do much better in examinations. . . . What yet these experiments are seeking to prove (or disprove) is that, just as the genes are extremely impervious to environmental change (as distinct from their own mutation), so too memory, which is so much a part of the whole personality, can be in like or at least similar fashion substantially transmitted by transmigration, and so too is it of a chemical character. Thus Sir Julian Huxley, in an unexpected fashion, may be, after all, a reincarnation of Thomas Huxley. Despite Lysenko, the inheritance of culturally acquired characteristics remains improbable. But chemical modifications could be of another order. The trend of biological science is to assert a continuity of body and psyche (St. Thomas came near to this point: "soul is the form of body") and that no natural breach is to be supposed between heredity in animals and heredity in man.

One can suggest with some confidence the improbability that man biologically follows quite different rules, as a separate creation, from those that hold for his animal cousins. That great Welsh rhetorician, Aneurin Bevin, once scored a debating point with wit by remarking that surely "their Lordships' House would not wish to assert that noble lords could be bred in the same fashion as pigs," with hereditary prize advantages. But their Lordships could have asserted precisely this, with the reservation that, eugenically, many noble families were so ill-bred as to have few advantages. Constant inbreeding (as with many of the royal families of Europe, especially of Spain) and marriage of first cousins issues in quite definite and hereditary disadvantages.

Statistical studies in the United States indicate that about 9 per cent of the male population, and a yet higher percentage of the female, are, have been, or during their lives will be in mental institutions. The actual percentage clearly depends upon the availability of institutions. But it appears questionable whether the entire liability is solely a matter of cultural or environmental influences. Some years ago studies in the United Kingdom by Sir Cyril Burt, of the Institute of Education, London, showed that the majority of the population was unlikely to advance mentally beyond the capacity of an eleven-year-old child. Nor did Sir Cyril assign this to cultural or even environmental factors in retardation. (On the other hand, the late Bronislaw Malinowski, in conversation with this writer, expressed his judgment that as much as 80 per cent of homosexuality was simply a matter of current cultural smart fashion, often in a brilliant, if decadent, intellectual society, and was not predetermined by hereditary, physical, or early environmental factors.) Are we, then, in summary to agree with the published view of the late Professor J. B. S. Haldane (incidentally sometime chairman of the board of the British *Daily Worker*) that "in a scientifically ordered society innate human diversity would be accepted as a natural phenomenon like the weather"? Or with the statement by Professor Sir Julian Huxley that "our new idea-system must jettison the democratic myth of equality: human beings are not born equal in gifts or potentialities, and human progress stems largely from their inequality." " 'Free but unequal' must be our motto, and diversity of excellence, not conformist normality or mere adjustment, should be the aim of education." Are we to say, with Josef Stalin: "Do we stand with Marx and Lenin or with the bourgeois egalitarians? I say we stand with Marx and Lenin," under the aristocratic Bolshevik system with its "pedagogic" society. The greatest single asset of Communist society may be that, on a base of proletarian applause, it is profoundly aristocratic or clerical.

One can indeed turn to Professor T. V. Smith's *American Idea of Equality,* which expounds the frontier and Jacksonian tradition and which relies unduly on the rather too facile philosophy of Locke, and to the late Professor R. H. Tawney's well-known book, *Equality.* Tawney had the merit of being, at least in much of his discussion, strictly empirical. It used to be said that the outward and visible sign of the (exaggerated) class system in Britain was apparent in terms of physical height. Tawney points out that the average height of children, of a given age, of middle-class parentage in so middle-class a resort as Brighton differed measurably by several inches from the height of like-aged children of manual workers in the East End of London. Thanks indeed to the welfare efforts of such men as Tawney, his Fabian colleagues (the Fabians always sought to be factual), and others, these differences have today been largely equalized out. Much of the alleged mental inferiority of some peoples, some Africans for example, will, on investigation, be found in fact to be a matter of nutritional deficiency. This important argument, however, so frequently urged, e.g., by the British Labor Party in wars on poverty, is concerned with environmental and consequent cultural factors and does not touch the issue of differences of heredity and stock, unless indeed these differences are asserted not to exist.

Historically many of the campaigns for human equality can, indeed, rather be seen as campaigns against specific forms, functionless and morally unjust, of social *in*equality—which is not at all the same thing. There was increasing scepticism (about which perhaps Aristotle himself even had some doubts) concerning the Aristotelian doctrine of "natural" (white) slaves, who were not so much obvious "inferiors" as people who had the misfortune to be prisoners of war. The African chiefs of the Slave Coast exported their potential Opposition as slaves, and such stout Protestants as John Hawkins transported them overseas in his ship, the *Jesus*. Although, as Talleyrand said, life might never have been "so pleasant" as in those days, the aristocracy of eighteenth-century France did little, in their lives of pleasurable fornication, to warrant their privileges. The crude Birmingham industrialists, of the nineteenth century, with their talk about "economic laws" and their practical concern with "brass," spurred to just revolt that "other nation" of the industrial workers who wanted a bigger slice of the spoils. Plato had prophesied that this would happen. Before Christ Plato had noted that, in political functions, women were not inferior to men; but then not until our own century were male patriarchal prerogatives to be re-examined. In each case, thanks to power and prejudice, a legitimate social function, as well as respect for what the other man was and could do, has been denied. Revolution has followed with the transfer of power.

We have yet still to ask whether, in a rational community, the ideology of total equality, with its apparent denial of the selective quest for excellence and of individual initiative and diversity of function, is really what we want. One of the most tricky and unanalyzed phrases in political theory and common discourse is "equality of opportunity." What purpose does the demand for it serve? Patently there may be, socially and functionally, unjust inequalities. What, however, is the point of urging "equality of opportunity" if the rewards of opportunity are or ought to be equally distributed anyhow? Are we, in the classical phrase, "to give equal things to non-equals"? Or is the real purpose of "equality of opportunity" to give to the more able man, among the so-called (and the phrase is subtly significant) "under-privileged," the opportunity to show the superior ability, deserving of privileges and rewards, of which in a just society he can demonstrate himself to be capable? Is the slogan, "equality of opportunity," substantially the negation of the total equality of us all? And when we orate about "equality," which precisely is it that we mean? Are we to remove the environmental inhibitions to native superior ability?

One of the first difficulties that arises in discussions of ability comes from the term "general ability." This term is itself too general to define. Specific ability is another question. It may be that here latent ability or capacity, as with physical stamina, and even with mathematical or musical gifts, may be in some measure hereditary, although perhaps not so much so as blue eyes or hemophilia. It "runs in the family." Because we have never yet defined "genius," no adequate work (despite Galton) has yet been done on whether genius is hereditary in families or whether, with appropriate cultural stimuli, we can not only "scrape the bottom of the barrel" of the second rate but also mass produce geniuses to order.

Of course Smith and Jones will always be flattered to be told that they are potential geniuses—and actual ones in a more just world. This is of interest to the biological scientist and to the specialist. The political theorist (who is himself a specialist) will tend to ask: What bearing has this upon politics or sociology? It would be more relevant were "general vitality" hereditary, or were a latent tendency to moral and criminal delinquency likewise a matter of genes.

There is a school, not least among American educationalists, that regards outstanding academic ability and its encouragement with suspicion. It does not seem consistent with encouraging the community spirit, "togetherness," the not negligible virtue of good citizenship, the absence of competitive jealousy and of feelings of inferiority. As has been observed since the days of the Greeks, the outstanding man may be a natural leader, but he is not, therefore, a good citizen. The sentiment is that "he loses touch with the community." As John Stuart Mill complained, there is always a bitter war between the second-rate, institutionalists who aim to make themselves safe, and the original or first-rate. There must not be common practices or prayers in a school (as distinct from the patriotic religious ceremony of saluting the flag), for those who voluntarily exclude themselves might come to feel like "outsiders" and inferior. Early examinations, or indeed any examinations, may have a deleterious effect, and we can, it is urged, say this without turning our attention to the source of the evil, in a too rigid, bureaucratic and wooden system of "educational channels." An eminent Princeton Professor of Sociology (July 16, 1965, *Philadelphia Bulletin*) recently stated that "classroom grades, grouping by ability and yearly promotion, should be dropped because they discriminate against dullards and slow learners." To say "You are not as good as Johnny so-and-so" is mortifying and creates a hostile attitude toward learning. How far then, should we go to encourage first-class ability and how far, to reiterate our earlier phrase, to "scrape the barrel" of second-class and third-class ability? Or can we do both? This issue is, of course, quite different from that of protest against suppressing—for reasons of money, status, or privilege—the ascertainable first-class ability that we have.

Several replies can be given to this argument. It is easy to ridicule the demand for neighborliness, "togetherness," fraternity, love, community. But the validity of the civic argument for mutual respect, as the basis for stable cooperation, remains. It is easy to exaggerate the role of the ignoble but human qualities of envy and jealousy of those who are objectively our betters, a jealousy and envy flattered by suggestions that really all are equal and, *sotto voce,* each of us rather better than his neighbor. (This is not yet to deny that vast rationalizations about class warfare and social justice can be constructed to give a more pleasant face to each individual human being's primal anxiety for power and fear of being powerless—a fear that would not be removed if all public social distinctions disappeared and if managers were replaced by commissars.) It is easy to overemphasize the austere stress for qualitative progress in human civilization without asking the contextual question: Excellence for what and in what respect? The weakness of modern Western civilization, and of "democracy" in one social sense (and that Platonic) of the term, is its lack of interest in, and even suspicion of, excellence and its *talk* about "the dignity of man," when in fact the undignified man, the unobtrusive cog of a man, is much preferred. But this surely does not mean that excellence and "Excellencies," being socially "on top," are identical.

There are today two major social issues upon which the

equalitarian campaign has a bearing. Most contemporary discussion of inequality in fact revolves around these issues. The one is the depressed condition, except in a few affluent societies of limited area, of the mass of the manual workers and indeed of some non-manual ones such as the unemployed college graduates and unplaced lawyers of Afro-Asia, severally points of discontent. The other, and interlocking, issue is that of depressed races, usually—but not always—non-"white" and chiefly African. (The Chinese, along with the Japanese, are members of a challenging race, but certainly do not feel themselves to be a depressed one. They represent the world's oldest, continuous high civilization. That they might be, in any significant sense except the industrial, "inferior" to the "hairy red barbarians" has never occurred to them.)

Mr. Robert Gardiner, in his recent Reith Lectures, has provided an admirable and incisive survey of the race problem.[3] It is, however, philosophically weak since his chief conclusion is that "interest" should prevail against the claims of "race." "Interest" is a word with a long history and with utilitarian overtones. It may spell merely being affluent, producing more and more, and having two cars each. This is yet psychologically far too narrow. If race loyalty be not itself regarded as a legitimate "interest," in a world where the *mystique* of community life and friendship is being increasingly developed, this is because, on analysis and in the hierarchy of loyalties, racial claims are not held to have priority. All the same, it may be alleged that community as such rightly takes precedence over individual affluence, even if its defenders do not make kith and kin (with or without segregation) the sole tests of community.

As to the "poverty issue," the disgrace in inequalitarianism has been the commercial exploitation of human beings as "hands," Aristotle's human machines, under a system where the working masses had small interest and less voice in the management. Here the spearhead of the movement to redress grievances has been not so much the proponents of class war (management being still required) as the trades union movement. This, however, is powerless in countries that are naturally poor in resources, dependent upon the market for primary products, and have no "cake" to be

---

[3] *The Listener,* London, November 18, 1965.

redistributed. Unless these countries are to be evacuated and their lands left untilled by a depleted population, the remedy lies in massive concerted aid from the wealthy until the "economic takeoff" is achieved. At present undoubted and objectively testable human ability, of a superior order, goes to the wall owing to lack of environmental facilities for its development. There is no equality of opportunity for the able.

The race problem arises from the inequalitarian depression of certain peoples, distinguished by color, cultural prejudice, or community resentment. Although the problem is different, some of the remedies are the same as before—but not all, for the problem itself is partly but not solely economic. It is indeed more economic, in terms of public or private provision of housing, health, and educational facilities, than is sometimes supposed. There are yet other prejudices and group fears at work.

Who rules whom? The strictly aristocratic response is that the more able must rule the less able and that issues of color, race, and the like must be ruthlessly disregarded as irrelevant. What is required, in the whole field from athletics to government, must be the objective test. Who does the work better? Who can do it better? To take one instance, the Japanese can beat the Westerner in many fields of skill, and this not only in terms of lower competitive wages. For one thing, he is less lazy and less self-indulgent. The Westerner sometimes thinks that it is the world's duty to feather-bed him, that he is *ipso facto* better than his neighbor. It is not true. The Japanese proved this, *inter alia,* by sheer force of naval guns when they reversed the trend of history since Marathon by thrashing the Russians.

This brings us straight up against the question of what we mean by "ability." Pride is the most precise psychological expression of original sin, which is unharmonized and irresponsible self-will and demand for immoral freedom. The demands of ability, in terms of certain gifts, frequently take the crude form, as argued by Callicles, that the men who think themselves abler than their neighbors should be on top. It is indeed not the prerogative of every lout to say that he is as good as his neighbors. The precise argument yet involves an ironic contradiction. It runs that, morals apart, those who are more able *are,* in the course of history, always on top or they *ought* to be. It ends with a sad complaint that, under democratic conditions, although they ought to be, they are not.

We may truthfully say, with Dr. James Conant, sometime President of Harvard, that "every honest calling has its own élite, its own aristocracy." Nevertheless, the ability or knack to produce a perfect tiddlywink is not of a high order of social importance. A machine can do it better—which fact, in certain contexts, humiliates the claims of fine mathematicians. (Besides, a man may have the highest mathematical ability and yet be a fool in household affairs or indeed in what is called "the art of life.") I would hesitate, however, to say that "God, the Great Mathematician" can best be worshipped by machines. Other qualities enter into our assessment. This general argument about the claims of ability usually ends in a discussion of claims of ability to govern. The reply to Callicles, as stressed by Plato, and to the claims of ability and meritocracy is not any flat denial of superiority or of excellence, fundamental to a high civilization, but is that it must be assessed in the context of community cooperation, harmony, the approval of the good man.

The radical objection to Nazi *Rassentheorie* is that it repudiates, not incidentally but fundamentally, the fraternity and community claims of the human race, which are the bases of universalist ethics. We are left with an enlarged tribalism; and although tribalism and clannishness are respectable within their limits, they are ridiculous and contemptible beyond those limits. They are the prerogative of low-grade peoples and of bad philosophers. (An Aristotelian contempt for "the barbarians," such as were our ancestors, which is a contempt shared by the Chinese, is in a rather different category.)

As to ability in government, this is not easy to define. Briefly, it can mean two different things. It can mean, as with Aristotle, the ability of the small farmer or of the common citizen to articulate his own private needs, to state what political goods he, as consumer, requires for his security or social and rational freedom, and to get his voice heard. Also, and quite distinctly, it may mean an ability that, under conditions of cooperative power, is largely administrative and expert. It would be a healthy thing if this latter ability were assessed in the same way as is executive ability in industrial management; and were it cut down to size from the pretensions of demagogues, dictators, "saviors of their country," and like messiahs. Undoubtedly, in this field, there are inequalities of ability, which should be not only recognized but also sought out. Be it said that the skilled politician is usually among the first to recognize the need to keep in touch with his consumer public and with community sentiment, or he will become bankrupt of support. His excellence is a recognizable and limited skill—that of superior social judgment, administrative or cooperative talent, as well as capacity to communicate. There is nothing grandiose in all this, although an age of television and popular entertainment, with political all-in party wrestling might lead to more dangerous conclusions. Advertising techniques here are, for the most part, not productive business, but parasitic.

The comment, made above, on the priority that must be accorded to the sense of community as against even the functional claims of political and like inequality, as well as against the nonfunctional assertion of racial inequality, applies also to economic inequality. Equality of opportunity may provide the opening for the man of greater ability "starting at the bottom of the ladder," to climb it and acquire a fortune. But, whereas the stimulus of profit and bonuses in production, as an alternative to increased compulsion, is justified in a strong economy, any extreme range of difference between rich and poor is not justified; breaks the community into "two nations"; and has to be remedied by distributive taxation. Without maintaining the principle of equality of incomes (expressed, if not practiced, by Bernard Shaw and condemned by Marx himself in his *Critique of the Gotha Program*), what is here affirmed about economic and social equalization is in no way inconsistent with what we have earlier said about human inequality and the need for the pursuit of excellence. It is dictated by reason.

Rhetoric about human equality is a vote-catcher that will always appeal to the mass of the jealous and envious and can be exploited in the name, for example, of the class war. It was urged in crude form as the primitive condition by the seedy Rousseau; although had he preached it among the primitive Zulus, he would probably have been impaled on the thorn bushes that the chieftain Tchalka reserved for those who raised such objections. Equality exists neither in the human nor in the related animal world; each has its "pecking order." It cannot be maintained by any political scientist of reputation, nor can a sound political science be based upon such bogus statements, however inflated. The equality of all men as "reasonable" is an affirmation of a different kind; it is really an affirmation about the nature of reason.

The affirmation, however, of functional inequalities in society and even of an order of command for specific purposes, of itself carries the condemnation of functionless or irrational inequalities. Against these, much of the equalitarian campaign has, historically and rightly, been directed. The ambition of powerful men to claim superior status, without agreement about rational function, has justified such flat statements of opposition as that all men are born equal and independent individuals. In society equality before the law and equality of opportunity can have their functional warrant. But the community, in terms of which we judge functions—although there are, of course, diversities among communities, about which there can be dispute—has a right of priority such that the pride stands condemned which stresses even a rational inequality beyond the social limit. An excess of external inequalities, beyond what is commonly accepted, destroys the fraternity. It is for this reason that alleged racial inequalities, beyond specific evidence, are not only scientifically suspect but also socially damnable. They deny alike the unity of humanity and the universality of ethics.

EGALITARIAN IMPLICATIONS AND
CONSEQUENCES OF BELIEF SYSTEMS

7

CHRISTIANITY AND EQUALITY

SANFORD A. LAKOFF

I

There is no such thing as Jew and Greek, slave and free-man, male and female; for you are all one person in Christ Jesus (Galatians 3:28). Even in the somewhat muted, donnish tones of the New English Bible,[1] the declaration of the apostle Paul keeps its dramatic ring. But drama apart, what did Paul mean?

---

[1] *The New English Bible, New Testament,* Oxford and Cambridge, 1961. Emphasis added. All quotations in the text from the New Testament are from this version, except as indicated. At least this modification is less troubling to the ear than "Pass no judgment, and you will not be judged" (Luke 6:37) or "Why do you look at the speck of sawdust in your brother's eye, with never a thought for the great plank in your own?" (Luke 6:41).

Was he suggesting that the new freedom purchased by the sacrifice of the messiah was already in itself an emancipation from the customary distinctions of the world and the flesh? Was he announcing a new doctrine of human equality, and did he intend it to stand as a challenge both to Judaic "chosenness" and to Graeco-Roman notions of the necessity for hierarchy in nature and society?

We have some help from Paul himself, but unfortunately not quite enough. The passage appears in the midst of an effort to explain to the backsliding Galatians how it is that they can consider themselves part of the issue of Abraham and, therefore, beneficiaries of the promises covenanted by God with the Jewish patriarch. It is not necessary, Paul contends, that they adopt the provisions of the Mosaic law. This law was promulgated, he points out, 430 years after the promise was made. To become the children of God and, therefore, his heirs, they must only have faith in Christ. Through faith they may achieve union with the messiah and thereby become themselves sons of God. Paul explains[2]:

> This is what I mean, so long as the heir is a minor, he is no better off than a slave, even though the whole estate is his; he is under guardians and trustees until the date fixed by his father. And so it was with us. During our minority we were slaves to the elemental spirits of the universe [or the elements of the natural world, or elementary ideas belonging to the world], but when the term was completed, God sent his own Son, born of a woman, born under the law, to purchase freedom for the subjects of the law, in order that we might attain the status of sons (4:1–5).

In offering this analogy, Paul is less concerned with describing the inheritance that now awaits the liberated believer than he is with persuading the insecure to pay no attention to rival evangelists. He urges them to ignore the "agitators" who insist that no one can enjoy the patrimony of Israel without assuming

---

[2] Though only under prodding from the dons: The prefatory phrase is absent from other versions. The King James has "Now, I say. . . ."

the yoke of the law, who warn that they cannot be considered
people of God unless they observe the holy days and circumcise
all male issue. (As for such circumcisers, Paul tartly observes,
"they had better go the whole way and make eunuchs of themselves!" [5:12][3]). It is only necessary, he insists, that they accept
the guidance of the spirit of God. Given a sincere faith and
righteous comportment, all may join in the hope that "if we do
not slacken our efforts we shall in due time reap our harvest"
(6:10).

It is a fascinating document, this epistle, especially as we now
have it in its new and more subtle English rendering. For all its
ambiguity, Paul's letter to the Galatians helps us understand not
only how the "good news" of Christianity contributed to the
development of egalitarian ideas but also how it came to inspire
an endless succession of movements for emancipation, from the
medieval mystics and sectaries to the modern secular rebels in
politics and art—all of whom have felt the yearning for a new
identity, a new wholeness, a new communion, in which the
frustrating and petty limitations of the human species would
somehow be overcome. Whatever the nature of the super-
natural "inheritance" Paul has in mind but does not specify, the
burden of his message is surely that this inheritance is available
to all, circumcised or not, and without regard to sex or station,
provided only that they rededicate themselves to a new life in
the image of God—a life exemplified in the savior who was God
in the form of man.

It was to prove a message of extraordinary force, particularly
among the Gentiles to whom, as Paul declared, he had been
called by God to proclaim the new dispensation. In some sense
it must surely have been received as a doctrine of equality. If, as
A. J. Carlyle could assert,[4] the Stoic doctrine of natural equality
stood in epochal contrast to the Aristotelian idea of natural inequality, how much more of an affront to received dogma must
the Christian conception have been? Not to the Jews, to be sure,
for Jesus was hardly the first Jewish teacher to announce that
the children of God ought to love their neighbors as themselves

---

[3] The King James: "I would they were even cut off which trouble you."
[4] *Medieval Political Theory in the West,* London, 1927, Vol. I, Chapter 8.

or that, as the children of Israel, they were all alike the progeny of a creator-God. This much of the Christian message was nothing new to them, and the rest struck fundamentally at the very roots of their existence—their ties as a people, the law embodying their relation to God, their expectation of a world transformation to be ushered in by the coming of the messiah. In the more fractious and unstable Graeco-Roman world, on the other hand, where narrow civic and kinship loyalties, evanescent cults, and exclusive mystery religions stood in embarrassing contrast to the unitary power of the empire, the universalism of the Christian doctrine was understandably attractive. Nor could its chiliastic egalitarianism fail to elicit interest in cultures where the myth of a golden age was a persistent theme.

The Graeco-Roman world had of course already developed in Stoicism a doctrine that served the same universalistic purpose as Christianity wished to serve and that also included a belief in equality. But the weakness of Stoicism as a rival to Christianity is nowhere more apparent than in their different ideas of equality. Although Stoicism too challenged elitist pretensions, it did so by using the same terms of argument that had traditionally served to support the belief in aristocracy. Thus, whereas Aristotle had argued that differences in rational capacity made some fit to rule and others fit only to obey, the Stoics asserted that the very possession of the capacity to reason made men more alike than different. Christianity in effect undercut the entire argument by contending that degrees of rationality made no difference. What mattered was that every man had a soul and that in the eyes of God all souls were equally worthy. In this respect, as in others, it is easy to understand why Christianity was more attractive to larger masses of people than Stoicism, which could only have had great appeal for an educated minority. Once the powerful edifice of Greek philosophy, which had already developed a concept of the immortality of the soul,[5] was fused with the revealed ethic of Christianity by the Neo-Platonists, the intellectual and moral appeal of the Christian conception of equality over that of Stoicism was assured. The message

[5] See Werner Jaeger, "The Greek Ideas of Immortality," *Harvard Theological Review*, Vol. LII, No. 3 (July, 1959), pp. 135–148.

of Paul could then become the firm belief not only of the Galatians but also of all the peoples of the great civilization that arose upon the foundations laid by Greece and Rome.

II

And yet, even as it triumphed in history, the Pauline Christian conception of equality was never a very clear guide to thought or action. It was one thing to proclaim that all human beings were equal in the eyes of God; it was another to assert that all should be equal in the eyes of the world. Was the Christian revelation to be considered a call for social and political equality? Or was it, like the Stoic conception of natural equality,[6] merely a wistful invocation of paradise lost implying no sanction of egalitarianism in the present? There have been plausible answers on both sides of the question. Indeed these answers can be divided into two broad theories of the Christian conception of equality: the *antipathetic* and the *anticipatory*.

The antipathetic view has been put forward both by politically conservative theological fundamentalists and by hostile critics of Christianity. In its mildest form, this interpretation maintains that Christianity is no sponsor of secular ideals. Insofar as the Christian revelation announces a doctrine of equality, the term is said to refer only to the inner soul and not to the external envelopes, which, in the eyes of the world, distinguish one soul from another. The promise of emancipation alluded to in Christian doctrine is, therefore, not to be taken as a prophecy of democracy, communism, or a liberal equality of rights, but simply and solely as a pledge that God loves all his creatures equally and holds out to all of them the hope of eternal life. As Bultmann says, succinctly if perhaps too dogmatically, "The negation of worldly differentiations does not mean a sociological program within this world; rather it is an eschatological oc-

[6] Cf. George H. Sabine and Stanley B. Smith, "Introduction" to Marcus Tullius Cicero, *On the Commonwealth*, transl. by Sabine and Smith, Columbus, Ohio, 1929, p. 25 and J. Plamenatz, "Equality of Opportunity," *Aspects of Human Equality, Fifteenth Symposium of the Conference on Science and Religion*, New York, 1957, p. 87.

currence which takes place only within the Eschatological congregation."[7]

Others have argued, on the same side of the question but with a still stronger belief in the opposition of Christianity to secular social reform, that a religious and a social conception of equality are incompatible. Kierkegaard contended that the effort to achieve an egalitarian social order was bound to be in vain. The world, he argued, is necessarily the realm of the separate and the diverse. In spirit, however, men are identical. In a Christian sense, therefore, there can be no distinctions among men, whereas, in worldly respects, differences are inherent and unavoidable. As a result, when Christian pietists hold property in common and a group of secular communists does the same, the contrast is fundamental, despite appearances, because in the one case the property is a thing indifferent (as a characteristic of worldly vanity and imperfection) whereas in the other it is all-important (as the desired good that is to relieve all suffering). Where material things are considered important, Kierkegaard suggests, there is bound to be contention and separateness of interest. Only insofar as the world is negated does equality become an appropriate standard for human relations. Christianity is, therefore, egalitarian but only in a spiritual sense. Otherwise it is opposed to all secular efforts at leveling—a phenomenon Kierkegaard condemned as a debasement of all higher values.[8]

Ironically, this rather fundamentalist and otherworldly interpretation of Christian egalitarianism is shared by the leading modern sponsors of atheistic alternatives to religion, Marx and Freud. In Marx's view, Christianity—indeed all religion—serves to deflect and dampen the outrage of the lower classes at the misery of their lot. Deluded by promises of far-off bliss (and revenge against their oppressors), they can be taught to accept

[7] R. Bultmann, *The Theology of the New Testament,* transl. by K. Grobel, New York, 1951, Vol. I, p. 309. Bultmann begs the question inasmuch as the "Eschatological congregation" may conceivably mean the community of believers or, more narrowly, the church. If the term refers to either one, the belief in spiritual equality can be quite legitimately understood as an injunction to institutional equality, either within the social structure in general or within the organization of the church.

[8] See Søren Kierkegaard, *On Authority and Revelation, The Book on Adler, or a Cycle of Ethico-Religious Essays* (1848), transl. by W. Lowrie, Princeton, 1955, pp. xxv–xxvi.

present exploitation with patient endurance. The Christian conception of an ultimate equality of souls is, therefore, precisely the enemy of social progress, an ideology that must be overcome rather than the inspiration of an ethical ideal that awaits implementation.[9] Freud held what amounts to a similar view. In a study of cohesiveness in the social system[10] he described the Christian doctrine of equality as a myth of order which serves to support the most hierarchical of social institutions by persuading adherents that God loves them all equally. Unlike Marx, of course, Freud could not conceive of a viable society that could in fact be built upon egalitarian principles, but he had no doubt that the Christian ideal of equality was, if anything, a barrier to egalitarianism of a structural kind.

Thus, despite other differences, Bultmann, Kierkegaard, Marx, and Freud all share a conception of Christian equality as at least indifferent to social equality and at most quite hostile to it.

According to the anticipatory theory, on the other hand, the Christian doctrine of equality is far from indifferent to society. Even though in itself it is a declaration of spiritual equality, Christianity is said to have clear implications for the social order—implications that have in fact been drawn in the course of Western history. By stressing the dignity of man, the immortality of the soul, and the promise of redemption held out to the low as well as the high, Christianity is said to have implanted the ethical seeds that ultimately blossomed in the various social conceptions of equality. The Christian idea of equality, according to this interpretation, should be understood as having anticipated a more explicitly stated ideal of social reform.

Ernst Troeltsch is perhaps the best exponent of the anticipatory theory. Troeltsch readily admits that there is nothing

---

[9] For a somewhat different Marxist view, however, see F. Engels, "On the History of Early Christianity" (1894–95), in L. Feuer, ed., *Karl Marx and Friedrich Engels, Basic Writings on Politics and Philosophy,* New York, 1959, pp. 168–194. Here Engels discerns parallels between early Christianity and the early history of working class movements but notes that limited as it was by its time, Christianity introduced the idea of another world as a "religious way out" (p. 184).

[10] *Group Psychology and the Analysis of the Ego,* transl. by J. Strachey, New York, 1949, p. 43.

directly socially revolutionary about the teachings of the New
Testament. "The message of Jesus," he points out, "is not a
programme of social reform. It is rather the summons to prepare
for the coming of the Kingdom of God. . . ."[11] But Troeltsch
also recognizes that in terms of historic impact, Christianity cannot be said simply to have issued a call for quietistic adjustment.
"At first," he observes, "the revolutionary power of the idea of
equality is hidden" in the Christian emphasis on inner, spiritual
equality, but in time "the realistic question" is bound to be
asked: "whether there are not grades and kinds of poverty which
make it impossible to rise to this kind of equality, and whether
external uplifting is not necessary."[12]

Unlike Bultmann, then, who argues that Christianity is in
intention a call to otherworldly values, Troeltsch holds that this
very summons was bound to raise the question of the need for
social reform in this world. There is, of course, no necessary
contradiction between these two interpretations. The one, which
is shared as far as it goes by both Bultmann and Troeltsch,
refers entirely to the inner logic of the Christian message; the
other refers to its reception and to the train of thoughts it inspired. And yet, the difference is important. If Christian doctrine
is in itself indifferent or even hostile to the reform of society,
any effort to achieve social equality of whatever kind may be
labeled unchristian or anti-Christian and, by some definitions,
idolatrous. On the other hand, if Christian ethics requires or
permits action to reform the world, then it may be the religious
duty of the Christian to promote the cause of social equality as
a means of infusing grace into worldly existence.

A variation on the same theme is what might be called the
proto-proletarian theory of the Christian concept of equality.
According to this point of view, Christianity was, virtually from
the start, a doctrine of mass emancipation. Inasmuch as the message of the Gospels was particularly addressed to the lowly, who
were promised bliss in the afterlife, whereas the rich and powerful were warned they would come to grief (see especially Luke
6:20–26), was it not in inception a doctrine of social equality—
or, at any rate, was it not bound to be understood as such?

---

[11] Ernst Troeltsch, *The Social Teaching of the Christian Churches*, transl.
by O. Wyon, New York, 1960, p. 61.
[12] *Ibid.*, pp. 77–78.

Nietzsche believed that it was. Judaism and Christianity were the very embodiment of the "slave morality" because both doctrines promised to turn the natural state of affairs upside down so that the meek and victimized could lord it over the high and mighty. The victory of Christianity, he maintained, was a victory for the slave morality because where Christianity was adopted, the belief in strength and glory was replaced by the exaltation of weakness and pity: "the wretched are alone the good; the poor, the weak, the lowly, are alone the good; the suffering, the needy, the sick, the loathsome . . . are to be saved, and not the powerful and rich."[13] Later on, the masses would turn upon the priests who had first persuaded them of this new morality and had inspired in them a wish for revenge. Not content with far-off satisfaction, they would demand immediate redress: They would become revolutionaries. Christianity, Nietzsche theorized, far from being indifferent to the social order, had actually been the source of all the egalitarian movements that, in modern times, were threatening to transform Western civilization into a mass society—from democracy and utilitarianism to anarchism and communism. He condemned them all, religions and secular philosophies alike, as agents of degeneration.

III

There is hardly much point in trying to decide between these two lines of interpretation. As is so often the case with major historical movements, even contradictory or incompatible theories turn out to have some plausibility. The Christian attitude toward the ideal of equality is certainly not wholly one of indifference or hostility; neither is it steadfastly and thoroughly sympathetic. Perhaps the best one can say is that it is profoundly dualistic. On the one hand, the identity of all souls and the equal promise of divine grace stand as the quintessence of the Christian revelation; and, on the other, the Christian is counseled to accept the inequalities of the worldly state as inevitable consequences of sin. From the start Christian doctrine combines both elements, either of which could be stressed to the virtual exclusion of the other. The monastic orders and the

[13] *The Genealogy of Morals* (1887), transl. by H. B. Samuel, *The Philosophy of Nietzsche*, New York, 1927, p. 643.

sectarian movements put the promise of ultimate equality at the very center of Christian teaching. To ignore this goal or to postpone its achievement, they believed, was to lead an unchristian life. To put aside all distinctions of rank, vocation, and dress, and to keep all goods in common was to demonstrate the possession of *pneuma* and to set an example for the sinful world without. But the fathers of the church and the canonists who came after them put the stress on the other element of Christian belief. Preoccupied as they were with the absorption of peoples ill prepared for perfection and apprehensive for the unity and the moral authority of the church in an unredeemed world, they venerated hierarchy as a synonym for order. All advocates of equality, whether obedient to the discipline of the church or disdainful of it, were bound to appear to them as either real or potential heretics.

In exhibiting this dualistic attitude toward human equality, Christianity was scarcely unique. The major Greek and Roman philosophers from Socrates on all looked upon equality either as the hallmark of some distant and irrecoverable past or as an ideal to which only the few best, Plato's Guardians, for instance, might aspire. Neither the democracy of Athens nor the ascetic communism of Sparta, in practice so important in the Greek experience, won favor with the philosophers. Equality might be recognized as a valid standard in the sphere of ideals— whether as an expression of the lost wholeness of humanity or of justice—but as a practical goal it was condemned for degrading the superior to the level of the inferior. Classical political philosophy, like Christianity, is a source of support both for those who believe in the ultimate merit of egalitarianism and for those who hold that as an immediate proposal it is impractical and pernicious.

With this ambivalence between ultimate and operative values, the Christian attitude was surely no radical departure from convention in the sphere of social philosophy. At the same time, it is easy to see how it might have been regarded as a radical departure by those who chose to consider only the ultimate side of its message. The Christian message *is* a doctrine of equality to the extent that it includes, as an extremely important element, the promise that in the victory over mortal limitations, the distinctions of the world are annulled and count for nothing.

The love feast celebrated by Christ and the apostles symbolizes this ideal of equality, as does the ethical injunction, adopted from Judaism, to love one's neighbor and to demonstrate this love by the performance of works of charity. The incarnation can also be understood as a token of the belief in equality inasmuch as the annihilation of the distance between God and man is evidence of the essential and common divinity of the human spirit. It raises, and it answers, the question whether, if there is no barrier between God and man, there should exist barriers between man and man.

This message, moreover, *was* directed especially to those who were both poor in worldly goods and deficient in the training that the priests of Israel claimed necessary to piety and the philosophers of the "pagan" world claimed necessary to virtue. Christianity was an appeal, as the King James translators awkwardly but perceptively put it, to the "poor in spirit" (Luke 6:20), to the vulgar "people of the land" *(am ha-aretz)*.[14] It could not have been received as anything but a revolutionary doctrine by those who were looked upon, and had come to look upon themselves, as the wretched and despised of the earth but whom Christ singled out for particular affection. The "poor in spirit" must surely have understood the radical social implications in the description of the original Christian communion in Acts 4:

> The whole body of believers was united in heart and soul. Not a man of them claimed any of his possessions as his own, but everything was held in common, while the apostles bore witness with great power to the resurrection of the Lord Jesus. They were all held in high esteem; for they had never a needy person among them, because all who had property in land or houses sold it, brought the proceeds of the sale, and laid the money at the feet of the apostles; it was then distributed to any who stood in need.

From this it might surely be concluded that the practice of Christian love required not only a belief in ultimate spiritual equality but also a willingness to put into practice the principle

[14] See George Foot Moore, *Judaism in the First Centuries of the Christian Era, the Age of the Tannaim*, Cambridge, Mass., 1962, Vol. II, pp. 72–73, *passim.*

of the abolition of social distinctions associated with the realization of perfect community in the kingdom of God.

Other Christians might nevertheless demur, understandably, from drawing such conclusions. Until the evils of the world were actually annulled by God, what right did any of its people have to pretend that they were already living in a state of redemption? While human relations remained under the curse of the fall, and were therefore inevitably imperfect, was not the obedient Christian obliged to accept inequities as God's judgment upon sinful humanity? The incarnation was experienced by one man for all, but to the believer it remained an achievement with which he could only identify indirectly and at a great distance. The new being exemplified by Christ would remain for other men only an aspiration and a hope. The ethical commandment to love one's neighbor was designed for, and would only be necessary in, a social structure riven with distinctions between the rich and the poor, the lettered and illiterate, the wellborn and the lowly. Because of the doctrine of predestination, moreover, even the promise of salvation was not unambiguously egalitarian. As Troeltsch has observed: "The idea of predestination cuts the nerve of the absolute and abstract idea of equality. . . . In spite of the equality of all in their sinful unworthiness and in their possession of grace . . . the equal claim of all to an equal share in the highest life-value through equal working out of vocation and destiny, is invalidated."[15]

Combined, however tenuously, both lines of thought were characteristic of early Christianity. There is no better statement of this dualistic attitude toward equality than that of St. Augustine, the most authoritative and the most influential of the fathers of the church. God, he declares, had originally intended that men should rule over "irrational creation" but not over other men: "the righteous men in primitive times were made shepherds of cattle rather than kings of men, God intending thus to teach us what the relative position of the creatures is, and what the desert of sin. . . ." Slavery and other forms of inequality were, therefore, not intended by the creator. Nevertheless, the inequalities in the world are ordained by God as "the result of

[15] Troeltsch, *op. cit.*, pp. 74–75.

sin."[16] Slaves are, therefore, not to revolt but to remain in subjection, not in "crafty fear but in faithful love, until all unrighteousness pass away, and all principality and every human power be brought to nothing, and God be all in all."[17] The Christian is expected to strive for justice in the earthly city, but he should entertain no illusions about the possibility of achieving it; the weight of his energies ought to be withdrawn from the world and concentrated on the love of God.

Even St. Ambrose, who is often celebrated for his denunciation of wealth, did not call for the abolition of private property. He merely offered a Christian gloss on the Stoic idea of a golden age in which there were no distinctions of rank and fortune, adding that present inequalities had come about through the fall from grace. Ambrose did not contend that these inequalities were unjust or that they should be done away with. Like Augustine, he was content to identify them as the consequence of sin. Ambrose's counsel was no different from that of the Stoics. A good man was obliged to behave charitably toward all, whatever their condition, but he was not compelled to pursue an unrealistic egalitarian goal. Equality, with paradise, would be restored by God in His good time.[18]

IV

Conditioned by feudalism and wracked by fear of disunity, Christianity underwent in medieval times an intensification of its antipathetic strain. Hierarchy was said by the spokesmen of the church to be as essential in human affairs as in the structure of the cosmos and the ordering of the personality. As the heavens rose above the earth and the soul was higher than the body, so the pope was superior to the emperor, the clergy to the laity, the secular nobility to its subjects. Thus refined and elaborated, Christianity could serve as a pillar of feudal aristoc-

---

[16] *The City of God,* transl. by M. Dods, New York, 1950, Book 19, Chapter 15, p. 693.

[17] *Ibid.,* p. 694.

[18] See T. Dudden, *The Life and Times of St. Ambrose* (Oxford, 1935), Vol. II, Chapter XX, pp. 502–554 and A. O. Lovejoy, "The Communism of St. Ambrose," *Essays in the History of Ideas,* Baltimore, 1948, p. 298 *passim.*

racy. Only with the revolt against hierarchy within the church, culminating in the Protestant Reformation, did the anticipatory egalitarian strain emerge again into the open as a respectable and widely held position. Until then it had been relegated to the eschatological underground—to the heretical sects in which the impatient and the thoroughly alienated sought release from earthly imperfections.

The Protestant Reformers were not all so radical in their intentions as these earlier heretics, but they, too, were moved to withdraw from the existing church, and in some instances from existing society, by what they felt was a scandalous disparity between the ideals of Christianity and the practices of Christendom. Given this perspective, it is not surprising that in elaborating a Christian conception of equality, the Reformers should have sought to make this ideal, no less than the others, operative as well as ultimate. This is not to say that all of them sought to reform the whole of society in an egalitarian direction. In most cases the Reformers' advocacy of equality was restricted to the church. But even in these cases, the reasoning advanced contributed to and prefigured the later development of the secular theory of equality in its three major variants: the liberal, conservative, and socialist.[19]

Luther, perhaps the foremost in influence, offered a view of Christian equality that in a number of crucial ways resembles and presages a modern liberal view. Much of what Luther had to say, in his conservative moods, about politics and society was quite conventional. But what is novel in his social theory tends in a distinctly liberal direction. In his celebrated advocacy of a "priesthood of believers," Luther squarely opposed the effort of the Roman church to distinguish among Christians according to their clerical or lay status and according to whether their vocations were "spiritual" or "carnal." In opposition to the Roman practice of hierarchical co-optation and designation, Luther argued that the congregation should ordain its own minister and that it should have the right to hold him responsible for the conduct of his office. Referring to the different treatment accorded clerics and laymen in law, Luther exclaimed: "Whence

[19] The development is traced in Sanford A. Lakoff, *Equality in Political Philosophy*, Cambridge, Mass., 1964.

comes this great distinction between those who are equally Christians? Only from human laws and inventions!"[20]

In economic and conjugal matters, Luther was similarly emancipated from the medieval association of the worldly with the demonic.[21] Max Weber has properly described his position as one of "inner-worldly asceticism" according to which the individual Christian is called upon to demonstrate the strength of his faith by a diligent pursuit of his calling and by pursuing a mode of life in which ordinary activities are regarded as opportunities and challenges for virtuous conduct. Although he generally stopped short of extending to politics and economics the egalitarian reforms he advocated for the church, Luther's reasoning is in principle quite close to what became the basis for the secular liberal doctrine of equality. Like Luther, liberals such as Locke and Mill would argue that all men were capable of governing themselves and that social life should be regarded as a kind of competition in virtue in which each individual was called upon to use his talents to the fullest extent possible.

Calvin used a quite different argument in his assault on Catholic hierarchy. At the center of Calvin's opposition to hierarchy was his belief in universal depravity. This pessimistic assumption contrasts sharply with Luther's relatively far more optimistic belief that all Christians were capable of spiritual discernment. Historically, Calvin's doctrine of equal depravity led to two rather different positions. Congregationalist disciples read his argument to mean that no one was to be trusted with prolonged or unlimited authority and that all matters of importance should be left to the disposition of the congregation at large. Presbyterians saw in Calvin's stress on predestination a profound modification of this concept of equal depravity and drew the conclusion that, in view of the sinfulness of most men, it was essential for the few saints who were God's elect to rule over the others in strict and unquestioned authority. Calvin him-

---

[20] *An Open Letter to the Christian Nobility of the German Nation, Concerning the Reform of the Christian Estate* (1520), in his *Three Treatises*, Philadelphia, 1943, p. 14.

[21] For Luther's novel views on "fleshly lust" see particularly his *A Commentary on St. Paul's Epistle to the Galatians* (1535), ed. by P. S. Watson, London, 1953, p. 503. For his economic views see, in addition to *Three Treatises*, his *On Trading and Usury, Works of Martin Luther*, Philadelphia, 1930, Vol. IV, pp. 12–69.

self had drawn a republican conclusion in theory (in his *Institutes of the Christian Religion*) but had provided a practical example, in his Genevan theocracy, of dictatorial elitism.

Neither of these groups of epigonic exegetes captured the essential logic of Calvin's argument, however, so well as did that most impious of political philosophers, Thomas Hobbes (even though he did so unintentionally). As Calvin and Hobbes both recognized, if men are equal only or primarily in the sense that they are all driven by their base passions and are all similarly incapable of achieving their egoistic goals, they are bound to be tormented by constant anxiety. Self-government will prove impossible; security or tranquillity will seem the most desirable of goals. The only way they could hope to put an end to their fears and perpetual insecurity would be to abandon all pretensions to self-reliance and to surrender themselves in utter and complete obedience to an omnipotent ruler, who alone can give them the greatest of gifts, the gift of life itself. It is only necessary to substitute for Calvin's God the conception of an all-powerful earthly sovereign—a *"Mortall God"*—and for his belief in salvation the ideal of security to see how this theological conception of equality can lead to a secular conservatism.

The Reformation also produced an incipiently socialist conception of equality in the doctrines of the so-called left-wing Reformers. Many of those on this left wing were pietists and mystics who wished only to escape society, not to reform it. The social activists, however, like Thomas Müntzer and Gerrard Winstanley, were left-wingers in the modern sense of the term. What sets them apart from previous sectarian advocates of Christian communism is that they do not simply wish to withdraw from society into communities of the perfect, there to await the transformation of the rest of the world, but instead see themselves as agents of social revolution.

Müntzer and his peasant army were convinced that they had been chosen by God to serve as the vanguard of millennium. As both Marx and Lenin of that movement, Müntzer offered to his followers a theory of the historical development toward the millennium and a justification for a revolutionary suspension of ordinary ethical standards. The spirit of God, he declared, had entered human history in the incarnation. It would grow stronger despite oppressions until it would finally topple the devilish powers of persecution. He and his followers, Müntzer declared, were instruments of the spirit whose mission was to bring about the kingdom of God, if necessary by exterminating the godless.[22] Winstanley, who was a much more pacifistic and democratic communist, also believed that the millennium would come in time and space through the work of the spirit of God in history, aided and put into effect by human effort. The time was approaching, Winstanley prophesied, when the spirit would begin to appear in the flesh and "every one shall look upon each other as equall in the Creation."[23] The new Jerusalem, he said, was not to be sought in the hereafter but in this world and this life. While man and the divine spirit are still alien to each other, man mistakenly imagines that redemption is to be achieved after death. But when the spirit finally succeeds in taking hold of him, "man is drawne up into himselfe again, or new Jerusalem . . . comes down to Earth. . . ."[24]

At the base of this socialistic conception of Christian equality is plainly a stress on the spiritual identity of mankind. It is this identity which, in the eyes of the radicals, calls for a total transformation—not only of the church but of secular society as well. The transformation must be guided by the effort to make the egalitarian example of the original Christian community the goal of all mankind. The similarity between the theological statement of this doctrine in historicist and dialectical terms and the later expressions of socialist egalitarianism is arresting evidence of the significance of the Reformation as a turning point in the history of social thought and of the links connecting seemingly diverse theories that are at bottom expressions of the same ethical impulse.

[22] See particularly T. Müntzer, *Sermon Before the Princes* (1524), in G. H. Williams and A. Mergal, eds., *Spiritual and Anabaptist Writers*, Vol. XXV of *The Library of Christian Classics*, Philadelphia, 1957. For a study of the entire left wing of the Continental Reformation see George H. Williams' monumental descriptive history, *The Radical Reformation*, Philadelphia, 1964. An interesting analysis of Müntzer and his movement is included in Norman Cohn, *The Pursuit of the Millennium*, London, 1957.

[23] *The New Law of Righteousness* (1648), in *The Works of Gerrard Winstanley*, ed. by G. H. Sabine, Ithaca, New York, 1941, p. 159.

[24] *Fire in the Bush* (1650), *ibid.*, p. 458.

V

As an ultimate ideal, then, equality was very much an element of Christian teaching from the outset. Just because it was regarded as an ultimate ideal, however, without bearing on life in the world, it was allowed to remain an abstract and un-differentiated goal. While Christian thought hovered uncertainly between heavenly hopes and earthly resignation, no significant effort was made to define the possible meaning of Christian equality in terms that would be relevant to society. Only when the demand for a socially relevant creed became a full-scale revolt with the Protestant Reformation, was such an effort under-taken by recognized spokesmen for large sectors of the Christian community. The outcome was not one Christian ideal of equal-ity but several. The Reformers thus provided a strong foretaste of the rival theories of equality that were to emerge in open contest only in the nineteenth century. Although these egalitarian principles were for the most part applied only within the church, the spectrum of possibility they represented was the same as that which was to define the pattern of political speculation in later times. The Reformers may, therefore, be said to have con-tributed to and prefigured the development of the liberal, con-servative, and socialist theories of equality.

To some present-day Christians this evolution of Christian doctrine will appear as a laudable effort to spiritualize social relations. To others it will appear as a decline into relativistic secularism. To the student of intellectual history, however, per-haps the most intriguing aspect of the matter is what is re-vealed of the parallel between religious thought and political philosophy. When political philosophy is dualistic with respect to equality, so is Christianity; when Christianity exhibits several ideas of social equality, so, not long afterward, does political philosophy. In matters of social ethics at least, the same tides seem to have carried both traditions in Western thought.

Indeed, it is tempting to speculate that what leads the socially sensitive religious thinker and the ethically sensitive political thinker to the same conclusion must be a fundamentally similar set of assumptions. What both wish to know, in the final analysis, is how to arrange human affairs in the way that best suits both the aspirations and limitations of the human species. There are optimists, pessimists, and meliorists among religious thinkers as there are among political thinkers. How understandable, therefore, that when they consider the possible shape of an egalitarian society, they should arrive at conclusions that reflect their various predilections. The very fact of the convergence should at least make us aware that the distance between religious and political ideals is not so great as is sometimes imagined. The apostles and their master may well have intended their message of equality to refer only to life in a world to come. But those who take this message of emancipation to heart are bound to wish to see it fulfilled in the world in which they live. Inevitably, they will also differ as to precisely how it ought to be realized. In this sense, the Christian dilemma with respect to equality is the universal and ever present human dilemma.

8

HIERARCHY, EQUALITY, AND CONSENT IN MEDIEVAL CHRISTIAN THOUGHT

PAUL E. SIGMUND

To the central problem of political theory, "Why should I obey?" the writers of the Middle Ages gave a variety of answers. Inasmuch as the society with which they were familiar was organized on the principle of hierarchy, it is not surprising that most of these answers were such as to justify unquestioning submission to one's superiors and acceptance of one's station in society. Yet one group of arguments concerning political authority did exist that was capable of subverting the entire medieval structure—those arguments based on the premise of human equality, as a natural, moral, or historical fact that must be taken into account in any discussion of political or religious authority. And by the fourteenth and fifteenth centuries—well before Locke's *Second Treatise* or the Declaration of Independence—equality and authority had been related to one another through a theory of consent that transformed the idea of equality from "the rule for an ideal state located in some distant or mythic past beyond recovery"[1] into the basis for representative institutions in both church and state. The demand for consent to government only emerged in the late Middle Ages, but the idea of natural equality on which it was based had coexisted with hierarchical theories since the beginning of political speculation in the West. An examination of some of the medieval conceptions of hierarchy, equality, and consent may be useful in understanding and evaluating more modern views.

THEORIES OF HIERARCHY

The prevailing theory of authority in most of the Middle Ages was a belief in a natural hierarchy in man, society, and the universe. This hierarchical scheme was ultimately derived from a Christianized neo-Platonism, which developed and extended to the entire universe Plato's vision of an ideal social organism in which each member finds his natural hierarchical place in a completely harmonious community.[2] In his *Timaeus* Plato had applied this hierarchical view to the structure of the cosmos and of the human body, but the complete systematization of the hierarchical outlook was carried out by a fifth-century monk, known to us as Pseudo-Dionysius (because of his claim to be Dionysius the Areopagite, the convert of St. Paul mentioned in Acts 17:32). In his works on *The Celestial Hierarchy* and *The Ecclesiastical Hierarchy,* he described the structure of the universe in ranks of three and nine descending from God down to the lowest level of creation. Basing his view on the writings of the neo-Platonist philosopher, Proclus (418–485), Dionysius outlined a system in which all existence was ordered in grades of value and each rank received its power from that above and transmitted it to that below. Differentiated inequality was the fun-

---

[1] Sanford Lakoff, *Equality in Political Philosophy*, Cambridge, Mass., 1963, p. 19. Lakoff holds that the idea of equality only became "operative" in modern times. This paper will argue that the myth of equality began to have institutional implications by the last part of the Middle Ages.

[2] Although the text of Plato's *Republic* was not available in the West until it was translated in 1422, a major part of his *Timaeus* was translated and preserved for the Latin Middle Ages in Chalcidius' *Commentary*.

damental characteristic of the created world, and existence and value issued from above in a "great Chain of Being."[3]

Dionysius did not apply this vision to politics, but medieval thinkers used his conception of a hierarchical order in the cosmos to justify a hierarchically organized society. An argument from the order of the angels was used to defend hierarchy in political and social life, and the hierarchical order among the angels became a model for political inequality on earth. Aegidius Romanus wrote in his *De Ecclesiastica Potestate*, published in 1302, "We can descend to the government of men through analysis of the natural phenomena which we can see in the government of the world."[4] Perhaps reflecting the influence of Aegidius, Boniface VIII in his bull, *Unam Sanctam*, also published in 1302, cited Dionysius in support of the derivation of the temporal from the spiritual power. "According to blessed Dionysius, the law of divinity is to lead the lowest through the intermediate to the highest things. According to the law of the universe, all things are ordered, not equally and immediately, but the lowest through the intermediate and the lower through the higher."[5] A generation earlier, St. Thomas Aquinas in the *Summa Theologica* had also asserted that just as there were three orders on each of the levels of the angelic hierarchy, as Dionysius had described them, so in every city, there is a threefold order, "Some are supreme as the nobles, others are lowest as the common people, while others hold a place between these, as the middle class *(populus honorabilis)*." The structure of the church follows the same model. "The ecclesiastical hierarchy is derived from and represents the heavenly hierarchy. By Divine Law, inferior things are led to God by the superior."[6]

[3] The history of this idea is outlined in A. O. Lovejoy, *The Great Chain of Being,* Cambridge, Mass., 1936. See also my *Nicholas of Cusa and Medieval Political Thought,* Cambridge, Mass., 1963, ch. iii.

[4] Aegidius Romanus, *De Ecclesiastica Potestate,* Book III, ch. 9, transl. by Ewart Lewis, *Medieval Political Ideas,* vol. II, New York, 1954, p. 383. The original Latin can be found in the edition by Richard Scholz, Weimar, 1929, at p. 190. Examples of "the argument from the angels" can also be found in Wilhelm Berges, *Die Fürstenspiegel des hohen und späten Mittelalters,* Leipzig, 1938, p. 32.

[5] Translated in R. W. and A. J. Carlyle, *A History of Medieval Political Theory in the West,* vol. V, London, 1938, pp. 391–392.

[6] *Summa Theologica,* I, 108, a. 4. For a similar argument, see also Gilbert of Tournai, *Eruditio Regum* (A. de Poorter, ed.) , Louvain, 1914, III, 2, p. 84.

Plato's defense of the rule of a selected elite with special qualifications and training thus became in its medieval form an elaborate argument from analogy, which was considered to have persuasive value because behind it lay the assumption of a purposive and rational God who had designed an ordered universe that revealed the proper patterns of authority to those who could perceive the hierarchical structure of the universe and of society.

Both the spiritual and temporal hierarchies were based on divine right, the intention of God, but the case of the spiritual authorities was the stronger, for it was based on scriptural texts. Christ had singled out twelve of his followers as apostles and given them power to bind and loose on heaven and earth. He had selected one of them, Peter, as the head of the church, when he said, "Upon this rock I will build my church and the gates of hell shall not prevail against it."[7] As neither Peter nor the apostles were to live forever, the theory of Apostolic Succession explained how their powers could be transmitted. With the belief that the apostles could pass on their authority by the laying on of hands, authority in the church was necessarily hierarchical, for only those who had been thus ordained had succeeded to Peter and the apostles in their positions in the government of the church.

The temporal ruler was also believed to govern by the intention of God. He was described as the "vicar of Christ," the "image of God," and ruler "by the grace of God."[8] Yet unlike the pope he could not appeal to an historical event that established his credentials, and his defenders were also compelled to refer to his superior wisdom, rationality, and justice as the basis of his claim to obedience.[9]

---

[7] Matthew, 16:18. The apostles are given the power to bind and loose in Matthew 18:18. The original or present constitution of the Church is a matter of disagreement among Christian denominations, but I cite these passages as they were viewed in medieval political theory and ecclesiology. There were also equalitarian tendencies, but for them to have any meaning in practice, the question of the transmission of orders from the apostles and of the primacy from Peter had first to be dealt with.

[8] For examples see Ernst Kantorowicz, *The King's Two Bodies,* Princeton, 1957, ch. III.

[9] See for example the arguments of St. Thomas Aquinas, *Summa Theologica,* I, qu. 96, a. 3 and 4, and John of Salisbury, *Policraticus,* Book V, ch. 6.

THEORIES OF EQUALITY

The principal arguments for authority in the Middle Ages were thus based on premises that began and concluded with inequality. Tradition, the divine will, qualitative differences in the universe, and the differences in wisdom among men, all seemed to point to obedience to one's superiors in church and state. Yet there was also another group of beliefs in classical and Christian thought which pointed in a different direction. In fifth-century Athens, the Sophists viewed men as similar in all important respects and used this view to demonstrate that political subjection is merely conventional, or even opposed to nature.[10] In Greece and Rome the Stoics argued for the natural equality of all men which they saw as derived from the common possession of reason, defined as the ability to know and do the good. Contrary to Plato, they asserted that all men are alike by nature: "if bad habits and false beliefs did not twist the weaker minds and turn them in whatever direction they are inclined, no one would be so like his own self as all men would be like all others."[11] Later Stoic writers such as Seneca, faced with the contrast between this concept of natural equality and the striking inequalities of imperial Rome, developed the notion of an earlier age of innocence—preceding the introduction of property, slavery, and government—in which men lived in a condition free from domination and coercion. This conception was taken over by the Roman lawyers and is reflected in the opening passages of Justinian's *Institutes,* "By the law of nature all men from the beginning were born free," as well as in the *Digest,* "According to natural law, all men are equal."[12]

[10] Different versions of the Sophist argument are presented by Callicles in Plato's *Gorgias* and by Thrasymachus and Glaucon in his *Republic.* The view is most clearly presented in the fragments from the Sophist, Antiphon, translated in Ernest Barker, *Greek Political Theory, Plato and His Predecessors,* London, 1960, p. 98: "[Those who are born of a great house] we revere and venerate; those who are born of a humble house we neither revere nor venerate. On this point we are [not civilized, but] barbarized in our behaviour to one another. Our natural endowment is the same for us all, on all points, whether we are Greeks or barbarians. . . ."

[11] Cicero, *De Legibus,* Book I, ch. 10.

[12] Justinian, *Institutes,* Book I, Title I, sec. 4; *Digest,* Book L, Title XVII, sec. 32. For a discussion of Seneca's political theory, see R. W. and A. J. Carlyle, *op. cit.,* vol. I, ch. 2.

Christianity adopted the Stoic belief in man's original equality, though on the basis of different premises. Christian equality was not related to a common rationality as in Stoicism but was based on a common faith in the fatherhood of God, common descent from the first parents and a sharing in their sin, and a common redemption by Christ. Yet the Christian ideas of religious equality were not applied to society or politics any more than the earlier classical theories had been. Just as for Seneca the age of innocence was lost forever, for the Fathers of the Church social and political equality had disappeared with the fall of man. Pope St. Gregory the Great, in a statement widely quoted in the Middle Ages, could insist that, "by nature all of us are equal"[13] and still urge Christians to accept both good and bad rulers as sent from God, for political subjection was considered a divinely appointed remedy for sin. The poor and the weak could only console themselves with Christ's words about the difficulties of the rich in gaining salvation (Mark 10:25) or the parable of the Rich Man and Lazarus, which indicated that worldly status might be quite the reverse of the status of souls before God (Luke 17:19–31).

When the study of law was revived in the twelfth century, medieval legal thought transmitted to the Middle Ages the idea of natural equality as it was found in Roman law. The texts of Justinian postulating the original natural equality of all men became familiar to the civil lawyers and were repeated by them. Bulgarus in his Commentary on the *Digest* speaks of the "natural law by which all men are equal" and Placentinus says that "as far as nature is concerned, all men are equal." Beaumanoir, the thirteenth-century French jurist, adds a religious note when he says, "Although there now exist several estates of men, it is true that in the beginning all were free and of the same freedom; for everyone knows that we are all descended from one father and one mother."[14]

The canon law was also a source of the idea of natural equality in the Middle Ages. The opening passages of the basic text, Gratian's *Decretum,* hold that the natural law includes possession

[13] Gregory, *Expositio Moralis in Beatum Job,* quoted in Carlyle, *op. cit.,* vol. I, p. 114, n. 4.

[14] For Bulgarus and Placentinus see the excerpts in Carlyle, *op. cit.,* vol. II, p. 35. Beaumanoir is quoted in Norman Cohn, *The Pursuit of the Millennium,* London, 1957, p. 202.

of all things in common and liberty for all men. Yet Gratian intended neither universal communism nor the abolition of slavery, for he specifically provided for the possession of property and slaves by the church. As in the writings of the Fathers, equality in the social order was described as a characteristic of the natural state of man before the fall. Thereafter slavery and property became necessary, Gratian explained, because of sin (of the slave?) and the greed of fallen man. The original natural state was an ideal that could not now be attained.[15]

By the thirteenth century, the original equality of all men was a commonplace of medieval thought. The following lines of the *Roman de la Rose* are typical:

> Naked and impotent are all,
> High-born and peasant, great and small.
> That human nature is throughout
> The whole world equal, none can doubt.[16]

FROM THEORY TO PRACTICE

However, it was only in the fourteenth and fifteenth centuries that the myth of original equality began to be applied as a standard to criticize or to justify existing institutions. In its most radical application, the leaders of the Peasants' Revolt of the fourteenth century used it to attack existing social and political inequalities. In a more moderate form, it was combined with the arguments from tradition, divine right, and superior rationality in a fifteenth-century conciliarist theory, which was the first to argue from equality to the necessity of consent to law and government.

Peasant revolts broke out in Flanders in the early fourteenth century, in France in 1351, in England in 1381, and in the Holy Roman Empire in the early fifteenth century. Only for the English revolt of 1381, however, do we have a detailed record of the views of the rebels: Two different sources indicate that

---

[15] The opening passages of the *Decretum* are translated in Ewart Lewis, *op. cit.*, pp. 32–36.

[16] F. S. Ellis translation, quoted in George H. Sabine, *A History of Political Theory*, 3rd ed., New York, 1961, p. 315.

John Ball, the leader of the revolt, drew from the tradition of original natural equality to argue for a drastic change in the social order.

Froissart, the French chronicler, gives a typical sermon of Ball's, "If we are all descended from one father and mother, Adam and Eve, how can the lords say or prove that they are more lords than we are. . . . Things can not go well in England nor ever shall until all things are in common and there is neither villein nor noble but all of us are of one condition. . . ." In England Thomas Walsingham describes a similar speech by Ball urging the common people to win back the freedom that evil men against the will of God had taken from them.[17] It is true that the peasants themselves were more concerned with specific economic grievances, but, from these sources, it appears that at least one of their leaders saw the revolt as part of a more general movement against inequality and used the by-then traditional doctrine of original natural equality to support his case.

The writers of the conciliar movement were not concerned with promoting political or social equality but with defending the superiority of the council to the pope. However, the argument for the council rested on the requirement that the whole church as represented in the council should give its consent to the pope and to church law. This in turn was defended in many different ways, some historical, some theological, and some legal. Marsilius, the conciliarist whose political ideas seemed to imply the greatest equality in practice, never based his arguments on original or natural equality but on the practical advantages of involving the people or "its weightier part as to quality and quantity" in the legislative process of both church and state.[18]

However, one theorist writing at the end of the conciliar period used the argument from natural equality as a central point in his defense of the requirement of conciliar consent to church law and

---

[17] See Cohn, *op. cit.*, ch. x for these and other examples of the use of the argument from natural equality in the fourteenth and fifteenth centuries.

[18] Marsilius, *Defensor Pacis*, D. I, ch. xii and xiii. Latin editions of the *Defensor Pacis* have been published by C. W. Previte-Orton, Cambridge, 1928, and Richard Scholz (2 vols.), Hanover, 1932-33. There is also an English translation by Alan Gewirth in *Marsilius of Padua*, vol. II, New York, 1956.

government. Nicholas of Cusa in his *De Concordantia Catholica* (1433) supported the council on the ground that the original freedom and equality of all men require that they give their consent to law and government:

> Accordingly since by nature all men are free, any authority, whether contained in written law or in the living law which is the prince, by which subjects are compelled to avoid evil and their freedom is directed to the good through fear of punishment, must come solely from the agreement and consent of the subjects. For if men are by nature equal in power and equally free, the properly ordered authority of one who is naturally equal in power can only be established by the choice and consent of the others, and also law is constituted by consent.[19]

Nicholas also referred to the canon law requirements of consent to various acts of church officers and to the Roman-law doctrine of the derivation of authority from the people, but his principal argument was based on natural equality. He does not identify its source, merely stating that natural and divine law include and imply equality. However, his references to original freedom and his usage of the term, *natura,* seem to indicate that he is drawing on the Stoic tradition as inherited through Roman and canon law and the writings of the Church Fathers. Like the Roman lawyers and the Fathers, though unlike the earlier Stoics, the emphasis is on the equality of all men in a state of original freedom, not, as in Cicero, on their equal capacity for the use of reason. This freedom is established by divine as well as by natural law because, in Cusanus' view, Christian faith confirms man's natural freedom. As he says at the end of the second book of the *Concordantia:*

> For those who before were completely free, by choosing a ruler over themselves, submitted themselves to him. Proper procedure requires free subjection on their part as a pre-

---

[19] Translated from Nicolaus Cusanus, *De Concordantia Catholica* (hereafter abbreviated as *DCC*) , Book II, ch. xiv, edited by Gerhard Kallen, Leipzig, 1941, p. 161. (A revised edition of Book II, by the same editor, has been published in Hamburg in 1965.)

requisite since both by the law of the Christian faith and by natural law, they should not be restrained beyond the limits of freedom.[20]

There is one additional element in Cusanus' doctrine of "free subjection" which merits comment. In addition to the argument for consent from the doctrine of man's original equal *freedom*, there is also the curious reference to the fact that consent is required for rulership because men are equal *in power (aeque potentes)*. At first glance, this appears to be an anticipation of a central point in the political theory of Hobbes' *Leviathan* (1651), which derived the necessity of consent from the equal ability of every man to kill any other man. It is possible to interpret Cusanus' statement in this way—and Christian thought has always contained an element that identifies government with coercion. However, I have translated *"aeque potentes"* as "equal in power," rather than as "equally powerful," in order to bring out the ambiguity in the Latin. *Potentes* seems to refer to political or moral authority rather than to physical force, and Nicholas thus is saying that by nature no man is endowed with any more intrinsic political authority than any other man. This interprets the reference simply as a reinforcement of the basic point of the whole passage, the natural equality and freedom of all men.

In itself, this doctrine was not new. What was new was the particular application it received in the *Concordantia*. The Roman lawyers had accepted the natural freedom of men and then proceeded to a discussion of slavery as a legal status about the existence of which there was no question. The Fathers had proclaimed the original equality of men but reconciled themselves to gross inequality as a consequence of sin. But in the writings of Cusanus equality is no longer simply a moral conception or a characteristic of a lost Golden Age or Garden of Eden. It is to be applied to contemporary political and ecclesiastical institutions. For if men are by nature equal and free, law and government must be based on their consent.

---

[20] Translated from *DCC*, II, xxxiv, 304. Other references to consent as based on natural and divine law (although without the mention of original equality and freedom) appear in *DCC*, II, xi, 143; II, xviii, 199; and vol. III (Hamburg, 1959), ch. iv, p. 346. The doctrine of Christian liberty was first set forth by William of Occam in his *Dialogus*, Part III, Book I, ch. v (ff. 183–4 in the Lyons edition, reprinted, London, 1962).

Inasmuch as it was impossible for each man to give his consent personally (and it is unlikely that in the fifteenth century one would even consider this possibility), another means had to be found for the institutionalization of consent. Here Cusanus moves to the next stage of his analysis—the principles of freedom, equality, and consent are held to entail representative councils in both church and state. About the church, he observes on this point, "if a right order is to be preserved, then the text of the council of Toledo should be observed, that local clergy be elected or at least that there be some suitable provision for consent regarding them . . . then the clergy should elect the bishop with the accompanying consent of the laity . . . and the bishops the metropolitan with the consent of the clergy . . . and the metropolitans of the church provinces with the consent of the bishops should elect the representatives of the provinces who are called cardinals to assist the pope, and these cardinals should elect the pope with the consent of the metropolitans in so far as possible . . . ."[21] In addition to the election of church officers, conciliar consent is required for all levels of canon law, and the law of the universal church should be made in the universal council. In the past, he says, the church agreed tacitly to the concentration of legislative authority in the papacy, but the council is the more appropriate institution for the purpose of ensuring consent.[22]

Concerning the temporal authority, Nicholas restricts himself to an examination of the structure of the empire as the expression of the temporal unity of Christendom. He recognizes that the emperor does not in fact rule all of Christendom but argues that he has a general pre-eminence as special protector of the church. He does not propose a conciliar structure for the lower levels of the empire, but he describes the imperial electors as "representatives of the German people and of the others who were subject to the empire at the time of Henry II" and bases their elective authority on "the common equal birth of all men." He is willing to admit hereditary monarchy, if it is initiated by the election of the king *cum successoribus,* but his preference is

---

[21] Translated from *DCC,* II, xviii, 200.
[22] This summarizes the argument of *DCC,* II, 8–12.

for a new election with each ruler—"by all or a majority, or at least by their leaders who represent all with their consent."[23]

Arguing that, in addition to electing the ruler, the people should have the right to depose him, Nicholas thus sums up the controversy among the Roman lawyers as to the ultimate power of the Roman people over the emperor: "It is the common opinion of all learned men that the Roman people can take away the power of making laws from the emperor, because he has received this power from them."[24] Although this principle is derived from a specific historical transfer of power, it could also be taken as an illustration of a more general power of the people to set up their governments, a power derived from the natural freedom and equality of all men.

At the beginning of Book III, in a preface influenced by his recent reading of Marsilius, Nicholas states that civil laws "should be made by those who are to be bound by them or by a majority agreed to by the others." However, the actual procedure outlined subsequently calls for the adoption of legislation by "a council of leaders and lords of both estates," and here Nicholas shows that he is thinking of the imperial *Reichstag*. Its members were not elected, of course, but as in the case of the electors of the emperor, Nicholas justifies their role on the basis of the tacit consent of the people. "For this arrangement is the rule according to which the subjects wish the power of the ruler to be directed."[25]

Beginning with the premise of the original freedom and equality of man, Cusanus developed an elaborate system of councils to give consent to law and government in both church and state. These conclusions could stand alone, but his major political work was intended to be a concordance of the political

---

[23] Translated from *DCC*, III, preface, 322. Cusanus' discussion of the universality of the empire appears in Book III, ch. vi, and the constitutional position of the electors is outlined in ch. iv of the same book.

[24] Translated from *DCC*, III, iv, 361.

[25] Translated from *DCC*, III, ch. xii, p. 375. On the relation of the preface to the rest of Book III, see G. Kallen, "Die handschriftliche Überlieferung der Concordantia catholica des Nikolaus von Kues," *Sitzungsberichte der Heidelberger Akademie der Wissenschaft*, 1963, no. 2, as well as my article, "The Influence of Marsilius of Padua on XVth Century Conciliarism," *The Journal of the History of Ideas*, vol. XXIII, no. 3 (July–Sept. 1962), pp. 392–402.

and ecclesiological theory of the Middle Ages, and therefore he also took account of the anti-egalitarian elements in medieval thought.

First, there was the theory of hierarchy of Christianized neo-Platonism. Counterbalancing the natural order of freedom and equality was a metaphysical vision of subordination and inequality in nature. In the first book of the *Concordantia,* Nicholas sets out the hierarchical pattern of the universe along the lines of Pseudo-Dionysius. Nearest to the Triune God are the nine choirs of angels, followed by nine spheres around and including the earth; then on earth all nature is divided into rational, sensate, and vegetable. The church is divided into the church triumphant in heaven, sleeping in purgatory, and militant on earth. The church on earth is divided into the sacraments (its spirit), the priesthood (its soul), and the faithful (its body). Within each of these ranks, there is a hierarchical qualitative differentiation. As to governmental responsibility in the church, the order again comprises three ranks of three—the subdeacons, deacons, and priests; the deans, archdeans, and bishops; and the archbishops, patriarchs, and the pope.[26]

The empire is organized in a hierarchy paralleling that of the church, so "that the emperor has rightful authority over the lower authorities in the empire as the Roman patriarch has over the bishops subject to the Roman church. And as the Roman patriarch is first among all the patriarchs, the king of the Romans (i.e. the emperor) is the same among kings. But compare the dukes to archbishops, counts to bishops and proceed for the rest. . . .[27] In the first rank are the kings and electors of the empire or patricians. Second are dukes, rulers, prefects, etc. Third come marquises, landgraves, and similar ranks."[28]

On what basis are these ranks to be determined? The hierarchies in church and empire are based on two criteria—superior rationality and the intention of God. In the case of the church, the divine will is decisive. The pope, at the summit of the governmental hierarchy of the church, fulfills Christ's intention

---

[26] *DCC,* I, viii, 62. On the disputed question of the transmission of Dionysius' influence to Cusanus, see my *Nicholas of Cusa,* ch. x. Dionysius is mentioned by name in *DCC,* I, vi, 53 and II, xx, 232.

[27] Translated from *DCC,* III, i, 327–328.

[28] Translated from *DCC,* III, xxv, 421.

in conferring the primacy on Peter. Here Nicholas rejects the extreme conciliarism of Marsilius who denied that the papacy was of divine institution. The primacy was established by Christ "to maintain unity" and "to avoid schism." Disagreements as to the interpretation of church law are to be resolved by the pope as "judge of faith."[29] In the temporal sphere, the ruler also derives his authority from God. No historical legal case for this is given, as with the papacy. However, all authority is believed to come from God, the emperor functioning as "the minister of God" and the "vicar of Jesus Christ on earth."[30] Both pope and emperor can, therefore, be said to hold their positions by a kind of divine right. God intends that the world be ruled by two authorities, one in spirituals and the other in temporals. Bishops and priests also have their positions by direct divine institution, and the divine intention concerning the other ranks is implied in their conformity to the divinely ordained hierarchical and triadic structure of the universe.

A second basis for the allocation of rank in both hierarchies is the possession of superior rationality. In the preface to the third book of the *Concordantia,* which is concerned with the structure of the temporal power, Nicholas confronts the two different traditions concerning the allocation of authority—the one based on the original natural equality of all mankind and the other on the unequal distribution of reason among them. With the exception of Marsilius, all political thinkers before him had emphasized the inherent right of the naturally superior to rule—and had defined this superiority principally in terms of reason, which they equated with moral and political virtue. Marsilius alone had questioned the rule of the wise although he had given them a share in the framing of legislation. Characteristically Nicholas tried to have it both ways. Although he wrote the preface to Book III after reading Marsilius, he still believed that the wise should rule. Yet he also wished to base all authority on consent derived from the premise of original equality and freedom. He attempted to reconcile the opposing principles of

---

[29] *DCC,* I, vi, 57; II, vii, 124; xxiv, 303, 306. The council, however, is superior to the pope, for it represents the consent of the whole church and is made up of the bishops who are successors of the apostles. Cf. *DCC,* I, xv, 81; II, xviii, 188–189; xx, 218; xxxiv, 292.

[30] *DCC,* III, v, 354.

authority by positing a natural and divinely intended harmony between the rule of the wise and the consent of the ignorant: "Almighty God has imposed a kind of natural servitude on the stupid and foolish in accordance with which they readily believe the wise so that they may thereby be ruled with their assistance and preserve themselves. . . . And thus by a certain natural instinct the rule of the wise and the subjection of the ignorant are brought into harmony by common laws which the wise initiate, preserve, and execute, with the voluntary consent and subjection of the others."[31]

In the second book of the *Concordantia*, we find a similar argument used in analyzing consent as the basis for authority. In the same chapter in which he derives the necessity for consent from the original equality of men, Nicholas presents an argument for the rule of the wise and attempts to harmonize the two principles as follows: All law is based on natural law. Natural law is known by reason. Therefore, "those better endowed with reason are the natural lords and rulers of the others." However, "the wiser and more outstanding men are elected as rulers by the others to make just laws by their aforesaid natural clear reason, wisdom, and prudence, and to rule the others by those laws."[32] Cusanus makes this point in arguing the case for conciliar participation in the making of church law. However, it is a general statement about all law, and would, therefore, apply to the civil as well as to the ecclesiastical authorities. As in the argument from the divine will, there is a parallelism between the basis of legitimacy in the two hierarchies—and a pre-established harmony between the divinely intended rule by those of superior rationality (in the sense of capacity to know the law) and the consent of all of their subordinates.

Yet in fact, there was no assurance that such a harmony would prevail. Merely because at one point someone was recognized as having superior moral and intellectual capabilities was no assurance that he would rule wisely and well. As later history demonstrated, representative institutions are necessary not only to express consent but also to withdraw it when the ruler abuses

---

[31] Translated from *DCC*, III, preface, 315, 317. Compare this with Marsilius' rejection of the argument concerning the ignorance of "the many" in *Defensor Pacis*, D. I, ch. xiii, v. 1.

[32] Translated from *DCC*, II, xiv, 160–161.

his power. Despite the fact that the Council of Constance had deposed the rival claimants to the papacy in 1417, Nicholas never discussed the council's power to depose an errant pope, although, as noted above, he referred in passing to the right to depose the emperor. Conversely he also never faced the problem of abuse of power by a council. This problem was posed a few years later when the Council of Basel began, in his view, to exceed its authority. At that time (1437) Nicholas abandoned conciliarism for the side of the papacy.

For Nicholas the problem of good government could be solved by harmonious cooperation of pope and council, emperor and *Reichstag,* and ruler and ruled. It was possible for him to believe in such a harmonious agreement for two reasons. First, underlying the doctrine of *concordantia* was Nicholas' belief in the action of God in bringing it about. This is revealed in the references, in the preface to Book III, to natural instinct and divinely ordained subjection, as well as in his repeated association of consent with divine presence.[33] Second, he introduced a sufficient number of qualifying phrases in his description of the institutionalization of consent so that it did not depart too radically from contemporary practice. Consent in most cases was tacit or lost in historical myth. Thus the German people were presumed to have consented to the establishment of the electors of the emperor and the faithful to the role of the college of cardinals in electing the pope. Local priests were appointed with the consent of the faithful but not directly by them, and Nicholas did not propose to implement consent on the lower levels of the empire.[34]

Yet, although consent was mainly tacit and representation virtual, more than a rationalization of the status quo had been achieved. For the first time, a political theorist had used the Roman and patristic belief in the equality of all men to support a form of universal participation in law and government through councils and elections. After his transfer of allegiance to the

---

[33] *DCC,* II, x, 138. "Ibi enim est Deus, ubi simplex sine pravitate consensus. . . ." The identical statement is repeated in *DCC,* II, xix, 205.

[34] However, see Erich Meuthen, *Das Trierer Schisma auf dem Basler Konzil,* Münster, 1964, for discussion of the influence on Cusanus' theory of the practice of consent by estates in the election of the prince-bishop of Trier.

papacy, Nicholas himself did not urge this program, but in a proposal for the reform of the church that he submitted many years later to Pope Pius II, there are references to the necessity of consent to government.[35]

EARLY MODERN THEORIES OF EQUALITY

The conciliarist theory of consent on the basis of original natural equality was later taken up by writers of the early modern period. It appears in the *Vindiciae contra Tyrannos,* a Huguenot tract that was published in France in 1679 and exerted wide influence both on the continent and in England. In Part III of that work, the author argues that kings are not superior to other men by nature, and, therefore, they must be elected or chosen through a contractual agreement with the people. Richard Hooker's *Laws of Ecclesiastical Polity* (1594) is similar in general spirit to Cusanus' *Concordantia* in its combination of a belief in a universal hierarchical order and in consent to government. Hooker does not specifically relate consent to natural equality, but he speaks of "those times wherein there were no civil societies" and the movement therefrom "by common consent," and asserts that "without consent there is no reason that one man should take upon him to be lord and judge over another. . . ."[36]

In his *Second Treatise on Civil Government,* published in 1689, John Locke took the notion of original equality as a fundamental principle of government. In the second chapter he states that there is "nothing more evident than that creatures of the same species and rank, promiscuously born to all the same advantages of nature, and the use of the same faculties should

[35] In his "Reformatio generalis" (printed in Stephan Ehses, "Der Reformentworf des Kardinals Nikolaus Cusanus," *Historisches Jahrbuch,* XXXII [1911], 274-297) , written in 1459, Nicholas described the college of cardinals as embodying the consent of the church to papal actions.

[36] Richard Hooker, *The Laws of Ecclesiastical Polity,* New York, 1907, I, x, 4, pp. 190–191. As the quotation indicates, I disagree with Professor Lakoff's reading of Hooker's consent theory as simply a matter of keeping the ignorant content (p. 96) . For the argument for natural equality in the *Vindiciae,* see F. W. Coker, *Readings in Political Philosophy,* New Haven, 1938, p. 354. On the relation of conciliarism to the *Vindiciae,* see Francis W. Oakley, *The Political Thought of Pierre d'Ailly; the Voluntarist Tradition,* New Haven, 1964, pp. 229–230.

also be equal amongst one another without subordination or subjection." Unlike Cusanus and Hooker, Locke makes no reference to a natural ruler or natural hierarchies. All men are equal and hence political authority can only be justified by consent. As Jefferson wrote, following Locke, government derives its "just powers from the consent of the governed."

The consent for which Hooker argued was to be given only at the time of the establishment of government and could not be withdrawn. Locke defended the right to withdraw consent from a tyrannical government, but he did not advocate universal suffrage or social equality.[37] In the eighteenth century, however, the implications of the idea of original equality for the democratic form of government and the abolition of aristocratic privilege were demonstrated by the prominent role of the doctrine in the ideology of the American and French Revolutions.

It is a long way from the Peasants' Revolts and the Conciliar Movement to the American and French Revolutions. Both of the earlier movements ended in failure, and the political and social circumstances in which they emerged made the establishment of real equality and meaningful consent an impossibility. Yet the history of the doctrine of natural equality goes back to the time of the Greeks, and there is a continuity in its use in support of consent to government from its first appearance in the writings of Nicholas of Cusa to its most important implementation in the opening passages of the Declaration of Independence. There are important differences as well, notably in the application of the doctrine, in the one case to constitutionalize the church and empire, and in the other to justify revolution, but the similarities are sufficient to warrant the assertion that the doctrine of the derivation of legitimacy from consent and equality emerged in medieval rather than modern times.

EVALUATION

In conclusion, some evaluation of the argument itself should be attempted. The different versions of the argument from natural equality to consent agreed in asserting that man has a minimum rationality, or a fundamental moral quality of free-

---

[37] See the argument of C. B. Macpherson, *The Political Theory of Possessive Individualism*, Oxford, 1962, ch. V.

dom, or quite commonly both, which justify his consent or participation in government. Underlying these assertions was a claim that there are no essential differences that give one an inherent right to rule and the others the obligation to submit.

It is true that many medieval Christian thinkers spoke of "dominion" as a necessary result of man's sin. Yet the mere assertion that "sin" makes government and slavery necessary is not persuasive. In the case of slavery, there is no proof that a given slave deserved this fate because of his own sin; while in the case of government, presumably both ruler and subject are sinners—an argument that some Calvinist writers and more recently Reinhold Niebuhr have used to argue for democracy and equality.

Assuming, then, the above definition of the argument from natural equality as a denial of any claim to rule by virtue of essential differences among men, anyone who wishes to evaluate this argument must answer Plato's challenge. Are there not in fact some who are better qualified to rule than others—if not on Plato's basis of undifferentiated intelligence, certainly on the basis of moral and technical superiority? Is there not a natural hierarchy of the *ratione vigentes,* to use Nicholas of Cusa's term, —an unequal and basically hierarchical distribution of talent and virtue? And are not those endowed with capacity for rational insight and moral will entitled as such to authority?

There are standard replies to this objection. As Plato himself later recognized, the highly qualified man may be corrupted and, therefore, needs the check of election and representation. (Nicholas of Cusa saw this only dimly when he defended the right of all to participate in the enactment of legislation but asserted that the more rational should have the decisive voice.) In addition, the expert cannot know everything about the needs of his subjects (as illustrated in the "shoe pinches" argument of A. D. Lindsay). Marsilius of Padua made both these points early in the fourteenth century when he defended lawmaking by the whole citizenry (or its "weightier part") on the grounds that this would avoid partiality and that "the common utility of a law is better noted by the entire multitude because no one knowingly harms himself."[38] Finally, there is also the practical

---

[38] Marsilius, *Defensor Pacis* (Gewirth translation), I, xii, 5, page 47.

consideration that potentially qualified government officials cannot readily be found unless there is equality of opportunity (although possibly this could be done through some kind of examination by a moral aristocracy, as Plato proposed).

However, the argument from natural equality really seems to be pointing up something more than any of these practical considerations. It maintains that each individual has the capacity or potential to make political and moral choices and argues that this capacity implies a right to its exercise. It asserts that each man has sufficient intelligence and moral worth to make at least some of the decisions involved in the selection of personnel and policy for government. As Locke put it in the *Second Treatise,* "The freedom then of man, and liberty of acting according to his own will, is grounded on his having reason, which is able to instruct him in that law he is to govern himself by. . . ."[39]

Yet no one argues for the establishment of a completely equalitarian system, such as that of fourth-century Athens where the major offices were assigned by lot. Modern government requires expertise and modern democracy is not really democracy in the Greek sense but a mixed constitution—in which we have as much faith as did Nicholas of Cusa in a harmony of hierarchy and consent based on equality. We have no Holy Spirit in politics, but we believe in giving all the people an opportunity to participate in law and government while recognizing virtue, in the sense of political, administrative, and moral ability, as a necessity for government. We hope for a balance between the moral demand to give and withhold consent and the need for a functional hierarchy based on merit, neither levelling all to the lowest common denominator nor restricting governmental decisions to the highly qualified alone. Both elements of the balance, the moral requirement of consent based on equality and the technical requirement of authority and hierarchy, were already anticipated in medieval Christian thought.

---

[39] John Locke, *Second Treatise on Civil Government,* ch. vi, para. 63.

9

JUDAISM AND EQUALITY

EMANUEL RACKMAN

INTRODUCTION

Biblical Hebrew has no word for "equality." Nonetheless in the book of Leviticus the Jews were told, "Ye shall have one law for the stranger and citizen alike; for I the Lord am your God" (Lev. 24:22). Equality before the law, according to Judaism, was divinely ordained. By the same token Hebrew has many equivalents for "differentiate," and God Himself presumably ordained many of the differences—not only natural but also legal. Can such antithetical mandates be reconciled so that God's attribute of justice is not impugned and His role respected as "judge of all the earth" (Gen. 18:25)? Not easily, but the literature of Jewish law and theology reflects a continuing tension between the ideal of human equality and the many inequalities that result from differences for which the tradition holds

154

the Creator Himself responsible. In the emerging dialectic, values other than equality play their part, as do the different functions assigned to human beings in society as a whole.

The paradox encountered in the Biblical texts is aggravated by the fact that it is more than equality before the law that God had willed. Indeed, even at creation did He will human equality as a *fact*. Because of this extraordinary notion, Judaism's contribution to the idea of equality differs from that of Stoicism.

In Stoicism it is the possession of reason that marks man off from the external world. Men are deemed equal because the part of them that reasons, their "souls," is the same in all men. Judaism also held that God endows all humans with His image—the *Tselem Elohim,* which Jewish philosophers in the Aristotelian tradition often equated with reason. The dogma was so basic in Judaism that the fundamental rationale for executing a murderer was that he destroyed a divine image. He killed, in a sense, God's likeness. "Whoso sheddeth man's blood, by man shall his blood be shed; for in the image of God made He man" (Gen. 9:6).

Judaism, however, also derives human likeness from the fact that God had created only one man from whom all humanity is descended. No one could ever argue that he was superior in birth because of his genealogy. "Man was created alone. And why so? . . . That families might not quarrel with each other. Now, if at present, though but one was originally created, they quarrel, how much more if two had been created!" (Babylonian Talmud, tractate Sanhedrin, 38a.) That all men have only one progenitor, whereas animals were created by God in the plural number, was held to mean that all human beings are born equal. They enjoy this equality by virtue of the very fact that they were born, even if they never attain to the faculty of reason. This was the only source on which Thomas Paine could rely in his "Rights of Man" to support the dogma of the American Declaration of Independence that all men are created equal. And this dogma was basic in Judaism.

Augustine later modified the Jewish doctrine considerably and as a result Western civilization did not have the full benefit of its implications. Were it not for Augustine's introduction of the need for grace resulting from the Fall of Man and of the elitism of those who are blessed with grace, the merging of Jewish and

Stoic conceptions might have accelerated progress toward equality in all human affairs. There would have been no blithe acceptance of inequality as a punishment for sin, for historic Judaism had no dogma of the "Fall of Man"; consequently the Jewish and Stoic views might have complemented each other for a more rapid fulfillment of the ideal of equality.

Nonetheless, even as all men are born equal because they all descend from the one Adam, men do differ. "The creation of the first man *alone* was to show forth the greatness of the Supreme King of Kings, the Holy One, blessed be He. For if a man mints many coins from one mould, they are all alike, but the Holy One, blessed be He, fashioned all men in the mould of the first man, and not one resembles the other" *(ibid.)*. Men differ in voice, appearance, and mind; men differ in sex and color; men differ ethnically and nationally. What is more, God Himself willed that they shall differ in language and geographic distribution. Within their national groupings, there are freemen and slaves, kings and subjects, priests, levites, and prophets—and of all these differences the Bible takes note. To some it gives *de facto* recognition; to others even *de jure* recognition. Some differences it prescribes itself and it accords to the differentiated special duties and privileges. How can this be reconciled with the command to have one law for the citizen and the stranger? And how consonant is this proliferation of mankind with the prophetic protest, "Have we not all one father?"

To this very day the annals of Jewish history, the folios of Jewish law, and the apologetics of Jewish theologians, reflect continuing concern with this dichotomy. This essay purports to deal principally with the legal norms and parenthetically with the theology that undergirds them. The facts of Jewish history— a record of successes and failures in attaining the ideal—are beyond its scope. Too often the legal norms were ignored and the prophets inveighed against the oppressors; sometimes rabbis were progressive and at other times conservative and reactionary; communal leaders were often on the side of the status quo and often against it. As among all national and ethnic groups there were forces other than the law that precipitated or retarded the movement toward maximum social, economic, and political equality. Scriptures and Talmudic materials were quoted by all sides. Yet Jews have adequate cause for boasting that the ideal of equality suggested by the very first chapter of the Bible was fulfilled in their society to a greater extent than among the many peoples with whom they had contact in their millennial history, and today the collectives of the new state of Israel are not only living laboratories of the ideal's fullest fruition but also seats of very impressive philosophical discussion on the meaning of equality. Despite the absolutely equal sharing of goods in these collectives, there is growing concern that some members enjoy more prestige than others by virtue of their positions as decision-makers or of their greater ability to produce, think, or lead. Even this concern, this feeling of guilt, bespeaks an enduring preoccupation with an absolute ideal and the difficulty encountered in fulfilling it in practice.

MALE AND FEMALE

From the seemingly divergent accounts in Genesis describing how God created Adam and Eve, one derives at least, first, that a man leaves his parents to cleave to his wife—wife in the singular. Thus while polygamy was practiced lawfully by many Jews, as it is in some oriental countries even today, monogamy appears to be the ideal. Second, women share the divine image; their lives, limbs, and property are to be accorded the same respect accorded those of men. Third, men and women have different functions. Judaism is, therefore, less receptive to the idea of a natural hierarchy but accepts the legitimacy of functional inequalities.

Polygamy and Polyandry

That a man might lawfully wed many women while a woman was bound to one husband at a time was a flouting of the ideal of equality. But Jewish law was committed to another value—the importance of the identity of the father in the case of offspring. Therefore, it could not countenance polyandry, which would result in children's uncertainty as to who their father was. To abolish polygamy was not easy, for most men resisted change. It required a considerable moral and social development that finally, in about the year 1000, culminated for occidental Jews in the ban of Rabbi Gershom against the practice. The Biblical ideal of man cleaving to one wife gave impetus to this moral and social development. Whenever it did discuss the polygamy of the patriarchs, some special reason for it was given: Abraham impregnated Hagar at Sarah's request; Jacob married two sisters because of his father-in-law's fraud and took two concubines at the request of the sisters. Kings were warned in it, moreover, not to enlarge their harems unduly. Especially noteworthy is the word used in the Bible to describe the relationship between two wives of the same man; it is *Tzarah,* which also means "misfortune" and suggests that two wives of one husband can only bring grief to each other. Yet, as will be demonstrated, the advantage of the male over the female still predominates in the inequitous law of divorce.

Marriage and Divorce

Whereas males and females who had reached their legal majority were absolutely equal in consummating a marriage, they were not so in divorce.

Because the husband performs the formal act creating the marriage, the Law assumed that it is he who must give the order to write and deliver the bill of divorce. He who created the sacred bond must undo it. In Judaism, including the Kabbalah, the male is regarded as the active principle in the universe and the female as the passive principle. Therefore, in marriage and divorce it is he who must perform the legally operative acts.

Yet without the consent of the female, a marriage could not be consummated. But until the year 1000, her consent to the divorce was not required. The need for her consent was slower in coming because the Law assumed that it served no purpose to keep her wedded to a man who did not respect her. The Law sought only to provide for her maintenance after divorce.

Moreover, her right to sue for a divorce is suggested by the Talmud, not the Bible. The Law labored under a presumption that any woman would prefer a bad marriage to no marriage: "It is better to live with any other, than alone." Yet virtual equality is now achieved and today where there is mutual consent, no court approval is required and no grounds for divorce need be offered. If either spouse withholds consent, a court of competent jurisdiction is able to adjudicate and act against the will of either spouse.

Nonetheless an inequality, which begs for correction, persists. Because it is the husband who must give the order to write the bill of divorce, the court is still impotent to terminate the marriage when the husband is not subject to the jurisdiction of the court, when he is missing or insane, and especially in states in which rabbinic tribunals have no authority except such as the parties want to vest in them. Therefore, wives are often helpless in getting the necessary bill of divorce and without it cannot marry other men. In similar circumstances, however, men could remarry. They could, for example, deposit with a rabbinical court a bill of divorce for an insane wife. Because by Biblical law there is no objection to a man's being wedded to more than one woman at one time, a man can marry a second wife while his first is hospitalized. Or if a wife has disappeared, the husband can, again, deposit a bill of divorce with a rabbinical court. This inequity is very much the subject of discussion among modern rabbis who will have to promulgate new rules to solve a problem . whose incidence is greater now, particularly in the areas of separation, due to the greater mobility of peoples and to the increase in and easier recognition of mental illness.

During Coverture

The extent to which the separate property of wives survived the creation of the marriage relationship was extraordinary. What a woman brought into the marriage as dowry became the husband's, but he was obligated, in the event that he predeceased or divorced her, to return the full amount he received. His liability in this connection was that of an insurer. The loss of the dowry because of acts of God or non-negligent management was no defense. What a woman acquired during her marriage by gift from friends or inheritance from relatives remained hers. Her right to separate property was well established. The husband became trustee of that property, taking the income for himself and conserving the corpus for her in the event of a divorce or his predeceasing her.

However, the one significant inequality was that she was not an heiress of her husband whereas he was her sole heir. She acquired from his estate her dowry, all separate property received by her during the marriage, and support until her remarriage. However, if she predeceased her husband, he took all of her estate to the exclusion even of the issue of the marriage.

In rights of inheritance generally males had the advantage. It would appear that the advantage enjoyed by males was due to the central importance, in the wealth of the community, of land, which the men were expected to cultivate and defend. The role of woman was truly domestic; she was to serve spouse and off-spring. The rest of the family's economy was the responsibility of the man. Thus differences in function may have contributed to the advantage of males.

But the husband had no special privileges with regard to the life and limb of his wife. He could not kill her even if he ap-prehended her in the commission of adultery. He was also re-sponsible for torts committed against her person not excluding torts committed in the course of coitus.

THE EQUALITY OF OFFSPRING

Jewish law limited the right of the father to disinherit his children—or, for that matter, any of the heirs entitled to the succession. In his lifetime the father could dispose of his property as he chose. But even a written document altering the Biblical pattern of inheritance was a nullity. The Oral Law did permit him to alter the disposition among his sons, or among his daughters if he had no sons. He could prefer one to the others. Yet the rabbis frowned on such behavior; their rationale was based on the religious value of penitence. One had no right to disinherit a child in anger or resentment because the child might repent, or the child's offspring might prove worthy of the estate. Saints are often born to parents who are villains.

The rights of issue were so vested that it did not matter whether the children were born in or out of wedlock, or whether they were even legitimate. A child was deemed illegitimate only in the rarest situation when proof was incontrovertible that he was born of an adulterous or incestuous relationship—and to prove this was almost impossible. The child born out of wedlock was legitimate even if there was no subsequent marriage between its parents. And these children were heirs. They were not subjected to the indignity of proving that they were entitled to take a share of their father's estate so long as their paternity was either generally known or admitted by the father in his lifetime. Moreover, if an illegitimate son, and a fortiori one born out of wedlock who was not illegitimate, was the first issue of the father, he was entitled to all the rights of primogeniture.

The rights of the first-born were generally prescribed. The Bible had said that they were entitled to a double portion. Did that mean two-thirds of the estate in every case, or two portions of the estate after it was divided by the number of sons plus one? The latter interpretation was upheld. The Biblical verse was strictly construed in this respect, as it was with every other problem that arose.

The first-born took his double portion only of such property that the deceased actually possessed at the time of his death. Claims of the deceased were not to be included. In addition, the first-born had to prove beyond the shadow of a doubt that he was the father's first-born. If a stillborn preceded him, he forfeited his special position. He must also have been born before his father died—he did not acquire special privileges as a foetus, and thus could not take more than his twin brother born moments after him. Moreover, he must have been born naturally from the womb and not by a Caesarean operation. This was strict construction of a verse, proscribing a right which the Oral Law deemed anomalous and inconsistent with the ideal of equality.

Perhaps the institution of primogeniture should have been abolished altogether rather than only radically proscribed. Certainly the narratives in the book of Genesis reveal how much grief resulted from the deeply entrenched preference for the first-born—for example, the rivalry between Ishmael and Isaac, Esau and Jacob, Reuben and Joseph. The Midrash so dwells upon these rivalries that one wonders whether some of Adler's psychoanalytic theories did not derive from it. But the rabbis did not abolish the institution. The Bible had approved of it even if it did curtail its benefits, and the rabbis were not prepared to abolish it altogether as they might well have done. Perhaps they regarded the first-born as the bearer of special social, economic, and educational responsibilities in the family. The first-born had been the family priests until the tribe of Levi replaced them as religious functionaries. As the eldest in the family, they were also expected to provide leadership after the father's death and even during his lifetime. Perhaps as Philo suggested, the first-born was owed a debt of gratitude by the father. After all, he made the father a father. Therefore, some special consideration was accorded him in the distribution of the estate. But to that extent the ideal of equality remains compromised.

If rabbis frown upon a Biblical law but refrain from nullifying it, is their thought to be regarded as deontological and Kantian rather than as teleological and utilitarian? It would be more accurate to say that it was all of these: The Law was theocentric —divine in origin and with creative achievement ever oriented to the fulfillment of God's will. Never to lose sight of this commitment, the Law had its suprarational mandates not readily explicable in terms of human values and interests. Every branch of the Law had them. But the Law was given to people, who alone were responsible for its development. The Bible itself appeals to man to comprehend the justice-content of the Law. It also bids him to live by the Law, not to perish because of it. Thus suprarational norms remain the Law's theocentric roots and prevent it from becoming altogether positive in character. But rabbinic creativity had to be mindful too of ends and utility.

SLAVERY

Jewish law distinguished between slaves who were Jews and slaves who were non-Jews, usually called Canaanite slaves. Their legal status was not the same, and the inequality derived from religious values that conflicted with the value of equality.

The abolition of the ownership of one Jew by a fellow Jew was accomplished centuries ago. Those who heard on Mount Sinai that all Jews were God's servants were not to become further indentured to coreligionists who shared with them a common bondage to the same Master! But what is most significant about this result is that it represented the achievement of Jewish jurisprudence—that very legalism of the Pharisees which became the butt of Christian criticism.

No one became a slave for failure to pay a debt. The sale was permitted only for failure to pay for one's theft. Furthermore, a man could be sold only if he failed to pay the principal amount due on the theft. If he could pay the principal but not the double or quadruple or quintuple damages due, he could not be sold into slavery. Nor could he be sold as a punishment for false witness. The Bible said "theft" and theft alone it shall be!

Having become a slave, the person kept a status virtually like that of a freeman. He could not be disgraced by a sale at public auction. The work he could do for his master was not to be difficult or degrading. Wherever possible, he was to continue in his former occupation. He was also to enjoy the same food, clothing and shelter as his master.

His life and limb were as protected as the life and limb of any freeman. The master was as liable for homicide or mayhem as if the slave were an equal. The slave's wife and children were not sold with him, as was the custom in most other contemporaneous cultures. As a matter of fact, the master was obliged to support the slave's dependents.

The slave could acquire property and redeem himself to freedom. At most his bondage would last six years and out of any property he acquired he could pay for any part of his unexpired term. According to Maimonides, his wife could engage in gainful employment. None of her earnings belonged to her husband's master, even while the master remained responsible for her and her children's maintenance. If the slave were ill for any part of his term—up to one-half thereof—he did not have to serve any extended period to compensate for the time of his indisposition.

He could sue and be sued. He was also competent as a witness. In one respect only was his legal status different from that of a freeman. The master could compel him to take a Canaanitish slave woman as a wife. The progeny would belong to the master, for the status of the progeny was that of their mother. In an age when polygamy was quite prevalent, this was not a serious invasion of personal rights.

Even in those isolated instances where the master was permitted to cause the Jewish male slave to mate with a non-Jewish female slave—the only instance justifying the contention that the master owned the very body of the slave—the moral standards of a monogamous relationship were applicable. Promiscuous relationships were prohibited. The institution of slavery was never to place in jeopardy the lofty moral ideals of the Law.

To demonstrate the high value set upon freedom, a slave who refused to become free had his ear pierced with an awl. Unlike the Hamurabi code, which prescribed this penalty for a runaway slave, Jewish law prescribed it for the slave who did not avail himself of an opportunity to become free.

When the slave's term expired, the master was to give him a gift—severance pay. Talmudic jurists fixed the amount instead of relying upon the master's generosity. Moreover, they exempted the gift from execution by the slave's creditors to insure the slave of the wherewithal for a new start in life.

With this kind of legal development, it was to be expected that one would hardly ever want to become a master of a Jewish slave. And thus by a rigid legalism slavery was abolished—a result sermons and homilies could hardly achieve.

A Jewish girl could become a slave only if her father sold her into bondage prior to her reaching puberty. The sale, however, was less a sale than a betrothal, for she was automatically emancipated upon reaching puberty unless her master or her master's son wed her. If the master or his son did wed her, she had the status of a wife with all the privileges thereunto appertaining. Moreover, her consent to the betrothal was required.

In all other respects her legal status was that of the male Hebrew slave. And neither the male nor the female could be resold by the master to another.

The Oral Law did not permit even a non-Jew to be enslaved without giving him sufficient status as a Jew to insure the protection of his life and limb and his partial participation in the religious life of the family and community. As such, he had a higher status than even a free Gentile. If the non-Jew was bought with the express proviso that he should not be converted to Judaism, then he had to acquiesce at least in the observance of the seven Noahide laws.

It would appear, however, that non-Jewish slaves preferred Jewish owners. As a consequence of their becoming members of a Jewish household, pursuant to the performance of the appropriate rituals, they could not be killed with impunity. There was no difference whatever in the law of homicide, whether willful or accidental, as to whether the victim was a Jewish freeman or a non-Jewish slave. Torts committed against the non-Jewish slave by persons other than the master were actionable. Though the recovery was the master's, the injuring of slaves was deterred by the very fact that a tort against him was actionable. And the master himself did not escape with impunity for his own torts against his non-Jewish slave. Emancipation of the slave might be the consequence of the master's tort. Under certain circumstances the master would even pay the death penalty for having killed his slave, although the Law also sought to protect his disciplinary authority. If a master refused to feed his non-Jewish slave (presumably as a disciplinary measure), the community performed this obligation for the slave as it performed it for the poor generally. The rabbis even penalized a Jewish master for selling his slave to a non-Jew who would not respect the non-Jewish slave's right to observe Sabbaths and festivals. The master was compelled to repurchase the slave though the cost of the repurchase might be ten times the amount of the original sale. Moreover, the master could not sell a non-Jewish slave even to a Jew residing outside the territorial limits of the land of Israel. Such a sale automatically emancipated the slave.

True, the Law frowned upon the emancipation of the non-Jewish slave. Such emancipation would give the non-Jewish slave the status of a full-fledged Jew, and the Law did not encourage this way of increasing the Jewish population. The Law abhorred the less stringent sexual code prevailing among non-Jews. Many authorities even observed that the non-Jewish slave would prefer slavery, with its license for promiscuity, to freedom as a Jew with its stern limitations on sexual relationships. Not having been reared in a milieu stressing the high moral standards the Law imposed, the non-Jewish slave was not to be catapulted into a free society that would make him unhappy or that he would feel constrained to corrupt. Nonetheless, the rabbis ruled that if by emancipation a moral purpose was achieved, or a *Mitzva* (a religious goal) was fulfilled, one might violate the injunction against freeing the non-Jewish slave. If, for example, a non-Jewish female slave has been promiscuous with the people at large, the Law urged her master to free her in the hope that she might marry and establish a monogamous relationship with a husband, infidelity to whom would be less probable because of the threat of the death penalty.

SOCIETY AND STATE

In the liberal tradition equality is stressed as a means to freedom and inequalities are often justified when they promote freedom. In the Jewish tradition equality is not principally a means but rather a fulfillment of all men's "creatureliness" under God, the only Master. Despite inescapable functional inequalities, equality was achieved within the family and household. It had to be achieved also within society and state. Indeed, equality must be achieved for the sake of order as well.

According to Maimonides, society requires a ruler, "who gauges the actions of the individuals, perfecting that which is deficient and reducing that which is excessive and who prescribes actions and moral habits for all of them to practice always in the same way, until the natural diversity is hidden by the many points of conventional accord, and so the society becomes well-ordered."

Yet shall the goals of equality and order negate the possibility of differences, in intellectual and moral excellence or in economic productivity, which freedom makes possible? Freedom is also a means to serve God better and improve His earth and its inhabitants. The Law certainly cherished the value of freedom, but equality was to be safeguarded by many principles.

Equality before the Law

Judaism was committed to the general principle that all are equal in the eyes of the Law. This applied to kings as it did to commoners.

With respect to racial differentiation, Judaism always was, and still is, color blind. Males and females, except as previously indicated, were equal in all matters civil and criminal. Women could not be judges or witnesses because this was inconsistent with their primary household roles. This did not mean that their credibility was impugned. With respect to all matters in which strictly formal testimony was not required, they could impart information to religious functionaries and would be believed. It was in a trial that might lead to a capital or corporal punishment, or in the creation of a new personal status such as marriage or divorce, or in an action in tort or contract, that they suffered exclusion. Indeed, there were matters in which they might be the only or most readily available witnesses and the Law had to make exceptions and admit their testimony. A classic example is a tort action for an assault committed in the women's section of a synagogue where no men could possibly be present. Moreover, they could act as judges in a civil action if the parties consented. Thus their exclusion from participation in the judicial function was not a reflection on their inferiority—although many rabbis were unchivalrous enough so to hold—but rather on the need for keeping women unseen that men might be more chaste.

Paradoxically, the one great exception to the principle were persons who had achieved greater intellectual and moral excellence. They were held accountable to stricter standards in tort and contract. "A distinguished person is different." More is expected of him, says the Talmud.

Equal Right to Positions of Leadership

In their earliest history Jews maintained the idea that leadership was the responsibility of merit rather than the prerogative of a class or family. In the religious sphere one tribe did ultimately become responsible for the performance of specified rituals, and in the political sphere one family acquired an indefeasible right to kingship. However, this situation did not long endure and all of the most important opportunities for leadership in temporal and spiritual matters became available to all equally. Even Moses divided the temporal and spiritual authority between Joshua, of the tribe of Ephraim, and Aaron, his brother, of the tribe of Levi. The "Judges" were recruited from all ranks to deliver the people from oppressive invaders, and they founded no dynasties. The prophets especially championed the ideal of equality, denouncing as they did the exploitation of the poor by the rich and disregard of the Law, which sought to achieve economic equality by such institutions as the Jubilee with its redistribution of the land every fifty years. The prophets also gave the world the messianic vision of an age when there would be universal peace and justice and nature itself would become perfect. The rabbis, who succeeded the prophets as the "Law's doctors," were also recruited from all ranks and even from among converts to Judaism. The requirement that they take no remuneration for their services made their labor one of love with the result that as a group they wielded more authority over the people than did priests or kings whose limited authority was hereditary. Thus the Jewish community ever enjoyed the circulation of the intellectual and moral elite and there never was a bar to the emergence of new leadership.

The most effective safeguard against the evils of any kind of monopoly on spiritual or temporal authority was the fact that Judaism was an exoteric rather than an esoteric religion; the law was promulgated, taught, and interpreted by all. "Would that every man in the camp of Israel were a prophet," exclaimed Moses.

In this instance, equality advanced the cause of freedom.

Equality between Clergy and Laity

Despite the unequivocal establishment by the Bible of a hereditary priesthood, the virtual obliteration of the difference between clergy and laity was achieved almost two thousand years ago. This was a giant step in the direction of social equality.

The priests and levites of whom the Bible speaks were the only persons in the Jewish community who had special status by virtue of their birth. Even long before the destruction of the central shrine in Jerusalem, their claim to hegemony over the spiritual lives of the people was successfully challenged by prophets and rabbis who came from all classes of society. In the year 70 they lost their special roles and rabbis became the guardians and exponents of the Law. And a rabbi never had any special sacerdotal power. He is nothing more than a layman who has more knowledge of Judaism than most people and can, therefore, offer them religious guidance. He does not even conduct religious services except as a layman might.

How the Bible created the anomaly of a hereditary priesthood in the face of so much concern for equality is itself a revelation of its commitment to the ideal that men shall not crave power over their fellows. Students of political theory are well aware of the discussions from Plato to the present about citizens' avoidance of civic responsibility. The best people often choose not to hold political office. Particularly with regard to the performance of sacred tasks in God's shrine, one may expect that the truly pious and devout will shy away, deeming themselves unworthy in thought and deed of any special role in the public service of God. Failure to decline is itself proof of the lack of the humility necessary for the purpose. Therefore, one must be drafted and only one who is drafted can qualify. Thus one never chooses to be a priest or levite. One has the obligation thrust upon him, and this is the only way it could possibly be unless the temple was to be staffed by people driven by ambition to rise above their brethren.

The tradition regards Moses himself as a drafted leader. When Aaron, his brother, was asked to be the High Priest, he too hesitated. Moses had to order him to serve. Moses also had to seize the levites forcibly and ordain them keepers of the shrine. And because they were drafted, it did not mean that they were rewarded. On the other hand, they were told of the greater hazards that would be theirs because of their service of the Lord. They would have to fulfill prescriptions meticulously and risk punishment for sins of omission or commission. Furthermore, they were given no share of the Promised Land. Fear, perhaps, of the extensive land holdings of the Egyptian priesthood— whom even Joseph could not expropriate—may have been behind the Law's denial to the priests and levites of any territory in Canaan. The Law even hedged their statutory gifts and taxes with so many conditions and restrictions that their delivery was in effect voluntary. A Jew was required to set the tithe gifts aside, thus learning the discipline of self-denial, but if he chose to let them rot, there was no one to stop him.

The rabbis' role in classical Judaism was determined primarily by a long-felt need to prevent the surrogates of God from exploiting their position for personal aggrandizement. All the safeguards proved inadequate to stop the priests and levites from abusing their election to serve God. The prophets had to denounce them for aligning themselves with the rich against the poor and the Pharisees had to denounce them for their usurpation of political power as well. The rabbis ruled that no one might derive a profit by his pursuit of Torah. Rabbis were to be volunteers. If they did perform services for another, they could lawfully be compensated only for time lost from their non-rabbinic vocations (no fewer than one hundred named in the Talmud were artisans). Indeed the rabbis were not clergymen.

The measure of their authority was based principally on the confidence of the community of believers.

Equality of Converts

The Law assured equality of status to all non-Jews who embraced the creed and practice of Judaism. Although there were some minor restrictions, one can generalize that all converts enjoyed the same privileges and were subject to the same duties as Jews. Yet, whereas their legal status was one of equality, socially they were often subjected to discrimination and suspicion. By the same token many rabbis held them in higher esteem than those who were born Jewish, but not always did these rabbis prevail against popular prejudice. Notwithstanding the prejudice, several important rulings reveal that the kinship of Jews with each other is not the kinship of blood but the kinship of a common faith. This is shown by the fact that in prayer the convert, no differently from the priest who can trace his male lineage to Aaron the High Priest, addresses God as "the God of our fathers." The patriarchs Abraham, Isaac, and Jacob, are his progenitors too. Moreover, the convert speaks of the land of Israel as the land given to his forbears in a special rite connected with the Pentecost festival.

SOCIAL AND POLITICAL EQUALITY

Jewish society was like all other societies in that social inequality did exist, even though the Law regarded all persons as equal. Yet generally the tradition was no respecter of wealth and the only aristocracy recognized was that based on piety and scholarship. And those so recognized rarely received special privilege or power unless a majority in the community—and this was true especially in the Middle Ages—elected them to comprise the "Seven Good Men of the City" who handled the affairs of the public.

A considerable amount of self-government prevailed in the medieval Jewish communities and by the twelfth century their form of government was democratic.

"The Seven Good Men of the City" were presumed to have been elected by a majority of male constituents and exercised authority because Jewish law recognized that a majority could properly create authority. Yet their powers were circumscribed. On many matters they had to conduct referenda, referring decisions to majority vote of all the male inhabitants of the city. On the other matters they had to obtain unanimous approval. On matters involving taxation and property it was often held that only a majority of taxpayers or property-holders could make decisions. Interestingly enough, if women were among the taxpayers or property-holders, they too were entitled to vote.

If only taxpayers and property-holders were to vote on matters pertaining to taxation or to the use and distribution of property, then the achievement of economic equality under such a system would appear to have been an impossibility. The expropriated would have no political means for improving their status. Paradoxically enough, it was precisely through a non-democratic institution that they achieved amelioration of their lot. The Beth-Din—constituted of the duly recognized doctors of the law— had virtually unlimited power to legislate as well as adjudicate matters affecting property. They could impose taxes and coerce the rich to support the poor as well as all public agencies and institutions. They also adjudicated occasional claims that the "Seven Good Men of the City" had exceeded their authority.

Thus whereas there was no clear distinction between legislative and judicial functions, there was a diffusion of power and a mixed form of government created by the people. Their choice of members of the Beth-Din was limited because the persons chosen had to qualify as scholars. However, once chosen, they had broad power and in patriarchal fashion could protect rich and poor and balance equities. The "Seven Good Men of the City" had more limited power, but anyone could qualify for that position.

The democratic experience of Jews in their own self-governing communities from the Middle Ages virtually up to World War II in Eastern and Central Europe predetermined their total accept- ance of universal suffrage in the modern state of Israel. Its legislature has the broadest governmental power comparable only to that of a king, who was anointed by the prophets. The latter, however, was subject to the Law and the sovereignty of God. According to Judaism, all the people, not just a majority, are denied the right to violate the basic norms of God's revealed will. Modern Israel's legislature is not now so limited. Yet it does

represent the full blossoming of the seed of political equality—
"one person, one vote"—contained in the medieval sources.

ECONOMIC EQUALITY

It is doubtful whether the Levitical law of the Jubilee,
which provided for a major redistribution of the promised land
every fifty years, was ever implemented. However, the elimina-
tion of poverty was a Biblical injunction. It appears that a poor
person even had a legal right to demand support from the
community. But before modern times there were no significant
experiments with total economic equality such as prevail in
Israel's collectives. The Law itself is very respectful of the institution of private ownership of property. Limited the right to such
ownership was—much more so than in modern capitalist states.
Yet no measures were ever taken to limit incomes or restrict
acquisitions. Consequently Jewish communities always had their
very rich and very poor. They differed from other communities
only insofar as they cultivated and maintained a high degree of
responsibility for all their constituents. Jewish historians even
maintain that one cause for the failure of Christendom to win
more converts among Jews, aside from the suffering and humilia-
tion inflicted on them, is that Jews within their own communities felt more secure than they might have felt outside
ghetto walls that their basic needs would be fulfilled. Jews remembered that their exile was predicted by the prophets as a
consequence of the exploitation of the poor by the rich; for
social and economic inequalities, which were the root of all evil,
were to be eradicated in the Messianic era. Augustine regarded
inequality as punishment for sin. Judaism, by contrast, regarded
the continuance of inequality as sin and the cause for God's
anger and national disaster.

Economic equality was the goal. Economic freedom was great.
But it was weighted heavily with responsibility.

Giving and Taking Interest

The Bible denies Jews the right to give interest to, or
to take it from, Jews. To gentiles Jews were permitted to pay

interest and consequently they could also take it. Plato, in his "Laws," suggested the same dichotomy for Athenians and "barbarians." Apparently, within the family, so to speak, free loans were to be the rule. Or it may be that a particular type of economy was to be promoted for the in-group while the out-group could engage in other economic activities, usually more peripheral ones.

During the Middle Ages the inequality became virtually academic because legal fictions were developed and Jews paid interest to fellow Jews as readily as they did to non-Jews and vice versa. Contemporary Israel has as yet done nothing to revive the Biblical prohibition, and modern capitalism is as entrenched there as in most of the Christian world.

Taxation

The greatest tension between the ideal of equality and the imperative need for inequality is in the area of taxation. To justify the imposition of higher rates on the rich than on the poor, moderns have invented the notion of the equality of burden.

Jewish law also exacted more from those more able to pay. But in one instance the system of taxation so sustained the ideal of equality that few, if any, other rules of law gave the ideal comparable popularity and esteem. For the support of the temple, all Jews—rich or poor—gave the same half-shekel. This poll tax became one of the most cherished of all practices of Judaism. Vis-à-vis the central shrine, all were equal.

Theodore Herzl, founder of the Zionist movement at the turn of the century, evoked popular support for his cause by reviving the institution. Commitment to the belief that the solution of the Jewish problem was the establishment of a Jewish state was evidenced by the purchase of a "shekel"—cheap enough for all Jews, no matter how depressed their lot. Fulfillment of his objective required substantial gifts from affluent persons and an unequal burden on donors. Yet membership in the movement was based on a nominal gift, equal for all. The new state in the imagination of many Jews replaced the central shrine of yesteryear and the revival of a time-honored practice gave impetus to the ideal of equality set forth in the Bible's first chapter.

PAGANS AND GENTILES

In no area of Jewish law is the tension between antithetical ideas comparable to that which exists between Judaism's
theological notion that all men are possessed of the divine image
and its strict, sometimes seemingly inhumane, attitude towards
pagans and gentiles. The literature on the subject is so confusing
and the views of the authorities so disparate that only a few
guidelines can be indicated.

The Idea of the Chosen People

First, the "chosenness" of the Jewish people—no matter
how understood or expounded by prophets and philosophers—
never furnished a foundation for a legal norm. The basic norm
of the legal order was simply that pagans were "outlaws," for they
had not accepted the seven Noahide laws regarded as essential for
a society with a minimal morality. They would constitute no
threat to Jewish settlements or communities unless they resided
among Jews, and, therefore, when Jews conquered and occupied
the promised land, they had to get rid of these pagans or compel
them to submit to the seven Noahide laws whereupon their
status was changed to that of resident aliens with considerable
protection by Jewish law. Pagan nations or tribes that created no
problem for the Jewish people were not to be attacked, exter-
minated, or even coerced to change their way of life. Indeed, the
prophets had stressed the equality of all nations, and one prophet
was even forced to go to the Assyrians to deliver God's message to
them. God may have chosen the Jewish people (for whatever
reason or mission one can glean from the sources), but He is
the Father not only of all creatures as individuals but also of all
nations and ethnic groups, and He judges all of them con-
tinuously, especially in the Messianic age.

Even pagans who were outlaws could bring offerings to God
in the central shrine in Jerusalem. Their divine image was the
warrant for this privilege and gifts that they made to the building itself in perpetuity were never to be altered. In this respect
they enjoyed an even greater assurance of the perpetuity of their
donations than did Jews. Moreover, Jews were obligated to
deport themselves so honorably vis-à-vis even pagans that pagans
might exclaim, "Blessed is the Lord of Israel."

Yet Jewish law often "recognized" the rules of law prevailing among pagans. For example, their rights of inheritance were respected as were their claims to property personal and real. Jewish law even established special forms for their acquisition of title. In the law of tort there was even the notion of reciprocity—whatever wrongful acts non-Jewish courts regarded as actionable when committed by non-Jews against Jews, Jewish courts regarded as actionable when committed by Jews against non-Jews. This is a far cry from justice but it makes for some degree of equality.

Persons or peoples, however, who had accepted the seven Noahide laws were deemed civilized and it is to them that the Bible refers when it orders Jews to love the stranger.

But Jewish law itself—the written and oral law—was given by God to the Jewish people for the governance of Jews. This made the law "personal" rather than "territorial." And it applied to Jews no matter where they lived. It was to receive and obey this law that they were chosen whether for the purpose of being a light or a blessing unto the nations, or bearing testimony to the perpetuity of their personal relationship with God, or helping to establish His kingdom on earth. As a law for a Jewish society, it had only peripheral concern with those whose "personal" law was different. It did provide for rules of warfare when such war was forced on Jews or sought by them. In no instance was the massacre of the enemy justified if the enemy chose to live in peace and accept the seven laws of Noah.

Perhaps the mood of Jewish law can best be understood in the light of the dilemma of modern liberals in the United States who are torn between a respect for human life—even the lives of Chinese communists—and their anxiety that the free world has to reckon with leaders who have little respect for the rule of law within or without their borders. In such a situation one must be ambivalent. To respect life may require inaction. But to insure the survival of cherished values may require wholesale slaughter. This was the dilemma of Jewish law vis-à-vis those who would not abide by the seven laws of Noah, and the law did not move as rapidly or as dramatically in the direction of the equality of pagans with Jews as it did in the direction of the equality of resident aliens.

The Righteous of all Nations

So committed is the Jewish tradition to the equality of
the non-Jew who leads a righteous life that it accords to him the
coveted title of "Chasid" and assures him salvation just as it is
vouchsafed to righteous Jews themselves. Maimonides distinguishes between a righteous non-Jew who pursues righteousness
because it is the will of God and a righteous non-Jew whose
pursuit of eternal values and moral deportment is derived from
reason and natural law. The latter he calls a "Chacham," a wise
man; the title "Chasid" is reserved for those who are also God-
fearing. But whatever the title, the conclusion is that Jews did
not feel impelled to convert non-Jews to Judaism. Commitment
to Judaism was not the condition prerequisite for salvation for
anyone but Jews. Non-Jews could achieve it by righteous living
alone. And Judaism today is still fully committed to this view.

Freedom of belief thus emerged from the recognition of
universal equality. The freedom of Jews, however, was more
limited. Whereas they enjoyed a considerable measure of latitude
in connection with dogma and doctrine, they were held strictly
to the fulfillment of the Law. By observance of the command-
ments they were to play a special role in God's vision of human
history.

CONCLUSION

Since God had created all men equal, their natural inequality can only be justified with reference to His service, which
means the fulfillment of the very equality God had willed. Freedom does not serve primarily the purpose of man's self-fulfillment, as in the writings of John Stuart Mill, but rather God's
purpose—that justice and righteousness shall reign on earth. In
Judaic thought, therefore, freedom is more the means and
equality more the end.

10

INDIVIDUALITY AND EQUALITY
IN HINDUISM

A. H. SOMJEE

      Hinduism comprises a religious outlook, an ethic that is both religious and social, and a distinctive social organization. Unlike other religions, which foster human equality or contain an ideal of human brotherhood, traditional Hinduism is ambiguous with respect to the concept of equality. Its religious component remained partially isolated from its ethical doctrine. The insulation of religion from social organization, which was held to derive its rationale from this religion, was in fact even greater. Hindu social organization was largely the product of historical circumstances requiring the accommodation of diverse racial and ethnic groups, differentiated in their political position and economic function, within the framework of a stratified system. Hindu ethical doctrine combined religious individuality and the concept

of an organized and stratified society. The three components of
Hinduism—religion, doctrine, and social form—each embodied a
specific attitude on the question of equality. The religious component exhibited a remarkable degree of equalitarian tolerance,
owing to its commitment to a relativistic notion of truth itself;
ethical theory reflected an unresolved tension between an equalitarianism, coming from religion, and inequalitarianism, represented in the social order that was the world's worst example
of moral and social inequality. This composite character of Hinduism has been responsible, to some extent, in making it receptive to the social and political equalitarianism of the West.

First, I shall examine the implications for or against equality
in the basic tenets of the religion, the ethics, and the social organization of Hinduism. I shall then analyze the views of social
critics and reformers on aspects of the social organization where
social relations were directly affected by the inequalitarian
principles. The fact that the religious system remained detached,
to a large extent, from the social organization facilitated Hindu
acceptance of criticism and reforms toward social equality in
recent years. The equalitarian aspects of neither Islam nor
Christianity exercised much influence on the thinking of the
reformers, inasmuch as these two belief systems[1] also questioned
the religious basis of Hinduism. More acceptable to the reformers, therefore, were the secular ideals of equality as emphasized in Western social and political thought from Locke to
the Fabians. Apart from the powerful force of nationalism, with
its implied social self-criticism, the drive toward equality was
accelerated in recent years by the provisions of the Indian constitution, the general leveling process of democratic politics, and
legislation designed to introduce some form of directed social
change.

I

The religious system of Hinduism is almost incapable of
precise definition. In its evolution it has assimilated a large
number of ideas and beliefs and has at any given time meant

---

[1] I have used the term "belief system" to include the religious system,
ethical doctrine, and reference to social organization.

different things to different people. The four important features of Hindu religion, which have some bearing on the notion of equality, are as follows:

First, Hinduism puts extraordinary emphasis on religious experience of the individual. In a sense all religions are addressed in part to the individual person and in part to his conduct in society. The latter invariably contains a concept of society that may or may not constitute an integral part of the belief system. In the case of Hinduism, its social references, as contained in its ethical doctrine and as exemplified in its social organization, do not form an integral part of the belief system itself.

Its preoccupation with religious experience rather than with conduct of the individual in society has led Hinduism to emphasize, in the words of a leading Indian philosopher, Dr. S. Radhakrishnan, "the art of self-discovery." Because of its emphasis on inner knowledge and the profundity of divine experience, its ideal man is not the "doer" but the "experiencer" of rare experience. For the last forty centuries such has been the ideal man of the Indians.[2] One of the few exceptions to the emphasis on rare experience is the *Bhagavad Gita's* highly activist exhortation. Whereas the *Bhagavad Gita* has remained the central text of Hinduism, its call to action, save in the time of crisis, has had a limited appeal.

Concern with personal experience brought the uniqueness of the person to the center of religion. No discrimination was made among the *individuals* engaged in pursuit of religious experience. Theoretically speaking, because every human being was a center of experience and as such equal to any other, he was considered potentially capable of the highest religious experience.

Second, because the religious system tended to diverge from ethical doctrines, and because the latter were confined to the society and therefore of this world, there were references to another code of ethics in Hinduism. This, second code of ethics, was an integral part of the belief system. For the sake of convenience the former may be called social ethics, as it referred to one's existence in society, and the latter, religious ethics. The main emphasis of the latter fell on "inner perfection." Through

[2] S. Radhakrishnan, *Eastern Religions and Western Thought*, Oxford, Oxford University Press, 1940, p. 35.

vidya or enlightenment the individual came under a moral obligation to seek this goal.

Along with the need to seek "inner perfection," the religious ethics also emphasized the identification of oneself with others. The emphasis of *Brihadaranyaka Upanishad,* one of the major religio-philosophical texts of Hinduism, on *tat tvam asi* (that art thou) reminded people engaged in the art of "inner perfection" of the humanity around them. Translated into the Christian ethic, as it was by Paul Deussen, it meant, "you shall love your neighbour as yourself because you are your neighbour."[3] The religious ethics, despite their limited influence, tried to counter-balance the extraordinary streak of personal cultivation in Hindu belief system by a definite reference to a broad humanism.

Third, the emphasis on deep religious experience through enlightenment led Hinduism to recognize the similar pursuits of other religions and the relative validity of all religions. Such a recognition resulted in an equalitarian tolerance of other belief systems, a rare phenomenon in the history of religions.

When the apostle Thomas arrived in India in A.D. 52, the Hindu princes conferred upon him the privileges of the highest caste and allowed him freedom to preach and proselytize. Now, the Syrian Christians of south India claim to be the descendants of those he converted. Then there are two racial groups of the Jews, one fair and the other dark, who, in the distant past, came and settled in the southwest of India. They too enjoyed complete freedom of worship. Zoroastrians also received asylum in India. The case of Islam was complicated by unfortunate turns of history and politics. But there again Hinduism showed, in the past as well as in recent years, a high degree of tolerance. It is because of the basic tolerance of Hinduism that in India there are nearly fifty million Moslems today.

The Hindu tolerance of other religions was due to its absence of social commitments, on the one hand, and its philosophy of relativistic truth, on the other. Because Hinduism regarded religion as a personal affair, it did not fail to recognize the same fact for other religions. Its lack of group reference or group consciousness, so far as the religious system and not the social or-

---

[3] *Op. cit.,* p. 102.

ganization was concerned, made it tolerant even of religions that were deeply committed to congregationalism.

Its own philosophy of relative truth further facilitated such an approach. Dr. Radhakrishnan has admirably summarized this approach: "If the most we can hope for is a relative truth, a provisional hypothesis, we cannot claim finality or absoluteness for any view. Where nothing is certain, nothing matters. Where there is no depth of conviction, tolerance is easy to attain."[4]

Fourth, the absence of any dogma in Hinduism prevented it from classifying other religious systems into categories of right and wrong. Invariably such a categorization becomes a basis for treating people as superior or inferior. Its confusing plurality of ideas and beliefs helped it to refrain from harsh characterization of the non-Hindu. A term such as *maleccha* (foreigner, non-Hindu, etc.), no doubt derogatory, was used much more sparingly than have been such terms as gentiles or heathens or kafirs, by other religions. Whoever was not a Hindu was therefore not a part of the highly stratified society. He was merely an "outsider," though not necessarily equal. He was just different.

II

The social ethics of Hinduism suggested a fourfold pursuit of life. It was *kama* (feelings and desires), *artha* (material well-being), *dharma* (rules of right living), and *moksha* (salvation). Of these, *kama, artha,* and *moksha,* by their very nature, could be pursued individually. *Dharma,* on the other hand, became a significant meeting point of the individual and society. Its main concern was to encourage the consciousness of the consequences of one's actions on the society as a whole and thereby regulate them with the help of rules and regulations. *Dharma,* therefore, became the central concept of Hindu social ethics.

The pursuit of *kama, artha,* and *moksha* was to be undertaken by the individual as an individual. Social imperatives and limitations on what he did came with *dharma.* The first three pursuits continued the individualized character of the religious system. *As*

[4] *Ibid.,* p. 314.

individuals all were expected to pursue these values. *Dharma,* because of its social and political implications, became closely linked with social organization, on the one hand, and the state, on the other. Inasmuch as the social organization was basically inequalitarian in character, the doctrine of *dharma* put a seal of sanction on social inequality itself. Hindu social ethics, in other words, reflected the unresolved antithesis of the individualized equalitarianism of the religious system and the social inequalitarianism of the social organization.

The social ethics also indicated the four stages of life of the individual. These were *brahmacharya* (life of preparation as a student and bachelor), *grahsthashram* (householder), *vanaprastha* (forest recluse), and *sanyas* (renunciation of the world). These, however, need not detain us for long. We must go back to the significant doctrine of social ethics, namely, *dharma.*

Derived from the root word *dhri,* meaning to hold together or sustain, *dharma* as a concept was repeatedly interpreted in religious texts of the Hindus. In the Vedic literature it was identified with laws, moral laws, and duties in general. In the *Dharmashastras* it explicitly referred to the ramification of duties in the four-caste society. The *Mahabharata* referred to its function as one of "restricting creatures from injuring one another."[5] And so on. Because life and obligation in society remained the primary concern of the average Hindu, *varnashram dharma,* the framework of regulations that governs the four castes, with all its implied inequalities, came to be cited again and again. Even the state and the king in ancient India were charged with the task of implementing it.

III

This then brings us to the examination of the nature of its social organization—a colossal illustration of social inequality. This social organization was, in part, a consequence of the racial problem, created by the Aryan conquest of the indigenous people. The conquerors were fair-skinned, whereas the native population was dark. The initial stratification in the social organization, therefore, was based on *varna* or color. This stratification soon de-

---

[5] See B. C. Gokhale, *Indian Thought Through the Ages,* Bombay, Asia Publishing House, 1961, pp. 25-26.

veloped along the lines of occupational classes, gradually assimilating the aborigines at the lowest levels, and finally expressed itself in the form of the caste system with all its institutionalized inequalities and rigidities.

What the stratified social organization did was to *accommodate* people of diverse races and ethnic groups, with diversity in their political and occupational positions, within one single organic social system. In the words of Professor Hutton, "The subcontinent of India has been likened to a deep net into which various races of peoples of Asia have drifted and been caught." Further, "all these varied people have been enabled to live together, in conditions of comparative stability and forming what may be described as a multiple society, by the caste system, which must probably be regarded as having developed as a sort of organic response to the requirements of the particular case."[6] Having started off with the four basic castes or *varnas,* namely, *Brahmins, Kshatriyas, Vaishyas,* and *Sudras,* the social organization succeeded in giving rise to nearly three thousand subcastes or *jatis,* governed by strict regulations that prevented their merging with one another. In the earlier stages there was a considerable degree of mobility and individuals and groups were in a position to rise up the social scale. Such mobility decreased as time went by. Let us now briefly examine the support the stratified social organization, with its institutionalized inequalities, received from sacred texts and juridical theories.

The earliest book of the Aryans, which is now part of revered Vedic literature, is the *Rig-Veda.* Historians believe that it appeared between 1500 B.C. and 1200 B.C. What strikes one most in this work is the plurality of gods in "the vedic pantheon."[7] According to Amaury de Riencourt, author of the illuminating work, *The Soul of India,* which attempts a psychological interpretation of the Indian epic, the Aryan mind remained preoccupied with space rather than time. The Aryans were deeply impressed by the variety of peaks and valleys through which they passed in their move toward the peninsula. Some of these peaks became their gods and goddesses, swelling the already great num-

---

[6] J. H. Hutton, *Caste in India,* Bombay, Oxford University Press, 1963, p. 1.

[7] Amaury de Riencourt, *The Soul of India,* New York, Harper & Row, 1960, pp. 16–17.

ber of those they already had. This abundance of deities gave
rise to polytheism and subsequently became the basis for a
tolerant outlook on religions as such. Philosophers who were
dissatisfied with multiplicity of gods and goddesses sought mon-
istic explanations and philosophies. But so far as the religious
outlook of the masses was concerned, it remained polytheistic in
character.

The *Rig-Veda* also made specific reference to the origin of the
four classes in the social order. According to the text they emerged
from the different parts of the body of Purusha, the primeval
man: "The Brahmin was his mouth, of both his arms was Ra-
janya (princely families: later on this came to be known as
Kshatriya) made. His thighs became the Vaishyas, from his feet
the Sudra was produced (10.90)."[8]

On the face of it, this appeared to be a reference to the organic
unity of the four social classes arising out of the same body and,
therefore, constituting a vast social body. Nevertheless, the fact
that these different classes emerged from the high, the middle,
the low, and the lowest parts of Purusha's body was subsequently
used to justify the increasingly hierarchical character of the
society. From then on, with few exceptions, the Brahmins who
wrote most of the sacred texts, gave themselves extraordinary
privileges. They accorded few of them to the Kshatriyas, fewer to
the Vaishyas, and imposed disadvantages of all kinds on the
Sudras.

The *Upanishads,* written in the sixth century B.C., mark the
end of Vedic literature. They represented a revolt of the thinking elite against the excessive emphasis on the rituals at the
hands of the Brahmins. They placed great stress on the individual
qua individual seeking his own salvation without the aid of the
Brahmins.

Difficult to read, the *Upanishads* were largely addressed to the
elite and well over the head of the average man. What the masses
needed, in fact, was a highly simplified religious doctrine and
above all a code of conduct rather than abstract philosophical
arguments as contained in the *Upanishads*. This need was met by
the two great epics of Hinduism, namely, the *Ramayana* and the

---

[8] See the text in *Hinduism,* edited by Louis Renou, New York, George
Braziller, 1962.

Mahabharata, and particularly within the latter by the *Bhagavad Gita.* Nevertheless, so far as the establishing of actual rules of conduct was concerned, the priestly caste continued to dominate. In most of its writings, it carved a special position of privilege for itself. We shall now examine some of them.

The Dharma Sutras, which appeared between the sixth and the third century B.C. attempted to institutionalize and to justify positions of the four castes in matters relating to initiation, the list of mortal sins, the numbers of wives one could possibly have, and taxes. According to the Sutras the Brahmins were required to go through the ceremony of initiation in their eighth year, and the Vaishyas in their twelfth year after conception (1.1).[9] Inasmuch as the Sudras were not considered to be twice-born, they did not have the privilege of being initiated.

Apart from the differences in the age of initiation, the definition of the five mortal sins listed by the *Dharma Sutras* greatly favored the Brahmins. These were: violating the bed of a guru (teacher: usually a Brahmin), slaying a learned Brahmin, stealing his gold, drinking liquor, and associating with the low castes. Three out of five mortal sins referred to the security of the Brahmins (1.1-46).[10]

Privileges were also claimed in matters relating to the number of wives one could possibly have. A Brahmin was permitted to have three wives, a Kshatriya two, Vaishyas and Sudras one each.

The *Dharma Sutras* permitted the kings to take one-sixth of the income of their subjects by means of taxes. The Brahmins, however, were exempted from this obligation. In return for the privilege, the king was assured that "after death bliss awaits the king who does not oppress the Brahmins."[11] The Kshatriyas too were promised a great deal if they listened to the Brahmins. "Kshatriyas who are assisted by the Brahmins, prosper and do not fall in distress (11.1-26)."[12]

The *Manu-Smriti,* a classic juridical exposition concerning conduct in general, contained a firm statement about the inequalities of various social groups. Unlike the *Rig-Veda,* which provides a cosmogenic explanation of how the four classes origi-

[9] *Ibid.,* p. 109.
[10] *Ibid.,* p. 113.
[11] *Ibid.,* p. 114.
[12] *Ibid.,* p. 115.

nated from an unequal source therefore to remain unequal, and
the *Dharma Sutras,* which promised rewards of all kinds in order
that the Brahmins might be well treated, the *Manu-Smriti* legal-
ized the relative positions of various groups in the social hierarchy. Having appeared during the second or the first century
B.C., it reflected the crystallized inequalitarian character of the
caste system in Hindu society.

The major premise of the *Manu-Smriti,* so far as the present
topic is concerned, is the consequence of what it describes as a
sinful act. The sins of the body result in rebirth in the form of
an inanimate object, those of the speech in the form of bird or
beast, and those of the mind in the form of low caste. The assumption behind the last was that the low caste was the product
of mentally debased acts of the previous birth. Not only was the
Manu-Smriti deeply committed to the doctrine of *karma,* but it
also implied a punitive attitude toward the low caste.

Based on these assumptions, its story of creation asserted that
in order "to protect this universe," different duties and occupations were assigned to different groups. The Brahmins were assigned the task of studying and teaching the Vedas, the Kshatriyas
that of protecting the people, the Vaishyas that of tending cattle,
and the Sudras that of humbly serving the three other castes.

The *Manu-Smriti* charged the king with the task of maintaining the purity of castes. The king was advised not to hesitate in
administering punishment to attain this goal.

This brings us to one of the greatest epics; namely, the *Mahabharata,* believed to have been written between the third century
B.C. and the first century A.D. It once again raised the problem
of the origin of castes. Rejecting the *Rig-Vedic* argument, it
maintained that the consequences of one's action determined
one's caste. Its argument ran as follows:

> There is no difference of castes: This world, having been
> created by Brahma entirely Brahmanic, became afterwards
> separated into castes in consequences of works. Those Brah-
> mins, who were fond of sensual pleasure, fiery, irascible,
> prone to violence, who had forsaken their duty, . . . fell into
> the condition of Kshatriyas. Those Brahmins who derived
> their livelihood from kine, . . . who subsisted by agriculture,
> and who neglected to practice their duties, entered into the

state of Vaishyas. Those Brahmins who were addicted to mischief and falsehood, who were covetous, who lived by all kinds of work . . . , had fallen from purity, sank into the condition of Sudras. Being separated from each other by these works, the Brahmins became divided into different castes (17.24) .[13]

For the first time past actions and their consequences explained the origin of *all* castes, not only of the Sudras. Even the Brahmins were pronounced as "not Brahmins" if they did not live up to the standard set for them.

Action itself became the cardinal principle of the *Bhagavad Gita,* one of the most important texts of Hinduism. An integral part of the *Mahabharata,* the *Gita* heavily emphasized its underlying action-orientation.

Despite its acceptance of caste differences, the *Gita,* by virtue of its extraordinary emphasis on reason, harmony, and universal sympathy, contained a strong undercurrent of humanism. This is evident in the following: "even those who in faith worship other gods, because of their love they worship me (Krishna) (9.23) ."[14] To different castes with different stations and even with different gods, the *Gita* held out great promise of becoming one with the creator. As it said, "they (the four castes) all attain perfection when they find joy in their work (18.45) ." Further, "a man attains perfection when his work is worship of God, from whom all things come and who is in all (18.46) ."[15]

The *Gita* thus gave hope to every caste, irrespective of its place in the social hierarchy, of attaining great heights of perfection. It provided each group with a sense of equality so far as the goal of attaining perfection was concerned. "Greater is thine own work, even if this be humble, than the work of another, even if this be great. When a man does work God gives him, no sin can touch this man (18.47) ."[16]

The doctrine of *karma* weighed heavily on the minds of men of the lower castes. The *Gita* gave them the hope of redemption in its unqualified equalitarian appeal for salvation. "Leave all

[13] *Ibid.,* p. 142.
[14] See the text in *The Bhagavad Gita,* translated by Juan Mascaro, Baltimore, Md., Penguin, 1963, p. 82.
[15] *Ibid.,* p. 119.
[16] *Ibid.*

things behind and surrender all to me; and come to me for thy
salvation, I will give thee liberty from the bonds of thy past sins
(18.66)."[17]

Having examined the various texts' explanations and sanctions
for inequalities that had already grown in Hindu society, I shall
now very briefly point out how the temporal power in ancient
India sustained the inequalitarian social structure. The sacred
texts required that the king, among his major moral obligations,
maintain the social order on stratified lines. In the words of
Professor A. L. Basham, "in general the king was not the arbiter
of morals; he merely enforced the existing moral codes of the
classes and the castes in his kingdom, as interpreted by the
learned Brahmins of his court."[18] The preservation of *varna-
shram-dharma* (the moral law concerning the four castes) was,
therefore, one of the primary duties of the government. Professor J. H. Hutton voiced a similar opinion in his distinguished
work on *Caste in India:* In matters of the caste system, "the
ultimate controlling authority is secular."[19]

Apart from the fact that the state in ancient India was morally
obliged to maintain the stratified social structure, the widely
accepted, cyclical theory of civilization left little or no scope for
projecting an equalitarian ideal in social life. According to this
theory the civilization gradually declined and with it degenerated
the social and moral life of the people. Under the circumstances
the king was the only "savior from anarchy." Neither the social
organization nor the political community of ancient India could,
therefore, become the focal point for projecting an equalitarian
ideal. Only the religious system itself could do this, particularly
in its concern for personal experience.

IV

Attacks on the inequalitarian character of the Hindu
social order came from Buddhism, Islam, Christianity, Sikhism,
and so forth. They also came from a number of religio-social

[17] *Ibid.,* p. 121.
[18] See A. L. Basham, *Politics and Society,* in "Some Fundamental Political
Ideas of Ancient India," edited by C. H. Philips, London, George Allen and
Unwin, 1963, p. 13.
[19] J. H. Hutton, *op. cit.,* p. 93.

protest movements. Because the former, and to some extent the latter, also attacked the Hindu religious system, which they could not dislodge, they achieved no significant influence on the social order. Those who actually succeeded in influencing the social order had little or nothing to say about religious belief. These were mostly the social reformers and the nationalist leaders of the last two hundred years. To their ideas we now turn.

Among the social reformers in the modern period, Raja Rammohun Roy was one of the few who expressed great admiration for Christian moral philosophy. Study of the New Testament, he believed, might have a desirable effect on the stratified Hindu society. In his view, the Christian "code of religion and morality is so admirably calculated to elevate men's ideas to high and liberal notions of one God, who has equally subjected all living creatures, without distinction of caste (s), rank or wealth."[20] While he had a great deal of influence in reforming certain ritual practices of Hinduism, a great deal of his mature thinking was devoted to refuting the arrogant claims of Christian missionaries in India.

With Dayananda Saraswati, the founder of the protestant sect of *Arya Samaj,* came a pointed denunciation of social inequality. He rejected the post-Vedic Hinduism, which had assimilated the caste system, and went back to the religion of the Aryans. He also rejected the notion of untouchability and maintained that no one should be debarred from the study of the Vedas.

With Ramakrishna and Vivekananda, the two most influential reformers, began the emphasis on recognition of the basic humanity of every person and the need to make it a central theme in religious worship. This view was formulated in terms of Christian ethics. Vivekananda argued that, "if you cannot love your brother whom you have seen, how can you love God whom you have not seen."[21] Further, "I shall call you religious from the day you begin to see God in men and women."[22]

Among the nationalist leaders, the earlier political agitation centered on the theme of equality between Indians and Europeans before law. In later years, most of them participated as much in

---

[20] Cited in *Sources of Indian Tradition,* edited by W. T. de Barry, New York, Columbia University Press, 1964, p. 577.

[21] *Ibid.,* p. 648.

[22] *Ibid.*

social reform movements as in the movement for political independence. Justice Ranade, who himself was deeply involved in social reform, called for "a general recognition of the essential equality between man and man."[23] Gokhale directed the attention of thoughtful Indians toward the need to improve the lot of the low castes. He saw that lot as "deeply deplorable," and believed "it constituted a grave blot on our social arrangement."[24] In his opinion, "modern civilization has accepted greater equality for all as its watchword, as against privilege and exclusiveness, which were the root ideas of the old world, and the larger humanity requires that we should acknowledge its claim by seeking the amelioration of the helpless condition of our downtrodden countrymen."[25]

Gandhi did not fully go along with those who were trying to bring about social equality in the caste-ridden Hindu society. On the one hand, he went a step further than they in his desire to remove the disadvantages from which the untouchables and other depressed communities suffered. He even fought for the rights of women and succeeded in influencing the social climate so that subsequently their participation in public life became possible. On the other hand, he was not prepared to abandon the ideal of *varnashram dharma* and work for the radical reordering of social relationships. For him the social code of *varnashram dharma* "satisfied the religious, social and economic needs of a community."[26]

V

In contemporary India's drive toward equality, a number of forces have played their part. Inasmuch as these were largely concerned with the status and opportunities of the individual, they did not come in direct conflict with the religious system itself. Once again, the basic tolerance and adaptability of the religious system facilitated the assimilation of the changes

[23] *Ibid.*, p. 685.
[24] *Ibid.*, p. 698.
[25] *Ibid.*, p. 700.
[26] Cited in *Indian Nationalism and Hindu Social Reform*, Charles H. Heimsath, Princeton, N.J., Princeton University Press, 1964, p. 345.

brought about by these forces. Briefly speaking, these forces are as follows:

The constitution of independent India has been the greatest single factor in generating, directly and indirectly, the drive toward equality. The framers of the Indian constitution were divided over the question whether the village or the individual should be the unit of Indian polity. Those who expressed their view in favor of the former had come under the influence of British and Indian writers, particularly of Gandhi, who had idealized the village republics of ancient India. Those favoring the latter were steeped in the nineteenth-century European liberalism, and their voices ultimately prevailed in the making of the Indian constitution.

In the constitution itself various kinds of freedoms were guaranteed to the individual, and greater equality was achieved. The constitution also sought to abolish various disabilities that were traditionally imposed on the depressed section of Indian society.

Associated with these changes was the declaration by the Congress Party of its intention to establish a "casteless and classless" society. This kind of declaration also had echoes in the other political parties of India.

A significant step in the direction of an equalitarian society was undertaken by the Democratic Decentralization Program of community development in recent years. The basic aim was to loosen the existing network of hierarchical relationships by creating popular institutions at different levels in rural India. This was expected to provide an opportunity for rebuilding the community on democratic lines.

Then there was the inevitable leveling effect of democratic politics. At the national, state, and regional level, greater participation by the masses is now in evidence. Whereas they still do not participate as individuals or as members of political organizations but as caste or kin groups tending to become affiliated to electioneering individuals and political parties, the fact remains that these groups, drawn from the masses, however socially inferior and economically depressed, have improved their bargaining position in politics. In rural communities particularly, the decision-making processes within social groups or among them are increasingly dispersed. The introduction of universal adult suffrage has caused a ferment in social and political life and has triggered a chain reaction that may even alter the character of society.

Finally, the introduction of social legislation that sought to remove inequalities between the sexes and between groups, industrialization, urbanization, compulsory primary education, professed faith in change and development—all these are helping the ossified social order to regain its dynamism.

These equalitarian forces have not brought into question or tried to alter the religious component of the system. What they have attacked is its implicit social order. The attack on the latter is not an attack on the former, and, therefore, the resultant changes have been assimilated without any serious threat to the inherited religious culture. The problems created by the equalitarian forces are of a different order. India has a highly personalized religious system and a group-oriented social order. The equalitarian forces have undermined the latter. But they have also posed the problem for a highly individualized people to think in terms of the wider community composed of aspiring and increasingly autonomous personalities.

11

EQUALITY IN EXISTENTIALISM

HERBERT SPIEGELBERG

To my knowledge the place of human equality in the social and political thought of the existentialists has not yet been the subject of special attention. In view of the urgency of the issue, this seems to me a regrettable omission. My immediate purpose in contributing this paper to the present volume is to collect some of the relevant evidence and to discuss its significance critically and reconstructively.

EXISTENTIALISM: CORE AND FRINGE

All generalizations about existentialism, amorphous as this movement is in its philosophical, literary, and political expressions, are apt to be misleading. But if one limits its circumference to the core of what is sometimes called the Paris group, i.e., Jean-Paul Sartre, Simone de Beauvoir, the late Maurice Merleau-Ponty, Francis Jeanson, and most of the staff of Sartre's

Les Temps Modernes, one statement about its political line needs
no qualification: It is unequivocal in its stand for human equality. This stand is part of the struggle of these existentialists for
the liberation of human existence from all types of discrimination
and oppression based on class, race, and sex. Thus they have
fought "colonialism," old and new, in Vietnam, Madagascar, and
Algeria. They have also denounced discrimination in the
American South and in totalitarian dictatorships, both fascist
and communist.

The situation becomes less clear if one includes, as most intro-
ductions to existentialism do, all those writers who have used the
term "existence" in a Kierkegaardian sense even before 1944,
when the label "existentialism" became the fashion, among them
such major inspirers of the core group as Kierkegaard, Nietzsche,
and such contemporary philosophers of existence as Karl Jaspers,
Martin Heidegger, and Gabriel Marcel, who violently reject the
label of "existentialism," and Nicolas Berdjaev, Martin Buber,
and Paul Tillich, who seem to be less allergic to it.

Søren Kierkegaard, who first gave the word "existence" its
existentialist ring, was for all practical purposes a *homo
apoliticus,* even in his philosophizing; hence for him the question
of social equality in existence did not arise. One might argue,
however, that inequality in the form of aesthetic individuality
belongs to Kierkegaard's aesthetic "stage on life's way," while
equality is at least compatible with the ethical and religious
stages.

If Friedrich Nietzsche is to be included among the philosophers of existence (to my mind one of the more dubious inclu-
sions if only because the term "existence" as such does not mean
anything special to him), then existentialism would indeed be
saddled with one of the most violent denouncers of human
equality, the "lie" invented by the envious resentment of the
revolting slaves.

Karl Jaspers, politically a staunch antitotalitarian and democratic liberal, finds it necessary to reinterpret the idea of equality
along Kantian lines: "The idea of equality of all men is palpably
false, as far as their specificity and endowment as psychologically
knowable beings is concerned. . . . The essential equality of all
men resides solely in that depth where to each one freedom opens
a way to approach God through his moral life. . . . This equality

means: respect for every man, which rules out the treatment of any man as means only and not at the same time as an end in himself."[1] Besides, Jaspers' fascination with greatness and great men, not only in philosophy but in other fields also, clearly expresses his aristocratic taste.

Heidegger's notorious, though short-lived, involvement with Nazism may well make him suspect of sharing its contemptuous rejection of the unity of the human race and its segregation into superior and inferior races. But an examination even of his most sickening pronouncements from that episode does not reveal any explicit repudiation of the doctrine of human equality. As to his philosophy and specifically his analytics of existence, one of the chief inspirations of the core existentialists, it is so absorbed in questions of the ontological structure of *Dasein,* rather than with concrete ontic existence, that anthropological questions such as that of human equality never arise. Heidegger's concern here is with the common plight of man as such in his relation to Being, not with men in their qualitative individuality and their differences.

Another problematic case among contemporary philosophers of existence is Marcel. Whereas he is an unequivocal enemy of all totalitarian degradation of man, he denounces equalitarian "fanaticism" as the basis for modern mass-mindedness and as originating not only from the sinister "spirit of abstraction" but also from the egocentric envy of the masses toward the privileged, at which point he even invokes Nietzsche and his theory of *ressentiment.*[2]

AN EXISTENTIAL OUTSIDER: VLADIMIR JANKÉLÉVITCH ON EQUALITY

I am familiar with only one case of an explicit plea for equality based on a concept of existence. It comes from a highly

---

[1] *Der philosophische Glaube,* München, R. Piper & Co., 1948, p. 56f.; Engl. transl.: *The Perennial Scope of Philosophy* by Ralph Manheim, Philosophical Library, 1949, p. 69f.

[2] *Les Hommes contre l'humain,* Paris, La Colombe, 1951, p. 119f.; Engl. transl.: *Man against Mass Society* by G. S. Fraser, Chicago, Gateway, 1952, p. 160f. Also *La Dignité humaine,* Paris, Aubier-Montaigne, 1964, p. 172; Engl. transl.: *The Existential Background of Human Dignity,* Cambridge, Harvard University Press, 1963, p. 131f.

original French philosopher, usually not associated with existentialism but clearly sympathetic to it in spite of his chiefly Bergsonian inspiration. Even his case is stated only incidentally. But it is unusual enough to merit a brief digression. It occurs in an article of 1939, hence is still a case of existentialism "avant la lettre," and runs roughly as follows:

Being, which Jankélévitch identifies with "ipseity," is absolutely contingent and in this sense a mystery. The "that" of this being is also the foundation of *human* being and the true foundation of its dignity. It is also equal for all human beings:

> Being does not require any particular aptitude. Here is a chapter where everyone is competent, since all men are equally and sufficiently initiated in the affairs of destiny. All are specialists. There are no laymen, no more or less gifted ones—for being represents the great equality of the unequals. Here everyone is housed under the same sign, and the hereditary princes are not ahead of the guardsmen. We are all equal according to our *being,* but doing makes us unequal (p. 25, translation mine) .[3]

Such equality proves to be the primary explanation of equality before the moral law and of the "ecumenical democracy of the men of good will. For the good is something which everyone can do without any handicap or initial privilege (p. 27)."

Certainly not all the steps of this sketchy argument are cogent. True, the fact that we are all equal in the contingency of our being is a plight worth remembering and considering. It is less clear whether it is sufficient ground for defending the kind of equality that is at stake in the philosophical and political debate about human equality. But what is most relevant in the present context is that Jankélévitch does not distinguish between being in the universal and classic sense and existence in the new Kierkegaardian sense of a specifically human way of being. Hence his equality of being in general is apt to "prove" too much: It would make us equal to sticks and stones and every form of life, granting them equal rights. Besides, it is by no means clear whether the *fact* of being implies any *right* of being. The con-

---

[3] "De l'Ipséité," *Revue internationale de philosophie,* Vol. II (1939) , pp. 21–42.

tingency of being may be a mystery, but hardly in a sense that gives it any special dignity and claim to our respectful awe.

Nevertheless, here is at least an explicit attempt to link an existential approach with the problem of human equality. What is more, the idea that contingency has something to do with the demand for equality is worth developing.

EQUALITY IN THE THOUGHT OF JEAN-PAUL SARTRE

However, the best defenders of human equality in social and political life remain the hard-core existentialists of Paris. It is all the more surprising that their theoretical writings in particular do not seem to include any explicit pleas and arguments for equality as a principle. I have no ready explanation for their apparent reluctance to speak out on this issue. Is it because of their general rejection of absolutes? But then why is freedom such a basic concept of their ethico-political ideology? Nevertheless, their writings contain enough evidence of their implicit equalitarianism. This deserves explicating.

I shall attempt to do this chiefly in the case of Jean-Paul Sartre, still the central figure of the Paris group, although he now seems to be ready to contribute his existentialism to a pool of diluted Marxism purged of its objectivism and materialism. I shall also comment on a pertinent elaboration of the general pattern by Simone de Beauvoir and an important variation by Merleau-Ponty. Next, I shall raise some critical queries about the foundation of this equalitarianism. And finally, I shall make some suggestions about possible ways of strengthening the existentialist case, even though these may not quite fit into the framework of orthodox existentialism.

Sartre's equalitarianism, as practiced in concrete situations both political and literary but not preached in his philosophical theory, can be derived as a corollary from some of his basic ideas. But before turning to his philosophical works, one might do well to seek them in his nonphilosophical writings. There is special reason for this, related to the strangely unfinished condition of Sartre's existentialist ethics. Sartre developed this ethics, and in fact proclaimed existentialism as a comprehensive philosophy, only after he had published the "essay in phenomenological ontology," which still contains his major claim to philosophical fame, *Being and Nothingness,* of 1943. Its "Conclusion" discusses some of the "Ethical Perspectives" of his philosophy, which were to be further elaborated in a book tentatively announced as *Man (L'Homme)*, which never materialized and apparently is no longer expected to do so for reasons never fully explained. In fact, Sartre's existentialism, in the sense of the term that developed after the liberation of France from the Nazis, has thus far been formulated mostly in literary documents, in such philosophical manifestoes as his lecture on existentialism as a humanism,[4] with its surprising changes in position,[5] and in his plays. The "manifesto" and even the political essays are strangely unenlightening on the equality issue. But there is one play in which it is at least skirted, *The Devil and the Good Lord.* Using as background the revolt of the German peasants against their feudal lords in the Reformation period, Sartre introduced into his plot some of the levelers of the time under the leadership of a sinister character by the name of Nasty, who poses as a religious equalitarian;[6] but quite apart from his odd name, he is certainly not Sartre's mouthpiece. So too, the egalitarianism that the main hero, Goetz von Berlichingen, tries to espouse during one of his existential conversions, also turns out to be a failure. When he sides with the embattled peasants he first wants to fight alongside them as their equal but finally finds himself forced, in view of the incompetence of the peasant leaders, to become their dictatorial general in the fight for the freedom of all men.

But, as happens only too frequently in Sartre's literary productions, the author's own explicit answer remains ambiguous and enigmatic. The only way to determine the foundation of Sartre's equalitarianism is, therefore, to examine the principles of his earlier ontology. I shall try to present, as briefly and nontechnically as I can, those relevant for the deduction of equality and to show their significance for the equalitarian position.

[4] *L'Existentialisme est un humanisme,* Paris, Nagel, 1946; Engl. transl.: *Existentialism* by B. Frechtman, New York, Philosophical Library, 1947.

[5] "French Existentialism: Its Social Philosophies," *Kenyon Review,* Vol. XVI (1954), pp. 446–462.

[6] *Le Diable et le bon Dieu,* Paris, Gallimard, 1951, p. 104; Engl. transl.: *The Devil and the Lord* by Kitty Black, New York, Alfred A. Knopf, 1960, p. 54.

Equality in Existence

Sartre's slogan for existentialism: "existence precedes essence" (which incidentally is not acceptable to the other philosophers whom he wants to include as existentialists) has a meaning that is anything but clear. One of its simplest interpretations is that man exists before he achieves a specific essence as a result of his choices. More specifically, there is no such thing as human nature before man "chooses himself" and in choosing himself also chooses for all humanity.[7]

What does this imply for the problem of equality? In contrast to essence with all its diversities, existence is here conceived as an indeterminate stage preceding all differentiation. But such indeterminacy cannot fail to be equal for each existence. Consequently the doctrine of an essenceless existence preceding human nature implies indeed an original equality at the very start.

Equality in Freedom

Human existence, as Sartre conceives of it, is not a merely passive condition, as is mere being, the opaque and massive state of unconscious reality, the "In-itself *(en-soi)*."[8] For Sartre, existence coincides with freedom. Now, according to one of Sartre's boldest pronouncements, freedom is either absolute or nonexistent. That it is indeed absolute is the challenge he flings into the face of scientific determinism. Now if all men's freedom is absolute, as Sartre asserts, then it is hard to see how they could be anything but equal. There could be inequalities in freedom only if freedom were a matter of degrees.

It should, however, be added immediately that from the very start Sartre warned against certain misunderstandings of this doctrine. For example, he never meant to assert that human freedom is omnipotent and that all human beings are equal in such respects as physical strength or social opportunities. As it turns out, man's unrestricted freedom concerns not factual possibilities but meanings and values. For no matter what his factual

---

[7] *L'Existentialisme,* p. 83f.; transl. p. 20f.

[8] For a discussion of the *en-soi,* see my *Phenomenological Movement* (2nd ed.), The Hague, Martinus Nijhoff, 1965, pp. 462, 469, 472.

limitations, man is always free to determine the meaning of the facts by choosing his projects and by relating the facts to these projects.

Equality in Responsibility

Whatever special meaning the term "responsibility" may have for Sartre—and indications are that it has many—he makes it clear that man is responsible not only for himself but for the world as a whole. In this sense his responsibility is, as he puts it, total. Now totality does not admit of any degrees. Hence the responsibilities of different "existers" would have to be equal.

Of course, one may wonder how anyone's responsibility can be total, if everyone else is also totally responsible. But being totally responsible does not necessarily mean to be responsible to the exclusion of everyone else. Whereas everyone may have responsibility for everything and each one may be responsible with his whole being, everyone else may be coresponsible in much the same way as, in the case of multiple insurance, all insurers are liable for the amount of the total damage, although they will eventually distribute their liabilities. The important thing is that, no matter how many bear the burden of responsibility, the field for which they are responsible is completely covered by their guarantees.

Equality in Facticity

To the philosophers of existence, all being is contingent. There is essentially no way to base being on a necessary being. This is also true of human existence or, as Sartre puts it, human reality. In fact, the contingency of human existence is even more acute. Man's "facticity," as Sartre called this condition, following Heidegger, is characterized by what the latter had called "thrown-ness" (Geworfenheit), and what Sartre calls "délaissement," i.e., abandonment. Besides, there are other aspects of his condition, such as anguish or despair (better, "non-reliance") that reveal the basic condition or facticity of human reality.

Now whatever differences there may be in the concrete forms of man's condition, basically it is the same for every exister. Each one is "thrown" into the world like an orphan, is existentially abandoned, no matter on what coast he is shipwrecked. In this respect at least our facticity is the same, although the concrete facts of each one's existence will differ. Thus our fundamental plight is equal.

Equality and Situation

Despite his insistence on absolute freedom and total responsibility, Sartre has always made it clear that such freedom is only freedom in concrete situations. Some of these may be common and equal, but most concrete situations differ and change constantly.[9] How far do these differences affect human equality?

In order to answer this question, one has to take account of Sartre's special conception of a "situation." For to him a situation is not simply an objective brute fact. Instead, he conceives of it as the joint product of the contingent "in-itself" *(en-soi)* and human freedom *(pour soi)*. There are therefore no such things as objective situations by themselves. Mere facts become situations only by their relation to a human consciousness with its freely chosen projects. Thus a wall may be a barrier to my project of walking or a challenging hurdle in an obstacle race.

How far then are the situations of different existers equal? This will depend partly on the factual element and partly on human freedom. Some of the factual elements are sufficiently common to be equal, but most of them are apt to differ enormously. However, to Sartre the decisive factor is the use that freedom will make of them. Will it try to equalize or "unequalize" the equal or unequal objective raw material of the situation? Even equal starting conditions can be "unequalized" by the societal goal of maximum variety, which may call for slaves and castrates. Even unequal starting conditions can be equalized by a society that grants equal votes even to citizens still uneducated. In other words, situations are essentially neither equal nor unequal. Their equality or inequality is in this sense a matter of choice.

But then what are concrete situations for Sartre's existentialism? In the main section on situation in *Being and Nothingness*, Sartre discusses five of them: my place, my past, my environ-

---

[9] It is significant that Sartre's essays on matters literary, aesthetic, and political have been republished under the title *Situations,* Paris, Gallimard, beginning 1947; Engl. transl. of Vol. IV by Benita Eisler, New York, Braziller, 1965.

ment, my fellowmen, and my death. He omits "my body," although elsewhere he assigns to it the role of a situation. Now for place, past, environment, and fellowmen there will certainly be plenty of differences in the factual elements. These differences will be less pronounced in the fact (though not in the form) of death, which however is for Sartre (in contrast to Heidegger) the situation discussed last and certainly not the ultimate "sense" of but rather the ultimate absurdity in human reality. But all these factors will always depend on their relation to the equalizing or "unequalizing" projects of freedom. The place where I am born can be fitted into the project of a prefabricated standard existence and thus become a monotonous situation. By the same token, my past, however humdrum, can become part of extremely different situations as I choose and follow a career.

This, then, would appear to be the basic pattern of Sartre's implicit philosophy of human equality: There is no total equality as far as the concrete facts of human existence are concerned, especially not in a society divided into classes and in a world composed of oppressors and oppressed nations. Whatever factual equality may exist is restricted to existence as it "precedes" essence and to freedom in its absolute power to decide upon the meanings of situations.

Such equality is certainly not enough to guarantee equal value and dignity to each man's existence. This will depend on whether men exist "authentically," choosing freedom for themselves and for others, or "inauthentically," escaping from it in bad faith and thus becoming cowards. But even then Sartre seems to believe that none of these choices is irrevocable. There are "conversions" like the metamorphoses of "Saint Genet," the kleptomaniac turned writer; yet according to Sartre's film *Les Jeux sont faits (The Chips are Down)*, there are limits to this freedom of reversing one's fate.

What is most obvious is Sartre's assent to equality in rights and duties. The concept of equality of duties is included in the thesis of man's total responsibility, which, however, need not imply equality of rights, a phrase not common in the vocabulary of the existentialists. But Sartre's stand for the oppressed as part of the struggle for universal liberation makes it amply clear that the equal freedom he claims for everybody also includes equal rights to freedom.

EQUALITY OF THE SEXES IN
THE THOUGHT OF SIMONE DE BEAUVOIR

As a philosopher Simone de Beauvoir reflects Sartre's position so completely that no special discussion of her version of existentialism seems to be called for. However, she deserves special credit for having spelled out, in her *For an Ethics of Ambiguity*, a little more clearly than had Sartre in *Being and Nothingness*, what his abandoned book on ethics might have contained—although the existentialist meaning of the term "ambiguity" needs considerable explaining. What makes her voice important in the present context is her discussion of the problem of equality between the sexes, a point about which Sartre himself in his philosophy is strangely silent.

The Second Sex is, of course, also an indictment of actual inequalities. And one might easily interpret it as just another plea for the equality of the underprivileged sex on existentialist grounds. But this is certainly not the whole story. Simone de Beauvoir does not even raise the problem of equalitarianism as such and is anything but a mere feminist. Most of this huge and learned work is diagnostic. The main finding is that there remains an enormous amount of inequality between the sexes, especially in social relations. This inequality has its chief root in the fact that woman finds herself, her life, and her world defined by man as "the other" or second sex, even where she is recognized as equal. However, her role as "the other" of man is by no means immutable and essential. On the whole "it is as absurd to speak of 'woman' in general as of an eternal 'man.' This explains why all comparisons, if one tries to decide whether woman is superior, inferior, or equal to man, are idle: their situations are profoundly different."[10]

There is thus a basic difference. But it is not a difference permanent in nature, "not a matter of brain or hormones," but of the situation.[11] Some of these differences, such as anatomical and physiological organization, are clearly permanent. But the decisive factor remains the interpretation of these situations; it

[10] *Le Deuxième Sexe* II, 454; Engl. transl.: *The Second Sex* by H. M. Parshley, New York, Knopf, 1952, p. 627.
[11] *Ibid.*, 422; transl. p. 597.

may emphasize or deemphasize, equalize or "unequalize" the meanings of these facts.

Even as far as the future and the ideal relation are concerned, Simone de Beauvoir raises no explicit demand for equality, and still less for uniformity. In fact, Stendhal's romantic offer of equality for women is one of those "myths" which do not satisfy her. What matters to her is that woman should become an "autonomous individual," able and entitled to define her own situation and not to have it defined for her by the "first sex." In the "liberation" she envisions, there will be not only equality in differences but "differences in equality."[12] Both sexes will be themselves but also "others" in reciprocity. In other words, each sex will be both first and second.

Thus even for the existentialist there will remain inequality in fact, based on the different situations resulting from the free choices that start from the biological differences. But such inequalities will not interfere with the equivalence in value and dignity, and least of all with the equality of rights and responsibilities, as far as these are not grounded in relevant biological differences.

HUMAN "UNIVERSALITY" IN THE THOUGHT OF MERLEAU-PONTY

Maurice Merleau-Ponty, whose phenomenological existentialism differs so much from Sartre's that the two should never be lumped together,[13] shared with him an apparent reluctance to discuss human equality explicitly and to refer to it as a political argument.[14] But one of his most original discussions of existentialism, the one on Hegel's existentialism in *Sense and Non-sense*[15] comes very close to spelling out existentialism's equalitarian implications in a way that improves on Jankélévitch's incomplete case.

[12] *Ibid.*, 576; transl. p. 731.

[13] "French Existentialism: Its Social Philosophies," *Kenyon Review*, Vol. XVI, p. 454ff.

[14] See, e.g., his "Sur l'Indochine," *Signes*, Paris, Gallimard, 1960, p. 403; Engl. transl. by R. C. McCleary, Evanston, Ill., Northwestern University Press, 1964, p. 323.

[15] *Sense et non-sense*, Paris, Nagel, 1948; Engl. transl. by H. L. and P. A. Dreyfus, Evanston, Ill., Northwestern University Press, 1964.

A first indication of such an argument is implied in a sentence in which Merleau-Ponty supports what his friend Jean Hyppolite used to say to his students during the Nazi occupation:

> We are all Jews to the extent that we are responsible for the universal, are not resigned to merely being *(être)*, and want to exist *(exister)*.[16]

Beyond this will to "existence" as a foundation for a common existential equality, the very consciousness of others, even as enemies, implies equality:

> My consciousness of another as an enemy comprises an affirmation of him as an equal.[17]

But the most explicit linkage of Merleau-Ponty's conception of existentialism with the idea of equality can be found in the first part of his final revision of its definition:

> A more complete definition of what is called existentialism than we get from talking of anxiety and the contradictions of the human condition might be found in the idea of a universality which men affirm or imply by the very fact that they *are* and at the very moment when they oppose one another; by the idea of a reason immanent in unreason; and by a freedom which becomes what it is by binding itself, and to which the slightest perception, the faintest movement of the heart, and the least action bear incontestable witness.[18]

I submit that this assertion of a (Hegelian) universality in the very fact of existing, i.e., of being-in-the-world as Merleau-Ponty conceives of it, constitutes a new and significant addition to the philosophy of human equality.

SOME CRITICAL QUERIES

This is not the place for a comprehensive appraisal of the existentialist position, its claims and its foundations, or even of its social philosophy. I believe that in all of these respects it is

---

[16] *Ibid.*, p. 133f.; transl. p. 67.
[17] *Ibid.*, p. 135f.; transl. p. 68.
[18] *Ibid.*, p. 139f.; transl. p. 70.

incomplete. But it is capable of development, particularly if it strengthens its phenomenological basis and overcomes its penchant to stun philosophers and laymen alike by its insistence on paradoxical overstatements of its case.[19] It also deserves such development in view of the fact that a sane existentialism may well break through and transcend the stalemated debates between liberal and communist ideologies. Signs of such possibilities have not been wanting, particularly in the case of as independent a thinker as the late Maurice Merleau-Ponty, especially in his *Les Aventures de la Dialectique* (1955).

However, certain fundamental points that have specific bearing on the existentialist philosophy of equality as explicated in the preceding sections can be raised profitably in this context.

(a) Sartre's conception of existence, linked by him with the scholastic distinction between essence and existence, rather than with Kierkegaard's conception, needs further probing. Not only ordinary usage and common sense but also conscientious phenomenology will balk at the idea that existence as the correlate of essence can occur, let alone act, by itself. This may at best be true of the "exister," of the existing ego. But Sartre never distinguishes between existence as a property (or "form") of a being and existence as the exister. It is on the latter that we would have to focus in order to make Sartre's view of existence as active tenable or at least plausible.

(b) The idea of such an existence as "preceding" all essence is certainly odd, especially ontologically, implying as it does that even in time there has been existence without essence or "nature." "The Man without Qualities" may be a suggestive and provocative title for a novel like Robert Musil's. But it certainly cannot mean that such a faceless being has no properties at all. How could such essence-less existence do any such thing as "choose" without having at least potentialities and the kind of structures underlying them that would allow it to actualize them? True, these "essences" could be fluid and impermanent. But they would have to be present all the same and allow a description of "existence" with regard to what it can undertake.

(c) Sartre's daring case for either absolute freedom or none at all is one he himself could maintain only with difficulty. Such

---

[19] See *The Phenomenological Movement*, pp. 509ff.

statements as the one that the French had never been as free as under the Nazi occupation[20] when every action had the weight of ultimate commitments were so paradoxical as to seem perverse. Since then Sartre's increasing sympathy with a humanistic Marxism that includes the thesis of historical materialism has made him admit by implication that this freedom is severely limited, not only because of the lack of economic foundations for its free use but also because of the limited range of choices for the underprivileged. In this sense it would of course no longer be possible to assert the equal freedom of every exister. All one might still defend is the contention that, like the fearless Stoic, everyone always has the possibility, though hardly the equal strength, to say "yes" or "no" regardless of the odds that confront him.

(d) Sartre's invigorating appeal to human responsibility is apt to become meaningless when he tries to make it "total." As long as man is a finite being, any insistence on infinite responsibility is not only paradoxical but bound to be self-defeating and paralyzing. How can we ever dream of living up to it? Besides, in view of Sartre's assertion that all values are of our own choosing, it seems strange that he should make us responsible not only for these but also for the whole universe into which we were "thrown" without having any choice. Responsibility in the genuine sense as expressed in ordinary language is bound to be proportionate to our actual powers. Any attempt to hold us responsible beyond these powers is not only unfair ("ultra posse nemo obligatur") but leads to the dilution of any genuine sense of responsibility. Thus our responsibilities will be equal only when our powers are equal. There is certainly no good reason for considering them "total."

ON CHANCES FOR STRENGTHENING THE EXISTENTIALIST CASE FOR EQUALITY

In making the following suggestions I do not want to imply that I consider myself an existentialist in any of the usual senses of the term. But I feel so close to some of the existentialist

[20] "La République du silence," *Situations* III, Paris, Gallimard, pp. 1–42.

views that I would consider it a loss if their potentialities should remain undeveloped. I feel the greater right to say so since I once presented a plea for human equality even before "existentialism" had appeared on the American scene, a plea in which I referred to a "deeper conception of our existence than usual as a necessary foundation for a vindication of the idea of human equality."[21]

But before connecting my earlier argument with the new existentialist position, I had better say in what sense and to what extent I am prepared to defend the equalitarian position.

a. Human equality as a fact, actual or potential, seems to me empirically indefensible (notwithstanding the intriguing exception of identical twins and doubles), even though I do not subscribe to Leibniz' principle of the identity of indiscernibles, which of course makes all absolute equality a metaphysical impossibility.

b. Human equality in value appears to me almost equally problematic, unless one is prepared to accept, as I am not, the position of complete subjective relativism, under which no objective comparison of value any longer makes sense. The only equality in value that I would admit is the potential equality of all moral agents with regard to those values based upon effort, where all depends on how large a portion of one's total energies, however unequal to those of others, has been spent on striving for the good within one's reach.

c. The case for equality of rights and duties seems to me strongest, at least as far as "basic" human rights are concerned. What is to be included among these is not easy to tell, although the recent convergence in the field of human rights (Universal Declaration of Human Rights) is a good indication, at least for a certain period. "Equality of consideration" and "equality of opportunities" seem to be some of the clearest candidates for a more permanent place.

However, the real philosophical problem is to find valid grounds for supporting the postulate of equality in rights and duties in the face of inequality in fact and in value. I discussed the difficulty and the ways in which other ethical theories have tried to meet it in my paper just cited (n. 21). I also sug-

[21] "A Defense of Equality," *Philosophical Review*, Vol. LIII (1944), pp. 101–124.

gested a solution that seemed to me partially new and, as I still believe, basically sound. What I want to do now is to show its possible connection with some of the theses of existentialism and to indicate how I think they may be strengthened.

Equality of the Existing Egos

In the preceding section I pointed out that one of the weak points of existentialism is not only its inadequate ontological conception of existence but also its failure to distinguish between existence and the exister. For what really matters is not so much existence as the exister. Although it is impossible to present here a full discussion of who this exister is, I submit that the primary candidate is the ego of Descartes' "ego cogito." If the existing ego., i.e., the concrete I-myself, is the real hub of a consistent existential position, then the question arises whether we have any right to assert the equality of all existing egos. Even the task of an epistemological justification of any assertion about the equality or inequality of such egos seems to be forbidding, considering the difficulty and limitation of all knowledge of egos other than our own. The difficulty is, by the way, quite different from that of knowing their individual personalities, their states and ideas. Perhaps the equal impossibility of certain knowledge in all these cases is one of the best reasons for the equal treatment of those whose inequality cannot be accurately assessed.

A more basic difficulty concerns the distinction between the ego and its properties. How far is the ego distinct from its body, from its endowments such as intelligence, or from its personality, including its temperament? Only insofar as such a distinction is possible at all does it make sense to raise the question of the equality of egos. If it is not possible, the inequalities are obvious. However, I do maintain that the distinction is defensible, at least to the extent that each ego can objectify these properties by reflection, consider them as distinct from itself, and even conceive of having others in their place. As far as the body is concerned, even Merleau-Ponty, usually considered one of the main protagonists of the identification of the subject with his body, has spoken on one occasion of the "metaphysical hypocrisy" of the person "who unreservedly pretends to be whatever it may be," for instance, a person who identifies with his hysterical symptoms

to the extent of deceiving not only others but himself as well.[22]
The clear implication is that even in hysteria the patient retains
enough freedom to keep himself distinct from his condition.

How far can we then assert that the various egos, as distinguished from their properties, are equal or unequal among each
other? If the ego itself has no actual qualities, has it at least
potentialities that could be equal or unequal to those of others?
I am afraid I cannot yet answer these questions with any confidence. However, there seems to me considerable evidence for
believing that different egos have different "ego-strength" and
even different powers for identifying with or dissociating from
their "personality." But these differences are hardly as pronounced as those between different personalities in their entirety.
Each ego is equal to every other ego at least in its plight of
having to face its existence and its fundamental situation.

Equality in the Accident of Birth and Circumstance

I shall now turn to the argument for equality in rights
and duties that I made in the previously cited paper and begin
by restating it in a slightly amended form as briefly as I can.

Its major premise was: All undeserved distinctions call for
equalizing redress; its minor premise: All inequalities of birth
constitute undeserved distinctions; the conclusion: All inequalities of birth call for equalizing redress. I called this conclusion
"the moral postulate of equality."

I placed the main stress of my argument on the minor premise's
assertion that inequalities of birth are undeserved distinctions.
This proposition seemed to me supported by the idea and
existential experience of the so-called "accident (or chance) of
birth," which includes such circumstances as sex, race, class, and
nationality. We refer to this accident even in our ordinary way
of thinking and talking without giving the matter much thought.
I submitted that it does, however, deserve such thought. So in a
later paper[23] I tried to show that what we mean by this phrase

---

[22] *Phénoménologie de la perception*, Paris, Gallimard, 1945, p. 190; Colin
Smith's English translation, *Phenomenology of Perception*, New York, Human-
ities Press, 1962, of this passage (p. 162) is misleading.

[23] "Accident of Birth: A Non-utilitarian Motif in Mill's Philosophy,"
Journal of the History of Ideas, Vol. XXII (1961), pp. 475–492.

is actually a *moral* chance, a condition not based on moral desert.

What I would like to suggest now is that existentialism can give further weight to this conception. One of existentialism's most characteristic motifs is that of the contingency of all being. For Sartre, as for David Hume, the idea of a necessary being is, therefore, a contradiction in terms. The most gripping expression of the experience of radical contingency occurs in Sartre's early novel *Nausea* (1938), especially in the episode at the root of the chestnut tree, where the realization of the complete irrationality of all being suddenly closes in on the hero:

> The essential thing is contingency. . . . Contingency is not a delusion, an appearance of which one can get rid. It's absolute. Consequently it is absolute gratuitousness. Everything is gratuitous, this garden, this city, I myself. If one comes to take account of this, it turns one's stomach, and everything begins to swim. . . . This is real nausea. The bastards try to conceal it from themselves with their idea of right. What a poor lie! No one has any right. They are completely gratuitous like everyone else. They don't get to feeling themselves as superfluous *(de trop)*. (But) within themselves, secretly, they know that they are superfluous. . . .[24]

Much of this is clearly literary overstatement. What seems to me significant about the passage is the emphasis not so much on general contingency as on gratuitousness, the absence of any moral right to existence.

Now what I mean by the accident of birth is actually nothing but a special form of this contingency. It is the contingency of the coincidence of two contingencies, the contingency of my being and the contingency of my "birth," i.e., my sex, race, physique, and so forth. In this sense it is actually a double contingency, a contingency to the second power. I believe that the existentialist stress on contingency as such can further heighten the poignancy of this experience. What existentialism does not seem to have done is to incorporate the original ex-

---

[24] *La Nausée,* Paris, Gallimard, 1938, p. 185f.; Engl. transl.: *Nausea* by Lloyd Alexander, Norfolk, Conn., New Directions, 1949, p. 176f.

perience of the accident of birth into its framework. Also, thus
far it has failed to spell out the full moral and social implications
of its doctrine of universal contingency and gratuitousness.

Equality and Human Dignity

Recently the idea of human dignity has developed into
one of the most powerful weapons in the struggle for equality,
especially racial equality. Yet it is an idea about whose meaning
there is surprisingly little clarity and agreement, both historically
and systematically. There are after all senses of the term "human
dignity" that may be expressions of blasphemous pride or
ridiculous self-importance. However, this is not the place to
explore the entire range of this fascinating idea.

What can existentialism do to clarify it? There is little discussion of the issue in the key existentialist writings. Actually, in
his *Nausea* and *The Flies* Sartre ridiculed the ideas of human
dignity among the bourgeois humanists. Only later, for instance
in the lecture on "Existentialism Is a Humanism," does one find
the claim that existentialism alone can give man dignity, inasmuch as it refuses to consider him a mere object, as materialism
does. However, there is no real development of the idea of dignity
in this or any other context. The only one who has tried this
is Gabriel Marcel in his William James lectures of 1961, *The
Existential Background of Human Dignity*.

But assuming that existentialism can add to the conception of
human dignity, what bearing has this on the postulate of human
equality? To suggest this connection one might raise a few
questions based on the experience of "indignities," of which our
age has provided so many appalling examples. Assuming that
any treatment of a person which does not respect his basic claims
to free development and expression offends his "dignity," is
there perhaps a basic indignity in the situation of a being from
whom equality is withheld? Is his dignity violated if he is not
treated on a par with others who have no better moral claims to
their own preferential treatment? I submit that in this sense
there is an element of indignity about every kind of inequality
that is none of the victim's fault.

However this may be, all I want to suggest here is that a deeper
consideration of the "human situation" may result in finding
new ground for the postulate of human equality. Existentialism is

well on the way to finding them. But it is certainly not the only way. Some ground may be found in such surprising places as the writings of John Stuart Mill. Perhaps the most fitting expression of the approach I am suggesting may be a quotation from Mill's diary, showing as it does that even a liberal thinker in favor of individuality could also be a friend of equality. For he based this view not only on utilitarian grounds but also on an appeal to the kind of nobility of mind which I consider congenial to the best existentialist temper:

> The passion for equality is an attribute either of the most high-minded or of those who are merely the most jealous and envious. The last should rather be called haters of superiority than lovers of equality. It is only the high-minded to whom equality is really agreeable. A proof is that they are the only persons who are capable of strong and durable attachments to their equals; while strong and durable attachments to superiors or inferiors are far more common and are possible for the vulgarest persons.[25]

[25] From "Diary," March 29, 1854, *The Letters of John Stuart Mill*, London, Longmans, Green & Co., 1910, Vol. II, p. 383.

POLITICAL AND LEGAL EQUALITY

12

A BRIEF DISCOURSE ON THE ORIGIN
OF POLITICAL EQUALITY

CARL J. FRIEDRICH

Men have always been politically unequal. Indeed, it
may be doubted that the expression "political equality" has any
basis in political experience. Why then could it become one of
the great battle cries of political oratory? In a reversal of the
famous question of the Academy of Dijon, it is possible to ask:
In what political situation does the argument about political
equality arise? To put it another way: Although it is a common
observation that men are treated differently and behave differently in all known political communities, the demand is made that
they should all be treated equally and should all act as if they
were equals. The patent political inequality is easy to understand.
It relates to the prevailing view in a given political community
as to the political qualities (virtues) required in various kinds

of political situations.[1] But political inequality not so related
also frequently occurs. When that is the case, people seeking
adjustments may couch their demand in terms of equality,
although what they really mean is appropriate differentiation.

Many aspects of egalitarian thinking are not specifically concerned with the political order. The argument here, however,
will be focused on the peculiar problems of political equality.
In a democracy where laws are adopted by a procedure providing
for popular participation in such legislation, any differentiation
between persons is likely to correspond to the prevailing views
as to what differentiating qualities are relevant to a determination of equality; thus, general equality is safeguarded by "legal"
equality (legal equality meaning that men are equal before the
law, but it may be at variance with political equality). A prevailing view does not, of course, exclude the possibility of differences
of opinion; often it is simply the majority view. (The matter of
what is prevailing may be complicated by federalism and other
varieties of constitutionally protected pluralism.)

In view of the fact that democratic communities—in line with
what has just been said—even though rendering homage to the
general principle of political equality, often not only accept but
also glorify inequality, it may be thought that political equality
is one of those vague, general notions which have no concrete
political content. This is far from true. Actually, notions of
equality intrude themselves continually into the political processes. If political equality is taken to mean, as it often is, that in
the field of political activities a similar condition can be presumed
to prevail as in a legal system providing for legal equality, that is,
that all men are "before politics" given an undifferentiated
opportunity to participate, then such "rights" as an equal vote
or an equal chance to compete for public office would constitute

[1] It is interesting to note that the great prophet of egalitarianism, Jean-
Jacques Rousseau, at the close of his *Discours sur l'origine de l'inégalité*
(1755) recognizes such natural inequalities as those of age, when he asserts,
for example, that it is manifestly against the law of nature for a young
person to give orders to an old one. Even Rousseau, then, does not appear
to believe that men are by nature politically equal. This is quite in keeping
with his general views, in which the rise of political community is related
to growth of civilization with its *amour-propre* (as contrasted with the
amour-de-soi of the natural state). Rousseau therefore distinguishes between
moral (I have called it general) equality, and political equality. General
equality is, in turn, related to "social justice."

political equality. Actually, the aforementioned rights and opportunities are only a special case of legal equality.[2] What is
presumed here is that no particular quality such as the capacity
for leadership, or for problem-solving, or for administering an
office is relevant for voting, or that if such properties are
relevant, they cannot be assessed by anyone. For as long as there
exists a prevalent belief that some quality or combination of
qualities is required or at least desirable for an effective participation in politics, there exists no adequate ground for offering an
equality of opportunity; it could not be used by those who lacked
the requisite quality. Democratic societies, ideologically committed to political equality, have often been involved in blatant
self-contradiction on this score. Many Americans have in the past
insisted, and quite a few are at present ready to insist, that
black men could not effectively participate in a free society.
Such patent inconsistencies apart, does full equality of opportunity in the broad sense ever exist in politics? If politics consists
in the acquiring and wielding of power, even when qualified by
considerations of justice, then surely such political equality is a
fata morgana, the pot of gold at the rainbow's elusive end. The
differences in vitality, intelligence, capacity to inspire, and other
such inborn qualities are, in themselves, as Hobbes rightly
insisted, power, or rather sources of power. But, it is said, the
opportunity only means that all men have an equal starting
chance, that "the least able and the most able are given an equal
start in the race for success."[3] But are such starts equal? And can
they be? Are, in other words, all political inequalities unnecessary, unjustified, and could they hence be eliminated, as they
deserve to be?[4] In the past, the situation has been complicated
by inequalities resulting from education, wealth, connections,
and so forth (all these in fact being to some extent interrelated).
But even if all these were largely eliminated, as has been attempted in Communist countries, does equality of political opportunity result? The concentration of power in a party elite

[2] In *Man and His Government,* 1963, especially pp. 292–3, I so stipulated
in defining political equality; the reflections here presented seek to go beyond
what is treated there.

[3] J. Roland Pennock, *Liberal Democracy,* 1950, p. 81. For Hobbes, cf.
Leviathan, Ch. X.

[4] This formulation is an adaptation of H. A. Bedau's starting point; cf.
Chapter 1.

(and bureaucracy) has, it seems, actually reduced political equality. As an ideological excuse, the Soviet leaders can cite Lenin (and Engels) who once stated that "any demand for equality which goes beyond the demand for the abolition of classes is a stupid and absurd prejudice."[5] It was a candid admission on the part of this outstanding leader that certainly he was "more equal" in Orwell's mocking sense.

What then are the political situations in which the argument about equality arises? Broadly speaking, they appear to be situations and constellations in which *disbelief* prevails concerning any manifest innate qualities justifying political inequality. Significantly, *more equality* is here sought because of *rising disbelief*. That it is a question of rising disbelief suggests that the situation was preceded by one in which belief in such manifest innate qualities (and hence political inequality) was present. In a sense, this goes without saying, but it is worth recalling, because the problem is linked to another one, namely a general propensity to believe that politics and government will be better handled, if greater political equality is granted. In other words, the rising disbelief in innate capacity to rule (whether based on heredity or some other factor) is linked to failure (or believed-in failure) of the pre-existing government. This reflection not only is important in itself but also directs attention to the fact that a failure of government and politics under conditions of maximized political equality *may* cause demands for its reduction, accompanied by possible revivals in the belief in innate qualities. The history of several European countries, including France and Germany, provides rather striking supporting evidence for this. In France a succession of failures from the *ancien régime* to the Fourth Republic has produced corresponding propensities to increase and decrease political equality, and to deny or assert the innate capacity of one man or a limited group. Similarly in Germany, the failure of the Empire led to the radical political egalitarianism of the Weimar Republic, and its failure in turn led to the reassertion of a belief in innate qualities of leadership; when the National Socialist regime failed dismally, a new wave of egalitarianism produced the rival regimes of the FRG and the GDR; the FRG having so far been accompanied by moderate

[5] Lenin, *Sochinenya*, Vol. XXIV (1935), p. 293. Lenin referred to Engels in making the point.

success, the egalitarian position has been reasonably consolidated; but wherever criticism is voiced, it tends to take the form of questioning the assumption of a disbelief in innate capacity to govern, accompanied by a variety of elite doctrines.[6]

If this then broadly defines the situation in which the argument about equality arises, it is important, next, to determine what might constitute an increase in political equality. Some answers are fairly obvious. The inclusion of ever larger classes of persons in such procedures as voting, being educated, competing for public office, having access to communications media (including the opportunity to speak one's mind—the "Hyde Park factor") obviously means more political equality. Looked at from the individual's standpoint, greater political equality is manifest in the refinement and extension of the procedures just mentioned: participating in the settling of specific policy issues through referenda and initiatives, having the education continue through life, making ever more offices competitive, and so forth. In terms such as these, there can be little question that the American Negro and the German worker are more equal today to other members of their communities than they were a hundred years ago. Political equality nevertheless remains elusive. The marked differences in inborn power cannot but affect the position of participants in a political society, and the consequences for the actual operation of politics and government are equally indeterminate (or at least not known in their determination).

What follows? Greater political equality increases the time and effort that members of the political community will devote to politics. Stated another way, the percentage of the social product put into political activities, such as elections, parties, and various forms of political communication (public relations), becomes larger. This is, incidentally, the reason why it has often been claimed that only a well-to-do community can afford political equality (democracy). The fact of such increasing absorption of human and other resources in the political process has served as a basis for some of the more pointed criticisms of equality. But are they justified? A definite answer would presuppose a convincing demonstration that the conduct of politics

[6] A striking illustration is provided by the writings of two German critics: Von Martin and Arnold Gehlen; the latter's *Der Mensch,* 1940 and later, is particularly symptomatic.

under conditions of increasing equality works no improvements. This kind of demonstration is almost impossible to make stick. Hence the argument remains highly inconclusive.

A second corollary and general proposition is that increasing political equality is compatible only with democratic legitimacy. This proposition can also be stated in the following form: Political equality is only compatible with a regime in which the right to rule is based on electoral procedures. It is often forgotten that the idea that the right to rule should be based on a majority vote is a curious one that has only recently found widespread acceptance. The right to rule (legitimacy) had in the past been based on divine (priestly) sanction, blood, descent, wealth, valor, and a variety of other notions. The reason for the truth of this proposition relating political equality to democratic legitimacy is not difficult to establish. Inasmuch as the proposition is (rightly) stated in terms of more or less, it might be desirable to restate it in the following form: Political equality is increased by the degree to which democratic legitimacy is embodied in the political order. As the idea of democratic legitimacy gains ground—and this is often a rather slow process—it is accompanied by the gradual increase in political equality. If there is a too rapid increase, the consequences can be quite serious. As ancient notions of legitimacy collapse all over the world, masses of persons often quite lacking the qualifications for political participation are permitted, indeed expected, to vote and even to seek election. That "all men are created equal," as the Declaration of Independence has it, constitutes an existential judgment hiding a normative proposition. The normative demand is that men ought to be provided with the opportunity to acquire enough equality in politically relevant respects to enable them to participate effectively in the processes which democratic legitimacy presupposes.

To the foregoing propositions relating political equality to democratic legitimacy and the use made of the total social product, a third can be added, relating political equality to the wielding of political power. This may be put as follows: Increasing political equality increases the fluidity of power. Power is fluid when it rapidly changes hands, and even in the same hands it increases or decreases within short periods.[7] Consensual power

---

[7] Cf. my *Man and His Government,* Chs. 9–11.

is more fluid power, and political equality produces more consensual power, i.e., it alters the ratio of consensual to coercive power in favor of the consensual. Recent work in American politics confirms the proposition.[8] The same trend may be observed in various European countries, including Germany where the fluidity of power has been strikingly increased in the course of this century. Here, as well as in Italy, France, and other countries, the destruction of ancient orders inherited from feudal times has facilitated the emergence of "elites of merit," as the beneficiaries of democratic politics are rather euphemistically called by those who have generalized the "elite" notion.[9] Such elites and the recurrent "appraisal" of their respective merit suggest the following corollary to the third proposition concerning political equality: Increasing political equality produces increasingly rapid circulation of the elites. If this corollary is correct, then it may be argued that a slowdown in the circulation of the elites, such as occurs with the establishment of one-party regimes, especially of the totalitarian sort, indicates a decline in political equality. This corollary is at the heart of arguments about the rise of a new class.[10] It is a moot question whether such greater fluidity is desirable or not, the arguments over it being at the heart of many of the political disputes between conservatives and progressives.

These three basic propositions are reinforced by the imagery of the "common man," as it has developed in the United States. It is, like all social myths, of considerable value in maintaining order, for it provides a rationale for intrinsically contradictory situations. I have argued elsewhere that this imagery has undergone substantial transformation; it may even be on the way out.

---

[8] Cf. V. O. Key, *Public Opinion and American Democracy*, 1961, especially Chs. 2, 3, 8, and 11. James W. Prothro and Charles M. Grigg, "Fundamental Principles of Democracy: Bases for Agreement and Disagreement," *Journal of Politics,* Vol. 22 (1960), pp. 276ff.

[9] The much-discussed notion of a "circulation of the elites" (Pareto) is, of course, closely related to what we call the fluidity of power; cf. Vilfredo Pareto, *The Mind and Society* (tr. Livingston), 4 vols., 1935, paras. 2026ff. A recent discussion has shown once again how controversial the "elite" concept remains; cf. Renato Treves (ed.), *Le Elites Politiche,* atti del IV congreso mondiale di sociologia, 1961. Cf. my article "A Critique of Pareto's Contribution to the Theory of a Political Elite," *Cahiers Vilfredo Pareto, Revue Européenne d'histoire des sciences sociales,* No. 5 (1965), pp. 259ff.

[10] Cf. Milovan Djilas, *The New Class,* 1957.

If so, it would create very serious issues for the maintenance of the established egalitarian order in the United States.[11] In any case, it is clear that one way of solving the problem posed by the patent differences of men in many spheres, especially intellectual and cultural ones, is to treat these differences as politically irrelevant. The political urgency of this need is to some extent responsible for the "anti-intellectualism" of the American democratic tradition, so annoying to all true intellectuals.[12] Lincoln's remark, "People who like this sort of thing will find this the sort of thing they like,"[13] is a droll expression of a mocking anti-intellectualism that has ever been popular in America. One only needs to recall Mr. Dooley, Josh Billings, and the rest of America's homespun philosophers of the pork barrel. For all of them share the characteristic outlook that eliminates from the belief in the common man "all matters of exceptional or rare value, more especially all matters of taste."[14] Furthermore, character is more important than intellect, because in matters of common concern, the steadfastness and dependability of character are a source of greater authority than intellectual prowess (*Washington* v. *Hamilton*). Views of this sort are, incidentally, by no means limited to Western egalitarian culture; Confucius taught that "character is the backbone of our human nature, and music is the flowering of character." (From *On Music*, Modern Library, 1943, p. 238.)

In a pointed critique of equality, the late Karl Llewellyn remarked that "in sum, we find gathered under the one label 'democracy' a 'refreshment' aspect in regard to policy which by no means coincides with that as to controlling personnel; a 'reasonable regularity' aspect which locks horns as often with

[11] Cf. my *The New Belief in the Common Man*, 1942, *passim*. The later German and Spanish versions transcend somewhat the original hortative phrasing.

[12] This aspect was given little attention by Richard Hofstadter in his otherwise remarkable and justly acclaimed *Anti-intellectualism in American Life*, 1963. It is indicative that Hofstadter's index contains neither the term "common man" nor that of "equality."

[13] Cf. G. W. E. Russell, *Collections and Recollections*, Vol. 1, Ch. 30.

[14] Cf. *The New Belief*, pp. 32ff. One reviewer in that tradition expostulated in a review of the book that "what this country needs is a Mr. Dooley to expound America's enthusiastic foster son, in the terms of Archey Road. . . . But oh, one misses an interpretation of it all by the philosopher of Archey Road." (*St. Louis Daily Globe-Democrat*, July 12, 1942.)

'democratic procedure' as with 'tyranny' or 'efficiency'; a 'downward distribution' drive in regard to product, suffrage, and opportunity both political and extra-political, countered by caste-building pressures; and an omni-competence attitude still at odds with needed specialized skills in government."[15] Equality is here treated as an "idealist" distortion of reality, democratic and other, without any regard for the *real* function of egalitarian thrusts.

One can speak of this political function as the "uses" to which equality can be put in the political process. When the equality of states is at issue, as treated in another part of this volume, the use of "equality" is not to be gainsaid; it serves as the foundation for all efforts to regularize, i.e., formalize, the conduct of states and their international relations in terms of international law. When the equality of groups or associations in pluralistic societies is at issue, it serves to provide the foundation for federal unions of cognate groups, on the one hand (federations of labor, of churches, of professions), and to regularize their status before the government, on the other; thus in legislation regulating their conduct, interest groups are treated as equal in spite of their striking differences in scope, power, and relatedness to the public interest. But of course the most interesting issues are presented by the political use of equality when such equality is claimed on behalf of individuals—in contesting various forms of discriminatory treatment, based on religion, race, sex, and so forth.

Ideological considerations aside, the political uses to which the egalitarian demand has been put are basically three, to wit: (1) increasing the size of the electorate for the purpose of favoring one or another political party, (2) broadening political awareness and understanding, and (3) discovering political talent, that is to say, potential leaders. The issues involved are complex ones, and there is no need to enter into them here. But the point is made to suggest that these uses are themselves an important part of the answer to the question: What is the political situation in which the argument about equality arises? For in the course of the intensification of the party struggle, astute political leaders, like Disraeli, will make themselves the

---

[15] Karl N. Llewellyn, *Jurisprudence—Realism in Theory and Practice*, 1962, p. 298; this critique is found in the essay "Common Law Tradition and Democracy."

spokesmen of demands for greater equality. At the present time, the clamor for lowering the voting age is often thus motivated, and a variety of more or less specious arguments are brought forward to support the proposition that because some youngsters eighteen years of age are quite interested and well informed on problems of public policy, it is sound to deny that most of them are still children who certainly are not the equals of the rest of the electorate.[16] Many of the new states are seriously troubled by such ill-considered claims of political equality that place the operation of any kind of workable democracy into jeopardy. This often desperate constellation leads in turn to frantic efforts at "educating the public," that is to say, to efforts at closing the gap between what is alleged and what is in fact true. And yet, there may be a partial justification, at least, for such precipitous extension of the electorate in the name of political equality, because of its use in discovering political talent. (Contrary to the egalitarian nonsense heard in the heyday of Jacksonian democracy, it is now generally recognized that politics and administration involve very special gifts—talent.)

Does this proposition bring the argument back to the "equality of opportunity"? It does not seem so to me. Looking at the problem from the viewpoint of the functioning of the political order, rather than from that of the rights of the persons involved in it (though one could say that it is the first right of everyone involved in a political order to have it function properly), political equality is provided, because it is not possible to know who are the politically gifted by other formerly recognized attributes such as birth, wealth, or even impressive intellectual gifts.[17] It is the obscurity of the indicators which makes it opportune to let many run; even then plenty of dopes and nincompoops get to be rulers.

In an interesting recent discussion, an American political scientist has put the preceding argument down as one of five "ways of thinking about equality," designating it as the argument from

[16] These arguments in favor of a low voting age fly in the face of what even a Rousseau believed to be obviously contrary to the natural law; see note 1 above.

[17] As Kant rightly pointed out against Plato, philosophers ought not to be kings or rulers because their talent for ruling is more than doubtful; cf. *On Eternal Peace* (in my *The Philosophy of Kant*).

utility. But he treats equality almost entirely in terms of a hortative proposition and in this connection observes that there is little to be said about this way of thinking, that "a utilitarian solution of a moral and philosophical problem is exactly that—utilitarian."[18] But as I have tried to suggest, the issue need not be a hortative one but can be existential and operational. There can be little doubt that men have put the argument about equality to political use, and that some important political gains have been secured for them by broadening the access to political functions, i.e., increasing equality. That being the case, the function of equality is related not only to prevailing values, interests, and beliefs in a given political community but also to the situational requirements in a particular political context.

In conclusion, it might be well to recall that apart from the functional aspects of political equality, the rise of political egalitarianism *has* a convictional and ideological root. The legal equality before the law is in a sense the secular version of the creaturely equality before God; both God and the Law transcend the individual and his needs. Yet, they suggest that in very essential respects, human beings are entitled to be treated as if they were equal. When Thomas Rainborowe cried out in the Army Debates at Putney (1647) that "the poorest he that is in England hath a life to live as the greatest he," he voiced dramatically this basic belief in men's equality. But it was and is the general equality, what Rousseau called the "moral" equality, which is so closely linked to the idea of freedom as the core of man's being. The freedom of participation, of taking part in the political life of the community to which one belongs, is part and parcel of the egalitarian premise of such freedom. But the extent to which such freedom calls for political equality is limited by the requirements for the well-functioning of the political order; for no one has a right to wreck the existence of his fellow-beings, and hence where political equality means political damage, or indeed catastrophe, the inequality of political gifts must set the limit to the exercise of political participation. *Videant consules, ne respublica detrimentum capiat!*

---

[18] John H. Schaar, "Some Ways of Thinking about Equality," *Journal of Politics,* Vol. 26 (1964), reprinted by UC Reprint Series (undated), p. 882.

13

EQUALITY OF OPPORTUNITY, AND BEYOND

JOHN H. SCHAAR

I

Equality is a protean word. It is one of those political symbols—liberty and fraternity are others—into which men have poured the deepest urgings of their hearts. Every strongly held theory or conception of equality is at once a psychology, an ethic, a theory of social relations, and a vision of the good society.

Of the many conceptions of equality that have emerged over time, the one that today enjoys the most popularity is equality of opportunity. The formula has few enemies—politicians, businessmen, social theorists, and freedom marchers all approve it— and it is rarely subjected to intellectual challenge. It is as though all parties have agreed that certain other conceptions of equality, and notably the radical democratic conception, are just too troublesome to deal with because they have too many complex implications, too broad a scope perhaps, and a long history resonant of violence and revolutionary fervor. Equal opportunity, on the other hand, seems a more modest proposal. It promises that the doors to success and prosperity will be opened to us all yet does not imply that we are all equally valuable or that all men are really created equal. In short, this popular and relatively new concept escapes many of the problems and pitfalls of democratic equality and emphasizes the need for an equal opportunity among men to develop and be paid for their talents, which are of course far from being equal.

The doctrine itself is attractively simple. It asserts that each man should have equal rights and opportunities to develop his own talents and virtues and that there should be equal rewards for equal performances. The formula does not assume the empirical equality of men. It recognizes that inequalities among men on virtually every trait or characteristic are obvious and ineradicable, and it does not oppose differential evaluations of those differences. Nor is the formula much concerned with complex chains of normative reasoning: It is practical and policy-oriented. In addition, equal opportunity is not, in principle, confined to any particular sector of life. It is held to be as applicable to politics as to law, as suitable for education as for economics. The principle is widely accepted as just and generous, and the claim is often made that application of the principle unlocks the energies necessary for social and economic progress.

Whereas this conception of equality answers or evades some questions, it raises others. Who is to decide the value of a man's talents? Are men to be measured by the commercial demand for their various abilities? And if so, what happens to the man whose special gifts are not recognized as valuable by the buying public? And most important, is the resulting inequality, based partly on natural inequalities and partly on the whims of consumers, going to bury the ideal of democratic equality, based on a philosophy of equal human worth transcending both nature and economics?

These are serious questions, and it is my intention in this essay to probe their deeper meanings, as well as to clarify some major assumptions, disclose the inner spirit, and explore some of the moral and political implications of the principle of equal opportunity.

II

The first thing to notice is that the usual formulation of the doctrine—equality of opportunity for all to develop their capacities—is rather misleading, for the fact always is that not all talents can be developed equally in any given society. Out of the great variety of human resources available to it, a given society will admire and reward some abilities more than others. Every society has a set of values, and these are arranged in a more or less tidy hierarchy. These systems of evaluation vary from society to society: Soldierly qualities and virtues were highly admired and rewarded in Sparta, while poets languished. Hence, to be accurate, the equality of opportunity formula must be revised to read: equality of opportunity for all to develop those talents which are highly valued by a given people at a given time.

When put in this way, it becomes clear that commitment to the formula implies prior acceptance of an already established social-moral order. Thus, the doctrine is, indirectly, very conservative. It enlists support for the established pattern of values. It also encourages change and growth, to be sure, but mainly along the lines of tendency already apparent and approved in a given society. The doctrine is "progressive" only in the special sense that it encourages and hastens progress within a going pattern of institutions, activities, and values. It does not advance alternatives to the existing pattern. Perhaps we have here an example of those policies that Dwight D. Eisenhower and the theorists of the Republican Party characterized as the method of "dynamic conservatism."

If this argument is correct, then the present-day "radicals" who demand the fullest extension of the equal-opportunity principle to all groups within the society, and especially to Negroes and the lower classes, are really more conservative than the "conservatives" who oppose them. No policy formula is better designed to fortify the dominant institutions, values, and ends of the American social order than the formula of equality of opportunity, for it offers *everyone* a fair and equal chance to find a place within that order. In principle, it excludes no man from the system if his abilities can be put to use within the system. We have here another example of the repeated tendency of American radicals to buttress the existing framework of order even while they think they are undermining it, another example of the inability of those who see themselves as radical critics of the established system to fashion a rhetoric and to formulate ends and values that offer a genuine alternative to the system. Time after time, never more loyally than at the present, America's radicals have been her best conservatives.

Before one subscribes to the equality-of-opportunity formula, then, he should be certain that the dominant values, institutions, and goals of his society are the ones he really wants. The tone and content of much of our recent serious literature and social thought—thought that escapes the confines of the conservative-radical framework—warn that we are well on the way toward building a culture our best men will not honor. The facile formula of equal opportunity quickens that trend. It opens more and more opportunities for more and more people to contribute more and more energies toward the realization of a mass, bureaucratic, technological, privatized, materialistic, bored, and thrill-seeking, consumption-oriented society—a society of well-fed, congenial, and sybaritic monkeys surrounded by gadgets and pleasure-toys.

Secondly, it is clear that the equal-opportunity policy will increase the inequalities among men. In previous ages, when opportunities were restricted to those of the right birth and station, it is highly probable, given the fact that nature seems to delight in distributing many traits in the pattern of a normal distribution, and given the phenomenon of regression toward the mean, that many of those who enjoyed abundant opportunities to develop their talents actually lacked the native ability to benefit from their advantages. It is reasonable to suppose that many members of ascribed elites, while appearing far superior to the ruck, really were not that superior in actual attainment. Under the regime of equal opportunity, however, only those who genuinely are superior in the desired attributes will enjoy rich opportunities to develop their qualities. This would produce, within a few generations, a social system where the members of the elites really were immensely superior in ability and attainment to the masses. We should then have a condition where the natural and social aristocracies would be identical—a meritocracy, as Michael Young has called it.[1]

Furthermore, the more closely a society approaches meritocracy, the wider grows the gap in ability and achievement between the highest and the lowest social orders. This will happen because in so many fields there are such huge quantities of things to be learned before one can become certified as competent that only the keenest talents, refined and enlarged by years of devoted study and work, can make the grade.[2] We call our age scientific, and describe it further as characterized by a knowledge explosion. What these labels mean from the perspective of equalitarianism is that a handful of men possess a tremendous fund of scientific knowledge, while the rest of us are about as innocent of science as we have always been. So the gap widens: The disparity between the scientific knowledge of an Einstein and the scientific knowledge of the ordinary man of our day is greater than the disparity between a Newton and the ordinary man of his day.

Another force helps widen the gap. Ours is an age of huge, complex, and powerful organizations. Those who occupy positions of command in these structures wield enormous power over their underlings, who, in the main, have become so accustomed to their servitude that they hardly feel it for what it is. The least efficient of the liberal-social welfare states of our day, for example, enjoys a degree of easy control over the ordinary lives of its subjects far beyond the wildest ambitions of the traditional "absolute" rulers. As the commanding positions in these giant organizations come to be occupied increasingly by men who have been generously endowed by nature and, under the equal-opportunity principle, highly favored by society, the power gap between the well- and the poorly-endowed widens. The doctrine

[1] Michael Young, *The Rise of the Meritocracy*, London: Thames and Hudson, 1958. Young's book imaginatively explores the conditions under which Jefferson's lovely dream of rule by the natural aristocracy turns into a nightmare of banality and outrage. The main condition, of course, is the dedication of virtually all creative energies to the goal of material abundance.

[2] Success is a function of both inborn talent and the urge to do well, and it is often impossible to tell which is the more important in a particular case. It is certain that the urge to do well can be stimulated by social institutions. How else can we account for Athens or Florence, or the United States?

of equality of opportunity, which in its origins was a rather nervous attempt to forestall moral criticisms of a competitive and inequalitarian society while retaining the fiction of moral equality, now ironically magnifies the natural differences among men by policies based on an ostensibly equalitarian rationale. The doctrine of equal opportunity, social policies and institutions based on it, and advances in knowledge all conspire with nature to produce more and more inequality.

This opens a larger theme. We untiringly tell ourselves that the principle of equality of opportunity is a generous one. It makes no distinctions of worth among men on any of the factitious grounds, such as race, religion, or nationality, that are usually offered for such distinctions. Nor does it set artificial limits on the individual. On the contrary, it so arranges social conditions that each individual can go as high as his natural abilities will permit. Surely, nothing could be fairer or more generous.

The generosity dissolves under analysis. The doctrine of equal opportunity, followed seriously, removes the question of how men should be treated from the realm of human responsibility and returns it to "nature." What is so generous about telling a man he can go as far as his talents will take him when his talents are meager? Imagine a footrace of one mile in which ten men compete, with the rules being the same for all. Three of the competitors are forty years old, five are overweight, one has weak ankles, and the tenth is Roger Bannister. What sense does it make to say that all ten have an equal opportunity to win the race? The outcome is predetermined by nature, and nine of the competitors will call it a mockery when they are told that all have the same opportunity to win.

The cruelty of the jest, incidentally, is intensified with each increase in our ability to measure traits and talents at an early age. Someday our measuring instruments may be so keen that we will be able to predict, with high accuracy, how well a child of six or eight will do in the social race. Efficiency would dictate that we use these tools to separate the superior from the inferior, assigning the proper kinds and quantities of growth resources, such as education, to each group. The very best training and equipment that society can afford would, of course, go to those in the superior group—in order to assure equality of opportunity for the development of their talents. It would seem more generous for men themselves to take responsibility for the matter, perhaps by devising a system of handicaps to correct for the accidents of birth, or even by abandoning the competitive ethic altogether.

Three lines of defense might be raised against these criticisms of the equality-of-opportunity principle.

It might be replied, first, that I have misstated the principle of equal opportunity. Correctly stated, the principle only guarantees equal opportunity for all to *enter* the race, not to *win* it. That is certainly correct: Whereas the equal-opportunity principle lets each individual "go as high as his natural abilities will permit," it does not guarantee that all will reach to the same height. Thus, the metaphor of the footrace twists the case in that it shows fools, presumably deluded by the equal-opportunity doctrine, trying to stretch hopelessly beyond their natural reach. But there is no reason to think that fat men who foolishly compete against Roger Bannister are deluded by a doctrine. They are deluded because they are fools.

These reservations are entirely proper. The metaphor of the footrace does misrepresent the case. But it was chosen because it also expresses some features of the case which are often overlooked. The equal-opportunity principle probably does excite a great many men to dreams of glory far beyond their real capabilities. Many observers of American life have pointed to the frequency of grand, bold, noble "first acts" in the drama of American life, and the scarcity of any "second acts" at all. The equal-opportunity principle, with its emphasis on success, probably does stir many men to excesses of hope for winning and despair at losing. It certainly leaves the losers with no external justification for their failures, and no amount of trying can erase the large element of cruelty from any social doctrine which does that. Cases like that of the footrace, and our growing ability to measure men's abilities, makes it clear that the equal-opportunity principle really is not very helpful to many men. Under its regime, a man with, say, an Intelligence Quotient of ninety, is given equal opportunity to go as far as his native ability will take him. That is to say, it lets him go as far as he could have gone without the aid of the doctrine—to the bottom rung of the social ladder—while it simultaneously stimulates him to want to go farther.

Secondly, it might be argued that the equality-of-opportunity principle need not be interpreted and applied, as it has been in this treatment, within a setting and under the assumptions of social competitiveness. The principle could be construed as one that encourages the individual to compete against himself, to compare what he is with what he might become. The contest takes place between one's actual and potential selves, rather than between oneself and others.

This is an interesting, and hopeful, revision of the principle. It would shift the locus of judgment from society to the individual, and it would change the criteria of judgment from social utility to personal nobility. This shift is possible, but it would require a revolution in our present ways of thinking about equality, for those ways are in fact socially oriented and utilitarian. Hence, this defense against the criticisms is really no defense at all. It is irrelevant in the strict sense that instead of meeting the specific charges it shifts the question to a different battleground. It is an alternative to the existing, operative theory, not a defense of it. In fact, the operative doctrine, with its stress on overcoming others as the path of self-validation, is one of the toughest obstacles in the way of an ethic of personal validation through self-transcendence. The operative doctrine specifies success as the test of personal worth, and by success is meant victory in the struggle against others for the prizes of wealth and status. The person who enters wholeheartedly into this contest comes to look upon himself as an object or commodity whose value is set, not by his own internal standards of worth but by the valuations others placed on the position he occupies. Thus, when the dogma of equal opportunity is effectively internalized by the individual members of a society, the result is as humanly disastrous for the winners as for the losers. The winners easily come to think of themselves as beings superior to common humanity, while the losers are almost forced to think of themselves as something less than human.

The third defense is a defense, though not a strong one. It consists in explaining that the metaphor of the footrace oversimplifies the reality that is relevant to an appraisal of the equal-opportunity principle. What actually occurs in a society is not just one kind of contest but many kinds, so that those who are not good at one thing need only look around for a different contest where they have a better chance of winning. Furthermore, there is not just one prize in a given contest but several. Indeed, in our complex and affluent society, affairs might even be so arranged that everyone would win something: There need be no losers.

This reply has some strength, but not enough to touch the basic points. Although there are many avenues of opportunity in our society, their number is not unlimited. The theory of equal opportunity must always be implemented within a set of conventions which favors some potentialities and discourages others. Persons who strive to develop potentialities that are not admired in a given society soon find their efforts tagged silly, or wrong-headed, or dangerous, or dysfunctional. This is inherent in any society, and it forms an insurmountable barrier to the full development of the principle of equal opportunity. Every society encourages some talents and contests, and discourages others. Under the equal opportunity doctrine, the only men who can fulfill themselves and develop their abilities to the fullest are those who are able and eager to do what society demands they do.

There is, furthermore, a hierarchy of value even among those talents, virtues, and contests that are encouraged: The winners in some contests are rewarded more handsomely than the winners in other contests. Even in a complex society, where many contests take place, and even in an affluent society, where it might seem that there had to be no losers, we know full well that some awards are only consolation prizes, not the real thing, and a bit demeaning to their winners. When the fat boy who finishes last in the footrace gets the prize for "best try," he has lost more than he has won.

The formula of equality of opportunity, then, is by no means the warm and generous thing it seems to be on first view. Let us now examine the doctrine from another perspective.

III

The equal-opportunity principle is widely praised as an authentic expression of the democratic ideal and temper. I shall argue, to the contrary, that it is a cruel debasement of a genuinely democratic understanding of equality. To argue that is also to imply, of course, that a genuinely democratic conception of equality is not widely held in the United States.

The origins and development of the principle are enough to throw some doubt on its democratic credentials. Plato gave the principle its first great statement, and he was no democrat. Nor was Napoleon, who was the first to understand that the doctrine could be made the animating principle of the power state. In the United States, the Jacksonian demand for equal rights was assimilated by the Whigs and quickly converted into the slogan of equal opportunity. It soon won a secure place in popular political rhetoric. Whig politicians used the slogan to blunt popular demands for equality—interpreted as "levelling equality"—while defending the advantages of the wealthy.

This argument from origins is, of course, merely cautionary, not conclusive, but other, more systematic considerations, lead toward the same conclusion.

The doctrine of equality of opportunity is the product of a competitive and fragmented society, a divided society, a society in which individualism, in Tocqueville's sense of the word,[3] is the reigning ethical principle. It is a precise symbolic expression of the liberal-bourgeois model of society, for it extends the marketplace mentality to all the spheres of life. It views the whole of human relations as a contest in which each man competes with his fellows for scarce goods, a contest in which there is never enough for everybody and where one man's gain is usually another's loss. Resting upon the attractive conviction that all should be allowed to improve their conditions as far as their abilities permit, the equal-opportunity principle insists that each individual do this by and for himself. Thus, it is the perfect embodiment of the Liberal conception of reform. It breaks up solidaristic opposition to existing conditions of inequality by holding out to the ablest and most ambitious members of the disadvantaged groups the enticing prospect of rising from their lowly state into a more prosperous condition. The rules of the game remain the same: The fundamental character of the social-economic system is unaltered. All that happens is that individuals are given the chance to struggle up the social ladder, change their position on it, and step on the fingers of those beneath them.

[3] *Democracy in America*, New York: Vintage, 1945, Vol. 2, pp. 104–5.

A great many individuals do, in fact, avail themselves of the chance to change sides as offered by the principle of equality of opportunity.[4] More than that, the desire to change sides is probably typical of the lower and middle classes, and is widely accepted as a legitimate ethical outlook. In other words, much of the demand for equality, and virtually all of the demand for the kind of equality expressed in the equal-opportunity principle, is really a demand for an equal right and opportunity to become unequal. Very much of what goes by the name of democratic sentiment—as that sentiment is molded within the framework of an individualistic, competitive society and expressed in the vocabulary of such a society—is really envy of those who enjoy superior positions combined with a desire to join them.[5]

This whole way of thinking leads effortlessly to the conclusion that the existence of hierarchy, even of oligarchy, is not the antithesis of democracy but its natural and necessary fulfillment. The idea of equality of opportunity assumes the presence of a mass of men of average talents and attainments. The talents and attainments of the superior few can be measured by comparison with this average, mass background. The best emerge from the democracy, the average, and set themselves over it, resting their position securely on the argument from merit and ability. Those on top are automatically justified because they owe their positions to their natural superiority of merit, not to any artificial claim derived from birth, or wealth, or any other such basis. Hence, the argument concludes, the workings of the equal-opportunity principle help the democracy discover its own most capable masters in the fairest and most efficient way. Everybody gains: the average many because they are led by the superior few; the superior few because they can legitimately enjoy rewards commensurate with their abilities and contributions.

So pervasive and habitual is this way of thinking today that it is virtually impossible to criticize it with any hope of persuading others of its weaknesses. One is not dealing with a set of specific

[4] Some civil rights leaders are suspicious of open enrollment plans to combat *de facto* segregation for precisely this reason.

[5] "The greatest obstacle which equality has to overcome is not the aristocratic pride of the rich, but rather the undisciplined egoism of the poor." Proudhon, as quoted in James Joll, *The Anarchists*, Boston: Little, Brown, 1964, p. 67.

propositions logically arrayed, but with an atmospheric condition, a climate of opinion that unconsciously governs articulate thought in a variety of fields. Something like this cluster of opinions and sentiments provides the framework for popular discussion of the origins and legitimacy of economic inequality. We are easily inclined to think that a man gets what he deserves, that rewards are primarily products of one's talents and industry, secondarily the consequences of luck, and only in small part the function of properties of the social-cultural structure. Somewhere around three-fourths of all personal wealth in the United States belongs to the richest fifth of our families.[6] There is no evidence, in the form of major political movements or public policies, that this distribution shocks the American democratic conscience—a fact suggesting that the American conscience on this matter simply is not democratic but is, rather, formed by the rhetoric of equal opportunity. Similarly, the giant public and private bureaucracies of our day could not justify for a minute their powers over the lives of men if the men so used did not themselves believe in the justness of hierarchy based on merit—merit always defined as tested competence in a special subject matter, tested mastery of a special skill or craft. Most modern writers on the theory of democracy accept this argument for elitism and point out happily that no serious moral or political problems arise so long as avenues for the movement of members into and out of the hierarchies are freely provided. The principle of equal opportunity, of course, does just that.

The basic argument is not new. What is new is the failure to appreciate the profoundly antidemocratic spirit of the argument. This failure is the specific novelty of the "democratic" thought and sentiment of our day, and it makes today's democrats as amenable to domination as any men have ever been. It is only necessary to persuade the masses (usually an easy task) that the hierarchs possess superior merit and that anyone (one naturally thinks of himself at this point) with the requisite ability can join them.

All that can be said against this orientation is that a genuinely democratic ethic and vision rejects oligarchy *as such*. The democrat rejects in principle the thesis that oligarchy of merit

[6] Oscar Goss, "The Political Economy of the Great Society," *Commentary* (October, 1965), pp. 31–37, at p. 37.

(special competence) is in some way different in kind from oligarchy of any other sort, and that this difference makes it nobler, more reasonable, more agreeable to democracy, than oligarchies built on other grounds. The democrat who understands his commitment holds oligarchy itself to be obnoxious, not merely oligarchy of this or that kind.

The argument for hierarchy based on merit and accomplished by the method of equal opportunity is so widespread in our culture that there seems no way to find a reasonable alternative to it. We automatically think that the choice is either-or: *either* hierarchy and orderly progress *or* anarchy and disorderly stalemate. But that is not so. It is hardly even relevant. The fact that it is thought to be so is a reflection of the crippling assumptions from which modern thought on these matters proceeds. It is thought that there must be hierarchies and masses, elites and non-elites, and that there can be no more democratic way of selecting elites than by the method of equal opportunity. The complexity of affairs demands elites; and democracy and justice require selection of those elites by merit and equal opportunity.

Of course there must be hierarchy, but that does not imply a hierarchical and bureaucratic mode of thinking and acting. It need imply no more than specialization of function. Similarly, the fact that complexity demands specialization of function does not imply the unique merit and authority of those who perform the special functions. On the contrary: A full appreciation of complexity implies the need for the widest possible diffusion of knowledge, sharing of views, and mutual acceptance of responsibility by all members of the affected community.

Of course there must be organization, and organization implies hierarchy. Selection of the hierarchs by the criterion of merit and the mechanism of equal opportunity seems to reassure the worried democrat that his values are not being violated. But hierarchy may or may not be consonant with the democratic spirit. Most of today's democratic thinkers soothe themselves on this question of democracy and organization with the assertion that everything that can be done is being done when organizations permit factions, provide channels of consultation, and protect individual rights by establishing quasi-judicial bodies for hearing and arbitrating disputes. Certainly these guarantees are valuable, but they have little to do with making organizations democratic. They are constitutionalist devices, not democratic ones.

Before there can be a democratic organization, there must first be a democratic mentality—a way of thinking about the relations among men which stresses equality of being and which strives incessantly toward the widest possible sharing of responsibility and participation in the common life. A democratic orientation does not grow from and cannot coexist with the present bureaucratic and "meritorian" ethic. It is an alternative to the present ethic, not an expansion or outgrowth of it. When the democratic mentality prevails, it will not be too hard to find the mechanisms for implementing it.

IV

I hope my argument will not be interpreted as some sort of mindless demand for the abolition of distinctions or as a defense of the ethic of mutual aid against the ethic of competition. The argument was mainly negative in intention, attempting to show that the idea of equality of opportunity is a poor tool for understanding even those sectors of life to which the notion of equality is applicable. It is a poor tool in that, whereas it seems to defend equality, it really only defends the equal right to become unequal by competing against one's fellows. Hence, far from bringing men together, the equal-opportunity doctrine sets them against each other. The doctrine rests on a narrow theory of motivation and a meager conception of man and society. It reduces man to a bundle of abilities, an instrument valued according to its capacity for performing socially valued functions with more or less efficiency. Also, the doctrine leads inevitably to hierarchy and oligarchy, and tries to soften that hard outcome by a new form of the ancient argument that the best should rule. In all these ways, the idea of equality of opportunity constitutes a thorough misunderstanding of a democratic conception of equality.

It is not the primary task of this essay to set forth a genuinely democratic conception of equality: that is a work for another time. Still, enough should be done in the second part of this essay to arrest the most obvious and most likely objections to the first part.

The equal-opportunity principle is certainly not without value. Stripped of its antagonistic and inequalitarian overtones, the formula can be used to express the fundamental proposition that no member of the community should be denied the basic conditions necessary for the fullest possible participation in the common life, insofar as those conditions can be provided for by public action and through the use of public resources. This formulation will take one some distance toward a democratic conception of equality, but it must be interpreted carefully, for it can easily turn into just another defense of the equal right to become unequal.

Still, the formulation does provide some useful guidelines. It obviously implies equality in and before the law. It also implies a far greater measure of economic equality than is the case today. The issue here is not material comfort. Nor does it have anything to do with the notion that justice is served when economic goods are allocated according to the actual work (in the customary definition) each man does. That is impossible. We may urge that each should contribute according to his ability; we must surely insist that each be provided for according to his need.

What the criterion of a substantial degree of economic equalization requires is the establishment of the material conditions necessary for a generous measure of freedom of choice for all members of the community and the establishment of the conditions necessary for relations of mutual respect and honesty among the various economic and social groups within a society. This is not some kind of levelling demand for equality of condition. It is no more than a recognition of the obvious fact that the great material inequality that prevails in America today produces too much brutishness, impotence, and rage among the lower classes, and too much nervous vulgarity among the middle classes. There is no assertion here that economic equalization is the sufficient condition for the democratic New Jerusalem. Rather, the assertion is negative. As Arnold put it, "equality will never of itself alone give us a perfect civilisation. But, with such inequality as ours, a perfect civilisation is impossible."[7]

---

[7] Matthew Arnold, essay on "Equality" (1878), in *Matthew Arnold: Prose and Poetry*, ed. by A. L. Bouton, New York: Scribner's, 1927, p. 362.

The equality-of-opportunity principle, as formulated above, also implies the equal right of each member to share in the political life of the community to the fullest extent of his interest and ability. But this is the point at which the principle, no matter how carefully formulated, easily leads one away from a democratic view. The equal-opportunity principle as employed today in, for example, discussions of representation and voting rights, really does nothing more than fortify the prevailing conception of political action as just another of the various steps individuals and groups take to secure and advance their own interests and advantages. In this view, politics is but another aspect of the struggle for competitive advantage, and men need political power in order to protect and advance their private powers. This conception of politics is drawn from the economic sphere, and never rises above the ethical and psychological possibilities of that sphere.

When it is understood that the principle of equal opportunity is in our time an expression of the competitive, capitalistic spirit, and not of the democratic spirit, then the boundaries of its applicability begin to emerge. To the extent that competition is inescapable, or socially useful, all competitors should have the same advantages, and this the equal-opportunity principle guarantees. In any competitive situation, some will do better than others, and it seems just that those who do well should be rewarded more generously than those who do poorly. This too the principle guarantees.

The basic question, however, is not whether competition should be praised or condemned, but where and under what conditions competition is a desirable principle of action and judgment and where and under what conditions it is not. Some kinds of competition actually draw men more closely together whereas others produce antagonism and isolation. The problem is to distinguish between these kinds, encouraging the former and discouraging the latter. Peace is but a euphemism for slavery unless men's competitive energies are given adequate outlet. Most people probably have some need for both inward and outward striving. Perhaps the struggles against other people and the struggles within the self can be brought to some kind of balance in each individual and in society as a whole. Ideally, we might strive toward a truly pluralistic society in which nearly everybody could find a specialty he could do fairly well and where he would enjoy friendly competition with others. Judged by this imaginative possibility, our present social order is a mean thing. It is a kind of institutionalized war game, or sporting contest, in which the prizes are far too limited in kind, the referees and time-keepers far too numerous, and the number of reluctant and ill-adjusted players far too high. We need a social order that permits a much greater variety of games. Such a social order could, I think, be based on an effort to find a place for the greatest possible range of natural abilities among men. The variety of available natural abilities is enormous and worth much more exploration than any of the currently dominant conceptions of social order are willing to undertake. In the United States today, the fundamental justification of the equal-opportunity principle is that it is an efficient means for achieving an indefinite expansion of wealth and power. Many men are unsuited by nature for that competition, so that nature herself comes to seem unjust. But many of the injustices we regard nature as having per-petrated on individuals are actually no more than artifacts of the narrow view we take of nature's possibilities and a consequent distortion of the methods and ideals by which we attempt to transcend nature. For example, in defining intelligence as what I.Q. tests measure, we constrict the meanings of intelligence, for there are many modes of intelligence that the tests do not capture —nature is more protean than man's conception of her. Further-more, having defined intelligence in a certain way, we then pro-ceed to reward the people who have just that kind of intelligence and encourage them to use it in the pursuit of knowledge, which they are likely to do by building computers, which in turn give only certain kinds of knowledge. Thus our constricted definition of nature is confirmed by the methods we use to study nature. In this special sense, there might still be something to say for the eighteenth-century idea that society should imitate nature.

We must learn to ask questions like these about the method of competition and the principle of equal opportunity. The task is to define their proper spheres of action, not to treat them as blocks to be totally accepted or rejected. At the outer limit, it seems clear that whereas every society is to some extent competi-tive and competition in some spheres is socially and individually valuable, no society ought to exalt the competitive spirit as such, and the equal-opportunity principle that implements it. Both conceptions tend naturally toward selfishness unless carefully controlled.

V

In addition to equality of opportunity, there is another kind of equality that is blind to all questions of success or failure. This is the equality that obtains in the relations among the members of any genuine community. It is the feeling held by each member that all other members, regardless of their many differences of function and rank, belong to the community "as fully as he does himself."[8] Equal opportunity, far from strengthening this kind of equality, weakens it.

When this point is reached, when the discussion turns to the meanings of equality involved in a democratic conception of membership and a democratic conception of ruling and being ruled, the equal-opportunity principle—no matter how carefully formulated—begins to mislead. A fuller conception of equality is needed, one stripped of the antagonistic and privatistic overtones of the equal-opportunity principle. That fuller conception, in turn, requires a broader view of politics than is afforded by the "who gets what, when, how" perspective.

Political life occupies a middle ground between the sheer givens of nature and society on the one side, and the transcendental "kingdom of ends" on the other. Through political action men publicly strive to order and transform the givens of nature and society by the light of values drawn from a realm above or outside the order of the givens. Men, acting together, define the ideal aims of the common life and try to bend realities toward them. Through acting with others to define and achieve what can be called good for all, each realizes part of his own meaning and destiny. Insofar as man is a being that wants not merely to live but to live well, he is a political being. And insofar as any man does not participate in forming the common definition of

---

[8] John Plamenatz, *Man and Society*, New York: McGraw-Hill, 1963, Vol. II, p. 120.

the good life, to that degree he falls short of the fullest possibilities of the human vocation. No man can assign to another
dominion over how he shall live his life without becoming something less than a man. This way of thinking about political
action leads to an idea of equality whose tone and implications
are very different from those of the equal-opportunity formulation.

Other features of political action lead in the same direction,
and, specifically, require a rejection of all claims to rulership
based on the ancient analogies between the art of ruling and
other arts. When one contracts with a carpenter to build a house,
he may assume that the carpenter's skills are sufficient to the
work that is to be done. But when citizens elevate some among
them to places of political authority the case is different. Politics
has so few givens and so many contingencies and complexities,
contains so many dangerous possibilities and so few perfect solu-
tions, and is such a baffling mixture of empirical, prudential, and
ethical considerations that no man or group of men has knowledge and skill sufficient for all situations. As John Winthrop
said, no man can "profess nor undertake to have sufficient skill
for that office."[9]

Winthrop's comment, grounded as it is on a solid understanding of the political vocation, is a just rebuke to all claims for
political authority based on technical competence. Relations
between politician and citizen are very different from those between craftsman and employer. Politicians cannot be said to
serve or to execute the will of citizens in the way that craftsmen
can be said to serve their employers. Nor can politicians claim
authority over their work and over other persons engaged in that
work on the grounds of technical competence. The relations
between politicians and citizens, in sum, are relations among
equals in a number of important senses. Above all, their relations
are built on premises that, when properly understood, encourage
genuine conversation among the participants, not merely the
transmission of information and commands up and down a line.
This way of thinking about the matter presumes equality among

[9] John Winthrop, "Speech to the General Court," July 3, 1645, in Perry
Miller, ed., *The American Puritans: Their Prose and Poetry*, Garden City,
New York: Doubleday Anchor, 1956, pp. 91–92.

citizens in the sense most basic to a democratic understanding of the relations among the members of a political community—in the sense of equality of being—and hence presumes the widest possible participation in and sharing of responsibility for the policies that govern the whole community.

Just as political authorities may not lay claim to superior rights on the ground of special merit, neither may ordinary citizens absolve themselves from partial responsibility for public policies on the ground that their task is done when they have selected those who will take active charge of the affairs of the polity. The democratic idea offers no such easy absolution from shared responsibility and guilt.

This sharing of responsibility and guilt may be one of the reasons why a genuinely democratic conception of equality is not easy to accept even by those who call themselves democrats. It is comforting to men to think that someone else is competently in charge of the large and dangerous affairs of politics: Somebody else rules; I just live here. Hierarchy and oligarchy provide subjects with that comfort and with easy escapes from shared responsibility and guilt. This freedom from political responsibility is very valuable to men who would much rather devote themselves to their private interests anyway, than share the burden of caring for the public good. The doctrine of equality of opportunity, tied as it is to the principle of hierarchy, easily leads to moral arrogance on the part of the winners and to the taking of moral holidays by the losers.

A proper view of equality still leaves wide scope for the existence of necessary and just superiorities and differences, but it brings a different mentality to their appraisal. Certainly, some things *are* better than others, and more to be preferred. Some vocations and talents are more valuable than others, and more to be rewarded. The implication here is only that the more highly skilled, trained, or talented man has no ground either for thinking himself a better *man* than his less-favored fellows, or for regarding his superiorities as providing any but the most temporary and limited justification for authority over others. The paradigmatic case is that of the relation between teacher and student. The teacher's superior knowledge gives him a just claim to authority over his students. But central to the ethic of teaching is the conviction that the teacher must impart to students not only his substantive knowledge but also the critical skills and habits necessary for judging and contributing to that knowledge. The teacher justifies his authority and fulfills his duty by making himself unnecessary to the student.

Perhaps this at least suggests the outlines of a democratic conception of equality and draws the boundaries of its applicability. The heart of such a view of equality is its affirmation of equality of being and belonging. That affirmation helps identify those sectors of life in which we should all be treated in a common or average way, so that the minimal conditions of a common life are made available to all: legal equality, equal rights of participation in political life, equal right to those average material provisions necessary for living together decently at all. It also stresses the greatest possible participation in and sharing of the common life and culture while striving to assure that no man shall determine or define the being of any other man.

This is what equality is all about, and it is a great deal.[10] But it is far from everything. Beyond the realm of the average and the comparable lies another realm of relations among men where notions of equality have no relevance. Hence, a fair understanding of equality requires a sense of the boundaries of that realm in which equalitarian categories do not apply.

Those boundaries begin where we try to define man himself. Every attempted formulation of equality stumbles on the mystery and the indefinability of the creature for and about whom the formulation is made. In the end, it makes no sense to say that all men are equal, or that any two men are, because it is impossible to say what a man is. It is easy to abstract a part from the whole, and define that part in terms that make it commensurable with the same parts abstracted from other whole men. Thus, one can define an American citizen in terms that impart perfect sense to the proposition that all American citizens are equal. But when it comes to talking about whole men and about man, the concept of equality is mute. Then there is only the mystery of being, the

---

[10] As Paine said, with permissible exaggeration, "inequality of rights has been the cause of all the disturbances, insurrections, and civil wars, that ever happened. . . ." Thomas Paine, *Works*, ed. by J. P. Mendum, Boston: 1878, 3 vols.; Vol. I, pp. 454–455.

recognition of self and others. Lawrence has expressed the idea perfectly, and he should be permitted the last word:

> One man is neither equal nor unequal to another man. When I stand in the presence of another man, and I am my own pure self, am I aware of the presence of an equal, or of an inferior, or of a superior? I am not. When I stand with another man, who is himself, and when I am truly myself, then I am only aware of a Presence, and of the strange reality of Otherness. There is me, and there is *another being*. . . . There is no comparing or estimating. . . . Comparison enters only when one of us departs from his own integral being, and enters the material mechanical world. Then equality and inequality starts at once.[11]

[11] D. H. Lawrence, "Democracy," as quoted in Raymond Williams, *Culture and Society, 1780–1950,* New York: Columbia University Press, 1958, p. 211.

14

EQUALITY IN THE ADMINISTRATION OF CRIMINAL JUSTICE

MONROE H. FREEDMAN

I

To a lawyer in the United States today, the concept of equality must appear as a potent force in our nation's progress toward the achievement of justice. Indeed, equality might well seem to be the essence of justice, since in so many critical areas of reform, equality has been the expressed legal-philosophical justification for change.

The most obvious examples, of course, are found in the dramatic movement toward justice for Negro citizens. There, under the constitutional banner of "equal protection of the laws," we have made significant progress, through all three branches of our government, in such critical areas as voting, education, employment, housing, and procedures relating to police investigation, arrest, and trial. In addition, there have been other important advances that, though not directly related to Negro rights, may well have benefited significantly from the momentum of the civil rights movement. These include such disparate matters as legislative reapportionment,[1] and the right of an indigent criminal defendant in a state court to have counsel appointed to defend him.[2] With less obvious relevance, even extension to the state courts of the privilege against self-incrimination appears to have been justified, in part at least, on a notion of equality.[3]

These recent developments apart, however, the concept of equality has not always fared well in American history. Despite the initial emphasis on equality in the Declaration of Independence, the Constitution itself had no equal protection clause.[4] Indeed, the only specific provision regarding equality was the malapportionment of the Federal Compromise, which gave equal state representation in the Senate regardless of population. At the same time, in the House, which was theoretically intended to be representative of population, slaves were to be counted as three-fifths of a person each. This is, of course, an anomalous antecedent to our present constitutional rule of "one-man, one-vote," formulated almost two centuries and one Civil War later.

Perhaps the American striving, embodied in our traditionally highly mobile society, has been less toward an ideal of individual equality than toward attainment of individual superiority. The classic American fantasy, after all, has not been of the disfranchised Negro who achieves the right to vote but of the boy from the log cabin who becomes President (or, updated, of the poor

[1] For an analysis of the relationship between Negro voting rights and legislative reapportionment, see my chapter on "Gerrymandering and Malapportionment," *United States Commission on Civil Rights Report*, vol. I, ch. 7, esp. pp. 113–117, 131–132 (1961).

[2] *Gideon* v. *Wainwright*, 372 U.S. 335 (1963). Cf. *Griffin* v. *Illinois*, 351 U.S. 12 (1956).

[3] "It would be incongruous to have different standards determine the validity of a claim of privilege based on the same feared prosecution, depending on whether the claim was asserted in a state or federal court. Therefore, the same standards must determine whether an accused's silence in either a federal or state proceeding is justified." *Malloy* v. *Hogan*, 378 U.S. 1, 1495 (1964).

[4] The conclusion that the Due Process Clause of the Fifth Amendment includes equal protection is a recent one. *Bolling* v. *Sharpe*, 347 U.S. 497 (1954).

immigrant, all of whose sons become President seriatim). The ideal, that is, is to start unequally low and to finish unequally high; insofar as it can be so described, of course, the American ideal is essentially non-egalitarian.

This attitude may be the basis for such observations as Justice Holmes', that the passion for equality is an "ignoble aspiration,"[5] and "a disguise for less noble feelings,"[6] specifically, of envy.[7] At any rate, it was from these premises that Justice Holmes, writing for the Supreme Court, deprecated the Equal Protection Clause as "the usual last resort of Constitutional arguments."[8]

Whereas Justice Holmes clearly underestimated the significance of equality in its relation to justice, it would also be inaccurate to credit equality with being more than a minimal aspect of justice. The concept of equality is capable of making a significant practical contribution in the search for justice, but this contribution is very limited.

II

We can gain some initial insights into the relationship between equality and justice by first considering the connections between equality and liberty. When we analyze the concept of equality with respect to liberty, we find its greatest significance in the relationship between those who are governed and those who govern. More specifically, we find equality between ruler and ruled to be a criterion of liberty—liberty is truly secure only where the rulers and the ruled are equal in subjection to the law. This is effectively illustrated by the contrast between the two following conceptions of governmental power:

> The Sovereign of a Commonwealth, be it an Assembly or one man, is not subject to the civil laws. For having power to make, and repeal, laws, he may when he pleaseth, free himself from that subjection, by repealing those laws that trouble him and making of new; and consequently he was free before. For he is free, that can be free when he will.

---

[5] Howe, M. DeW. (ed.), *Holmes-Laski Letters,* vol. I, p. 769 (1953).
[6] *Ibid.,* vol. II, p. 1089.
[7] *Ibid.,* vol. II, p. 942.
[8] *Buck* v. *Bell,* 274 U.S. 200, 208 (1927).

Nor is it possible for any person to be bound to himself, because he that can bind, can release; and therefore he that is bound to himself only, is not bound.[9]

In contrast is the following passage, which antedates Hobbes by over two thousand years:

It shall be, when [the king] sitteth upon the throne of his kingdom, that he shall write him a copy of this law in a book. . . . And it shall be with him, and he shall read therein all the days of his life; that he may learn to fear the Lord his God, to keep all the words of this law and these statutes, to do them; that his heart be not lifted up above his brethren, and that he turn not aside from the commandment, either to the right hand, or the left.[10]

Where the ruler's "heart is not to be lifted up above his brethren"—that is, where those who exercise governmental authority are themselves bound by the laws they enact and administer—liberty is secure. Remove the equality under law between governor and governed, as with Hobbes' sovereign, who "is not subject to the civil law," and no member of the governed community can be assured of his liberty. Equality under law is thus, for practical purposes at least, a *sine qua non* of liberty.

The relationship of equality to justice[11] is rather different. First, we can observe that equality is pertinent to justice not in the relationship between ruler and ruled but in the relationships among those who are governed. Here equality connotes not so much "equality under law" (liberty) as it does "equal protection of the law." The latter phrase expresses the idea that what government gives to or takes from one person or group of people it should give to or take from others similarly situated. The justice implied by equality is, therefore, a relational or comparative kind of justice, and therein lie both the significance and the limitation of equality in the quest for justice.

The concept of equality is, by definition, relational or comparative. A person can only be found to be equal *in relation to* or

---

[9] Hobbes, *Leviathan*, ch. xxvi.

[10] Deuteronomy 17:14–15, 18–20.

[11] I am using justice to mean the privileges, rights, and material benefits that a member of the community ought to be granted or permitted

in comparison with some other person who serves as a standard or criterion. Justice, on the other hand, is a less precise concept in that it does not intrinsically require a reference to any specific criterion.[12] What equality lends to justice is just such a criterion: I may not know precisely to which rights justice entitles me, but I do know that I am entitled at least to those rights enjoyed by my neighbor. Is he entitled to vote, to worship as he chooses, to own property, or to speak freely? Whether he should have these things at all is the difficult inquiry of justice. Whether, when he has been given them, I too should have them, is the narrower and simpler concern of equal protection of the law.

Equality, then, is considerably less than synonymous with justice. Indeed, it is possible to have equality without justice, and it is also possible to have justice without equality. Assume, for example, a concentration camp in which all prisoners are subjected to the identical deprivations and indignities. Surely there is equality among the prisoners and, just as surely, there is an absence of justice. Similarly, it would be just to free A from the camp (if one somehow had this limited power), even though B, C, and D were required to remain.

Further, there will be circumstances where justice requires inequality in treatment in order to remedy the injustice produced by previous unequal treatment or unequal status, inasmuch as to give equally may serve only to maintain inequality. It is interesting to observe that this idea is contrary to what we have earlier noted to be a strong non-egalitarian strain in the American ideal. The suggestion has been made, for example, that preferential (or, more accurately, compensatory) treatment should be given to American Negroes in order to adjust for the impact of decades of discriminatory treatment. Yet the creation of equality through preferential treatment, according to critics of the idea, "implies a solution far afield from the American dream."[13]

Despite the substance of this contention, the word "dream" must be read more literally, perhaps, than the writers intended. Preferential treatment has not seemed un-American to our

---

[12] Justice is "relational," of course, in the sense of *occurring* between persons, or in distributions to citizens from the state, and so forth. It is not relational in the sense used here, however: that is, it does not by definition involve a comparison with a criterion.

[13] Evans and Novak, *Washington Post* (Aug. 18, 1965), p. A19: 1–3.

farmers, small businessmen, labor unions, industries competing with imported goods, corporations with tax depletion allowances, and countless others.

Moreover, there are two major differences between these groups and American Negroes. First, most other groups receiving preferential treatment have been disadvantaged (if at all) by forces other than society and its laws (e.g., by market conditions). American Negroes, on the other hand, have been subjected to what President Johnson, in his speech at Howard University, called "the devastating heritage of long years of slavery, and a century of oppression, hatred, and injustice." Second, the concept of equality can be used effectively in making the case for compensatory treatment for Negroes but can be similarly used for only few, if any, of the others.

Significantly, the farmer tries to use the concept of equality in the idea of "parity." But his argument is deficient in that it is not based on equality between persons, *i.e.*, between the farmer and some other member of society. Rather, the equal treatment he seeks is measured by his own earnings in a given prior year. Thus, the farmer seeks justice defined in terms of what he himself once enjoyed in the past. The Negro, on the other hand, seeks justice in terms of what other people in society have been and are enjoying, which he has been denied.

For purposes of this analysis, the importance of the difference between the farmer's plea for justice and the Negro's, lies in the criterion provided by the concept of equality in the latter case. Whether the year selected for parity is really representative of justice is a readily debatable issue. However, it is far less easy to dispute that the rights, privileges, and material benefits enjoyed by the most advantaged group in society constitute a standard of what is just for all.

An irony implicit in the foregoing sentence emphasizes, however, the limitations of equality in the search for justice. The obverse of that sentence is also true: What is just for the least advantaged group in society may be just for all. Equality, therefore, can lead us either to preferential treatment designed to raise all to the highest standard or to a destructive levelling of all to the lowest standard.[14] Equality may be keyed to any

[14] It may well have been the latter connotation that moved Justice Holmes to view the quest for equality as ignoble.

number of criteria, but it cannot assure us that any criterion has more merit than another. The most—but also the least—we can say is that what is just for one member of society is prima facie just for another. This is the essential significance, and the essential limitation, of the concept of equality.

III

To summarize the main observations in the preceding section:

1. Equality is neither synonymous with justice nor capable of providing answers to such ultimate questions as what rights individuals should have in society.

2. However, once society decides to grant or permit certain privileges, rights, or material benefits to some, the concept of equality informs us that these are prima facie valid criteria of what privileges, rights, or material benefits society should grant or permit to others.

3. Furthermore, consistent with the ideal of equality, if not essential to it, is a recognition that inequality in treatment (compensatory treatment) may be necessary to provide an approximation of equality in status.

Although I am not aware that these propositions have been previously formulated just this way, they do not appear to be particularly startling or even controversial. Yet the recent debate over the American Law Institute Model Code of Pre-Arraignment Procedure (Preliminary Draft Number 1) has shown that even the Attorney General of the United States and the several "disinterested" legal scholars who participated in preparing the Draft[15] have failed to appreciate the significance of equality in the administration of criminal justice.

The problem arises in a number of provisions of the Code, but for convenience I will refer here only to one, dealing with the right to counsel. Section 4 provides for detention and interrogation of a citizen by police officers; it does not include the safe-

---

[15] It should be noted that the Reporter of the Pre-Arraignment Procedure Code, Professor James Vorenberg of Harvard University Law School, was also in the employ of the Justice Department as Director of the Office of Criminal Justice while the Draft was being prepared.

guard of prior presentment before a judicial officer whose function it is to advise the prisoner of his constitutional rights to counsel and to remain silent. Whereas a citizen who can pay to retain a lawyer may consult with him and have him present during interrogation, a citizen who cannot afford a lawyer would not have one provided.[16] Emphasizing the recognized importance of having a lawyer present at this critical stage of the criminal judicial process, the Reporter's Comment strongly urges against the exclusion of retained counsel from the interrogation.

In his letter to the Attorney General of June 16, 1965, Chief Judge Bazelon of the United States Court of Appeals for the District of Columbia Circuit made the obvious but significant point that the primary adverse impact of this and other Code provisions would fall upon "the poor and, in particular, the poor Negro citizen." This, Judge Bazelon noted, would "diverge greatly from the ideal that the administration of criminal justice should avoid invidious discrimination based on wealth." This point is, of course, consistent with the first two propositions set forth at the beginning of this section: Equality cannot tell us whether anyone should have a lawyer present during police interrogation; however, once we adopt the premise that justice requires a lawyer for the rich, the concept of equality informs us that counsel should be granted to the poor.

For Attorney General Katzenbach, however, the point is neither obvious nor significant. In his reply to Judge Bazelon, the Attorney General wrote that the impact of the Code on the poor, in general, and on the poor Negro, in particular, strikes him "as particularly irrelevant." Although recognizing that the "underlying assumption" of Judge Bazelon's point "appears to be some conception of equality," Mr. Katzenbach proceeded to miss the point entirely: "It would be ridiculous to state that the overriding purpose of any criminal investigation is to insure equal treatment," he wrote, adding, "I do not believe that regula-

[16] Similarly, former United States Attorney David Acheson has proposed that the police of the District of Columbia give the following legal advice to suspects: "You have a right to call a lawyer. . . . He may be present here and you have a right to talk to him. If you cannot afford a lawyer, one may be appointed for you *when you first go to court*." (Emphasis added.)

tion . . . of investigatory procedures should have as its purpose
to remedy all the inequalities which may exist in our society."

The question, of course, is not whether the purpose of criminal
justice is equality.[17] Rather, it is whether rights granted the
rich are equally to be granted to the poor. Yet even the *Washington Post,* in an editorial siding with Judge Bazelon, was in part
misled by Mr. Katzenbach's rhetoric. The *Post* editor wrote:
"There is an inequality, as Anatole France long ago pointed out,
even in laws providing that neither the rich nor the poor may
sleep under bridges or steal bread." Then, having completely
missed France's irony, he continued, "General Katzenbach rightly argues that the courts cannot confer equality on the citizens
who appear before them."[18]

Insofar as this contention has any relevance to the debate, it
is in the implication that society has no obligation to "confer
equality on . . . citizens" by providing counsel for the indigent
defendant. The issue then relates to the validity of the third
proposition at the beginning of this section: Inequality of treatment (compensatory treatment) may be necessary to provide an
approximation of equality in status. That is, although the rich
man must pay for his own lawyer, the poor man should have
an attorney provided at the expense of the government. Although
this is "preferential treatment," the only alternative consistent
with the ideal of equality is a levelling of all to the standard of
justice available to the poor.

Adoption of this latter alternative, however, is inconsistent
with the clear purport of recent decisions involving the right to
counsel. In *Gideon* v. *Wainwright,* the Court held:

> Precedents . . . reason and reflection require us to recognize
> that in our adversary system of criminal justice, any person
> haled into court, who is too poor to hire a lawyer cannot
> be assured a fair trial unless counsel is provided for him.
> This seems to us to be an obvious truth . . . the right of
> one charged with crime to counsel may not be termed
> fundamental and essential to fair trials in some countries,
> but it is in ours.[19]

[17] Following the Attorney General's lead, a number of newspapers and
magazines so stated the issue, e.g., *Time* (August 13, 1965), p. 41.
[18] *Washington Post* (August 6, 1965), p. A16: 1.
[19] *Gideon* v. *Wainwright,* 372 U.S. 335, 83 S. Ct. 792, 796 (1963).

Moreover, the Supreme Court has recognized that counsel may be equally essential during pre-trial proceedings and that the prisoner cannot constitutionally be interrogated for a confession while his lawyer is being barred from the interrogation room.[20] It hardly seems likely, therefore, that the Supreme Court would uphold the attempt of the Department of Justice and of the ALI draftsmen to permit interrogation of indigents lacking counsel, while permitting counsel, under the same circumstances, to those who can afford it.[21]

POSTSCRIPT

While the foregoing paper was in press, the Supreme Court decided the Confession Cases.[22] Consistent with the analysis set forth above, the Court held that every criminal defendant is entitled to counsel prior to interrogation and that there is an obligation on the government to appoint lawyers for those who cannot afford to retain their own.

The Chief Justice, who wrote the prevailing opinion, was not misled into believing that the issue was whether equality is the "overriding purpose" of criminal justice. Rather, he recognized that equality of treatment was offered as a criterion of justice. Having established that counsel must be present prior to interrogation in order to preserve the privilege against self-incrimination, the Court went on to hold that:

> The financial ability of the individual has no relationship to the scope of the rights involved here. The privilege

[20] *Escobedo* v. *Illinois,* 378 U.S. 478 (1964).

[21] It may be argued *ad absurdum* that the standard of equality is not met until the poor defendant is given counsel of quality equal to that available to the wealthiest defendant. One answer to this contention is that any absurdity lies in the realm of practicality rather than of the ideal. However, one can go much further. Society insures a minimum standard of competent representation by licensing the practice of law. Beyond this, there is a growing tendency to supervise the representation of indigents and to invalidate convictions in which the highest professional standards have not been met. Indeed, one hears complaints from members of the bar and bench in the District of Columbia that standards of representation are higher for the indigent than for the large majority of defendants who retain counsel of their choice. Although this complaint may be exaggerated, it tends to confirm that the practical limitations on equality in the administration of criminal justice are not as severe as might be supposed.

[22] *Miranda* v. *Arizona,* decided June 13, 1966, 16 L.Ed.2d 694.

against self-incrimination secured by the Constitution
applies to all individuals. The need for counsel in order to
protect the privilege exists for the indigent as well as the
affluent. . . . Were we to limit these Constitutional rights
to those who can retain an attorney, our decisions today
would be of limited significance. . . . While the authorities
are not required to relieve the accused of his poverty, they
have the obligation not to take advantage of indigence in
the administration of justice. Denial of counsel to the
indigent at the time of interrogation while allowing an
attorney to those who can afford one would be no more
supportable by reason or logic than the similar situation
at trial . . . struck down in *Gideon* v. *Wainwright*. . . .[23]

Having thus adopted equality as a criterion for justice, the
Court then applied the principle of compensatory treatment:

In order fully to apprise a person interrogated of the
extent of his rights under this system then, it is necessary
to warn him not only that he has the right to consult with
an attorney, but also that if he is indigent a lawyer will
be appointed to represent him. Without this additional
warning, the admonition of the right to consult with
counsel would often be understood as meaning only that
he can consult with a lawyer if he has one or has the funds
to obtain one.[24]

Thus, the principles of equality suggested above, including
the corollary of compensatory treatment, have been author-
itatively recognized and applied in this most critical area of
criminal justice.

[23] *Ibid.*, 16 L.Ed.2d 722–23.
[24] *Ibid.*, at p. 723.

15

NOTES ON THE RULE OF EQUAL LAW

GEOFFREY MARSHALL

In an obvious but notoriously diluted sense, a lawmaker is concerned ex officio with promoting equality of treatment. To deal with men by general rules rather than by individualized fiat is to treat them in at least one respect equally. But this is not saying very much, for a rule that applies equally to all may make different provisions for some as against others. This, among other things, would make it difficult for a modern legislative sovereign assembly to know whether it had complied with the recipe for legislative action that Rousseau prescribes in the *Contrat Social*. In that work Rousseau demands that the general will not only be respectably general in its origins but also aim at generality and equality in its substance. Equality and generality of aim are exemplified in a number of ways. "Law must be," Rousseau writes, "applicable to all." It must not seek to achieve

261

"a merely individual or limited end." It must not seek to "judge an individual person or an isolated fact." It must not purport to determine specific rights arising out of a situation not previously regulated by general agreement. It "changes its nature when called upon to pronounce upon a particular object." It must not lay "a heavier burden on any one subject than on another." And so on. "Every authentic act of the general will lays the same obligations and confers the same benefits on all." The sovereign "knows only the nation as a whole and does not distinguish between the individuals who compose it."[1]

So myopic a legislator, we may suppose, would make heavy weather in our own times. The lieges are not all of a lump. There are producers and consumers, private citizens and state officials, farmers and manufacturers, soldiers and civilians, married men and bachelors, adults and minors. What is to be understood by treating them all alike or imposing the same burdens on all, when their situations, capacities, duties, and obligations are different and ought to be so? Yet, is not constitutional theory replete with dim and less dim reflections of Rousseau's specifications? No Bills of Attainder. The rule of Law, not men. The equal protection of the laws?

Given, in particular cases, acceptable reasons for differences in treatment, the prescription of equality in law, as in morals, seems sometimes to fall away into an empty formality—namely that all deserve equal treatment unless there are good reasons to prescribe otherwise. Admittedly, at some times and places, tautologies may strike fire. Mr. Gladstone's famous truism of 1864 is an example: "I venture to say that every man who is not presumably incapacitated by some consideration of personal unfitness or of political danger is morally entitled to come within the pale of the constitution."[2] Lord Morley tells us that this "thunderbolt of a sentence" threw the House of Commons into an uproar. But the House of Commons was not listening very carefully. The question may be raised whether this Gladstonian formulation of the principle of equality, as absence of disqualification or of irrelevant discrimination, furnishes any informative or useful proposition in either morals or law.

---

[1] J. J. Rousseau, *Social Contract*, Book 2, Chap. IV.
[2] John Morley, *Life of Gladstone* (1908), Vol. I, p. 569.

EQUAL SUBJECTION TO LAW

It cannot be said that there are many startling similarities between the views of Albert Venn Dicey and Jean Jacques Rousseau. But one shared characteristic is an insistence on the equal application of law. By the rule of law, Dicey understood, among other things, "the idea of legality or of the universal subjection of all classes to one law administered by the ordinary courts." Equality before the law, interpreted as the equal subjection of all classes to a common rule, might at least be contrasted significantly with chaos or lawlessness, but it does not in itself imply any qualitative view about the sort of law to which all should be subject. At least three senses might be given to the "rule of law," of which this first would be the minimal sense. These three senses, or programmes, might be:

1. Everyone (equally) should be covered by, or subject to, general laws rather than exposed to chaos, individualized commands, or mob rule. Englishmen, as Dicey insisted, are ruled by the law and by the law alone. "A man may, with us, be punished for a breach of law, but he can be punished for a breach of nothing else."[3] No subject of Queen Victoria in 1885, it must be admitted, would have been much astounded by this proposition.

2. Everyone (equally) should be covered by some body of law which is impartially applied by an independent judiciary without fear, favor, or anything similar. In this sense South Africa and Southern Rhodesia are at present governed by the rule of law, although some of the law in question is in substance abominable.

3. Everyone (equally) should be covered by an impartially administered body of law which meets certain criteria of precision, equity, and justice. Professor Fuller, I think, would call these conditions the inner morality of law.[4] One might alternatively call them the ethics of legislation.

The rule of law in its English context has (like due process of law and natural justice) been mainly expounded in the senses mentioned in 1 and 2; primarily, that is to say, as a procedural concept. The rule of law is not, on Dicey's view, violated when

---

[3] A. V. Dicey, *Introduction to the Study of the Law of the Constitution* (10th ed.), p. 202.

[4] See L. Fuller, *The Morality of Law* (1964), Chap. II.

the King's most Excellent Majesty, by and with the advice of the
Lords and Commons enacts that the Bishop of Rochester's cook
be boiled to death without benefit of clergy,[5] or when the Queen
in Parliament makes a retrospective legislative adjudication[6] on
a claim so as to nullify ex post facto a judicial decision inimical
to the Crown.[7]

Nevertheless, in two ways, Dicey's doctrine was not merely
procedural. The equal rule of law, as he expounded it, involves
at least one substantive requirement. It must not permit wide
powers of discretionary action to be conferred on officials. It
prescribes also a requirement of equal access and subjection of all
private and public persons to the same judicial tribunals. It
omits, however, to register the truism that the law that all citizens
find when they get to the common courts may make unequal provision for some as against others. The same law that binds all may
say that the Crown cannot be sued in tort.[8] and that policemen
and state officials shall have powers, privileges, or legal defences
not open to private citizens. At the same time, the prohibition on
the creation of wide discretionary powers assumed in its original
expression that there could be no valid justification for such
powers, which might be based on relevant differences between
citizens and officials. Dicey's implied ideal is rooted in a situation
where the state and its agents confront individuals in a condition
of Rousseauite equipollence. Much of the English controversy
over the rule of law has concerned the workability of this assumption—the equality of public and private persons.

EQUALITY OF STATE AND INDIVIDUAL
BEFORE THE LAW

It is in one way plain that the state and the citizen, the
community and the individual, cannot be equals. One imposes
its will upon the other. What is not so plain, however, and can
be meaningfully debated, is the matter of which community

[5] 22 Henry VIII c. 9. "It is ordained and enacted by authority of this
present Parliament that the said Richard Rose shall be therefore boiled to
death. . . ."

[6] War Damage Act 1965.

[7] *Burmah Oil Co.* v. *Lord Advocate* (1964) 2 All E.R. 348.

[8] As it could not in Dicey's day.

purposes require the community's agents to be given significant legal privileges not shared by private persons or collectivities. It is especially necessary to put the question in this form in the common law world, where by theory and tradition the law knows only private persons. Secretaries of State, civil servants, and policemen are equally the Queen's subjects. "With respect to the argument of State necessity, or the distinction that has been aimed at between State offences and others, the common law does not understand that kind of reasoning, nor do our books take notice of any such distinctions." And "by the laws of England every invasion of private property, be it ever so minute, is a trespass."[9] Into this framework of private rights and private law, a statutory body of public powers and public law has had to be fastened. For reasons that do not surprise us, but perhaps ought to, this has not resulted in any great growth of official privilege or discretion in the area of civil liberties. The relations of policemen with citizens are largely conducted as relations between one citizen and another. Law officers make arrests, lay informations, and prosecute offences as private citizens, protected at vulnerable points by only a minimum of statutory armour. But in the field of economic and administrative relationships, a different kind of transaction appears. Where the use of natural resources (and particularly land) is concerned, the rules of the common law have changed. In the nineteenth century English courts may be said to have acted on the assumption that their business was to hold an equal balance between citizens and officials. An interference with the property rights of Englishmen often gave rise to disquisitions upon the two rules of natural justice (*audi alteram partem* and no man to judge his own case) . These rules rested on the assumption of a fairly conducted legal combat between two parties viewed essentially as equals by the arbitral tribunal. The analogy has become steadily less applicable to twentieth-century contests between the Crown and individual property-owning litigants. When governmental agencies initiate action, they are conceded to be judges of the merits of their own proposals. At least one of the rules of equal judicial combat cannot apply. Indeed, its disappearance may even imperil the application of the other (*audi alteram partem*) rule.

---

[9] *Entick* v. *Carrington* (1765) 19 State Trials, 1030 per Lord Camden C. J.

This did in fact happen in one sphere of English administrative jurisprudence, and the right to a fair hearing is still struggling for recognition as an independently valid claim of the citizen,[10] even when no longer conceived as engaged in an equal judicial contest with state officials.

Administrative justice in fact poses a dilemma. It can never be literally true that for all disputes between State and individual citizens, recourse should exist to an independent third party.[11] Yet we aim to provide such recourse in a significant, if vaguely delineated, set of cases. What should define such cases? An answer sometimes suggested is roughly that official action that affects all equally, for example raising a tax or recruiting an army, does not give rise to a dispute or a right of appeal (as distinct from political or electoral redress), whereas action affecting citizens in an individual capacity alters the case. But what is an individual capacity? A change in governmental policy or the cancellation of a defence contract may affect workers in a particular town or factory in a way not shared by the general population. But we do not admit these cases as creating a right of appeal or review. Nor can a sensible criterion be laid down in terms of State action that affects individual *rights* rather than privileges or concessions, inasmuch as the classification of a potential claim as a right will depend upon the remedies available to vindicate it. Historically the question may be put in this form: For which purposes have legislators been willing to subject governmental action to fixed rules, and for which purposes have they been inclined to leave the government free to formulate and enforce *ad hoc* policies? Typical of the first sphere is criminal legislation; typical of the second, diplomacy and foreign affairs. The latter sphere is necessarily marked by inequality of citizen and State (considered as government agencies). Some advocates of administrative justice argue or imply that the sphere of fixed rules ought to be as wide as possible. But this conclusion is not obvious. The sort of equality that exists between defendants and prosecutors does not fit every possible form of public-

[10] Its recent development was surveyed in *Ridge* v. *Baldwin* (1964) A.C. 40.
[11] This is sometimes implied. Cf. *The Economist* (July 27, 1957), "Every subject who has *a quarrel* with the Crown has a right to know that his case will at some stage be submitted to some *wholly independent person* for an impartial opinion." (Italics added.)

private relationship. Perhaps the only generalization that can be made here is that the analogy breaks down wherever government is both party to an issue and a protector of some admitted general or national interest such as scarce natural resources or national security.

DENIAL OF EQUALITY BY LAW

The traditional English rule-of-law man confined his concern for legislative ethics to a veto upon excessive delegation of discretionary power. Predictability of action and the avoidance of procedural privilege were the values he had in mind. As a good Austinian and loyal exponent of the sovereignty of Parliament, he had no truck—at least no professional truck—with the avoidance of substantive privilege in law. Let the Queen in Parliament clearly place unequal burdens on one class of subjects as compared with another and the subject knows where he stands. If where he stands is uncomfortable or unjust, that is no concern of jurisprudence or judges. It is a part of politics and a question of moral judgement, with which legal tribunals should have as little as possible to do. The traditionalist suspects that the issues raised by the rule of equal law in the American (as well as in the Indian, German, and Japanese) sense can only be answered by a tribunal that is openly legislative. Setting this aside as mere prejudice against judicial review in any form, there remains perhaps a question whether the application of equality guarantees does not involve a creative and legislative burden greater than that which a judicial tribunal ought to carry.

In the jurisprudence of equal treatment, as in thinking about equality outside the law, a certain indecisiveness can be seen about which of two positions to occupy. Argument begins with the acknowledgement that equality before the law does not require every person to be treated in the same way but only similar treatment for those in similar circumstances, or an absence of discriminatory treatment except for those in different circumstances. But sometimes this view treats equality as simply having this meaning (i.e., not to be understood as "treating all alike") whereas at other times it asserts that equality cannot be absolute, that it must be balanced against other requirements, that reasonable classification and discrimination may take place, and that when this happens, legislation may properly produce constitutional *inequalities*.

Whether we say that equality may legitimately be qualified or modified, or whether we say that acceptable departures from identical treatment do not detract from or qualify the principle of equality, the criteria upon which qualification of, departures from, or applications of the principle take place are obviously crucial. The notion of different situation or circumstance carries a certain ambiguity. A recent commentary on the Indian constitution[12] explains that legislative classifications or discriminations for those in different circumstances may relate to geographical differences or differences in time. Bombay may be treated differently from Madras. A reform may be introduced earlier for some persons or places than for others. It is clear, however, that the differences in situation do not consist simply in the different geographical or temporal situations themselves but in the way these situations are evaluated and related to the legislative facts in question. The briefest excursion through equal-treatment litigation reveals that this relationship and evaluation has been characterized in a number of ways. It being agreed that legislators may select different persons or groups for different treatment, inasmuch as "classification is inherent in legislation,"[13] various things may be said. To cite a few examples, it may be held:

1. that between classification and legislative objects there must be *some nexus;*
2. that classification must be based on an *intelligible* differentiation;
3. that classification must be based upon some *real and substantial* distinction;
4. that classification must be *relevant* to the object of the legislation;
5. that classification must be *rationally related* to the object;
6. that classification must be *fairly related* to the object;
7. that classification must not be *capricious or invidious;*
8. that classification must not be *arbitrary;*
9. that classification must be *reasonable;*
10. that classification must be *just.*

---

[12] G. N. Joshi, *Aspects of Indian Constitutional Law* (1965), p. 80.
[13] Mr. Justice Frankfurter, *Morey* v. *Doud*, 354 U.S. 457 at 472 (1957).

These formulae are plainly not equivalent. Arranged in this way they might be seen as a series of increasingly high hurdles. Roughly speaking and in ascending order three standards of criticism may be distinguished, i.e., that which is intelligible, that which is relevant, and that which is just or reasonable. A distinction between two persons or classes which is intelligible or real may not be for some purposes relevant, and a distinction which is relevant to the purpose in hand may not be sufficiently relevant to be reasonable, fair, or just. The use of the word "arbitrary" perhaps tends to conceal the difference between the second and third tests (i.e., between relevance and reasonableness), inasmuch as "arbitrary" is sometimes used to mean "irrelevant or capricious" and sometimes to mean "unjust or unfair." The distinction between the two tests is important. Compare, for example, a legislative proposal to tax red-haired men with a proposal to tax the owners of gambling clubs. In both cases the distinction between the tax-worthy and the non-tax-worthy class is existent and intelligible. In the red-haired case the tax would fail to pass the test of both relevance and reasonableness. In the gambling case the tax would pass the test of relevance but not necessarily that of reasonableness. There might be several reasons for not thinking it reasonable. Although having a high income, in this case from owning a gambling club, is a relevant reason for being taxed, one might still think the tax inequitable and unfair because other entertainments, vices, or sporting facilities are not taxed at all, or because the tax is too severe, or because the owners of gambling premises perform a service to the community.

When courts apply tests to legislative classification, it is not always clear what hurdle, higher or lower, they are requiring the impugned legislation to clear. Sometimes they seem satisfied with mere relevance; at other times more is demanded. Even if it is clear which test is being applied (though especially if it is the second), decisions are often unpredictable because of the different ways a large number of possible differences between persons or situations may be weighed.

Many Fourteenth Amendment cases illustrate this point. As Mr. Justice Jackson said, "The equal protection clause ceases to assure either equality or protection if it is avoided by any con-

ceivable difference that can be pointed out between those bound
and those left free."[14] Yet in this case *(Railway Express Agency*
v. *New York)* which involved an attack on New York traffic
regulations prohibiting advertisements on some vehicles but not
others, a number of differences between the two classes of vehicles
was pointed out. Some carried paid, others unpaid advertisements. Some were more of a traffic distraction than others and
so on. All these differences were relevant to the purposes of the
regulations but not necessarily thereby reasonable bases for the
discrimination. Another feature of the prohibited advertisements
was that they were less of a traffic distraction than displays on
Times Square. This feature, however, was ignored. (It was no
requirement of equal protection that all evils of the same genus
be eradicated or none at all). Which features of the situation
produced by legislative classification will strike a court as relevant and reasonable seems in many cases unpredictable. In
Goesaert v. *Cleary*[15] Mr. Justice Rutledge, Mr. Justice Douglas,
and Mr. Justice Murphy thought that a Michigan law prohibiting the licensing of female bartenders unless they were the
wives or daughters of the male owner of a licensed victualler
establishment made an invidious distinction between male and
female owners of bars. The majority of the court, however, whilst
conceding that Michigan could not "play favorites among women
without rhyme or reason," or produce "irrational" discrimination,
considered there to be a possible basis in reason (relating to the
hazards of unprotected barmaids) for Michigan's action, and
therefore upheld the regulation. This, perhaps, fell some distance
away from a test of reasonableness. To assess its reasonableness
would have meant considering and weighing the counterargu-
ments to Michigan's belief, which, however, the majority were
unwilling to do. The constitution did not require legislation,
they said, to reflect sociological insight or shifting social standards. So although the classification might rest, we may infer, on
outmoded social standards or lack of legislative insight, Michigan
could have had an intelligible and relevant, though possibly un-
substantial and unreasonable basis for its discrimination.

One of the features of the situation which is frequently re-

---

[14] *Railway Express Agency* v. *New York,* 366 U.S. 106 at 115 (1949).
[15] *Goesaert* v. *Cleary,* 335 U.S. 464 (1948).

jected as decisive in arguments for equal treatment is that the legislature has omitted to act in some similar situation alleged to be relevant. In an Indian case a section of the penal code was upheld although it penalized adultery by men and not women.[16] In Germany it has been held that the criminal punishment of male homosexuality does not violate equality by reason of not punishing lesbianism.[17] When apparently relevant features of a situation are discarded, it may be said that "mathematical" or "abstract" symmetry is not required by equality,[18] or that in determining the reasonableness of a classification, attention may be paid to "the established usages and customs and traditions of the people,"[19] (though this consideration has become unfashionable), or that equality does not demand an attack on all evils at once. At other times, however, omission to act in some other case deemed equally evil is stigmatized. "Sterilization of those who have thrice committed grand larceny, with immunity for those who are embezzlers is a clear, pointed, unmistakable discrimination."[20]

It has been suggested by Indian commentators that "frivolous" cases have sometimes been brought forward involving allegations of inequality. A sales tax on hides and skins, for example, is attacked because no tax is placed on other articles.[21] But it is not obvious why this contention is any more frivolous than any other disputes about denial of equality. Is it more frivolous than, say, the question whether a legislature would be denying equal protection if it provided for the taking over by the government of a particular firm or industry as compared with any other firm or industry?[22] To nationalize one industry and not another—coal, but not steel—is obviously a form of discrimination. But

---

[16] *Aziz* v. *State of Bombay,* 1954 S.C.R. 930.

[17] 6 B Verf G.E. 389 (1957). The relevant constitutional provision (Article 3 of the Basic Law) states that (1) All persons shall be equal before the law; (2) Men and women shall have equal rights; (3) No one may be prejudiced or privileged because of his sex, descent, race, language, faith, homeland and origin or because of his religious and political views.

[18] *Patsone* v. *Pennsylvania,* 232 U.S. 138 at 144 (1914).

[19] *Plessy* v. *Ferguson,* 163 U.S. 537 at 55 (1896).

[20] *Skinner* v. *Oklahoma,* 316 U.S. 535 at 541 (1942).

[21] *Syed Mohammed* v. *State of Andhra* 1954 S.C.R. 1117.

[22] This question has come before the Indian Supreme Court in a number of cases.

what sort of test can be applied to the classification problem here? What foothold has a judicial interpreter of equality between "abstract symmetry" and mere political preference? Perhaps this is unfair to judges. But is a guarantee of equality any different in its application to such cases from a guarantee of justice?

EQUALITY AND PRIVACY

A clash between equality on the one hand and liberty on the other occurs particularly where the equality concerned is that of access to publicly and privately supplied facilities of important kinds. The demands of equality and one sort of liberty (the liberty to supply and associate) reinforce each other. Equal treatment cases involving segregation of races or classes could equally well be argued in terms of a denial of liberty to each class to associate with each other. Nevertheless the demands of equality are potentially at odds with another sort of liberty—the liberty to withhold, withdraw, or dissociate. The United Kingdom, stepping cautiously into the field of race-relations legislation, is only now encountering the clash of principles long implicit in both the Fourteenth Amendment and American State and Federal antidiscrimination measures in employment, public accommodations, labor organization, and property disposal. The boundary between what is thought justifiable and what not is unsettled. There is, it is supposed, a sphere of private relationships which ought not to be subject to official enforcement provisions. The phrase "private relationships" is, however, liable to beg questions. Here (as in the argument about the enforcement of criminal sanctions in matters of private conduct or morality) "private" is used ambiguously both to describe a physical context ("in private") and to characterize activity as meriting immunity from public intervention. Although some matters of private morality, in the second sense, happen usually to take place in private, this second proposition is no guarantee of the truth of the first. Wife-beating or homicide within four walls is not immune from social intervention. Similarly, in arguments about discrimination, we may be told that "it is both possible and desirable for governments to make unfairly discriminatory practices, except in the sphere of primarily private relationships, illegal."[23] But criteria of privacy are badly needed to rescue this advice from vacuity. The limits or boundaries drawn in antidiscrimination programs tend to be a cluster of *ad hoc* exceptions. Small businesses or housing projects below a certain size or domestic employment, may be exempted from enforcement measures, and this exclusion is sometimes justified in terms of privacy and a right to free association. But if a right of free association or dissociation is a justifiable principle, why should it be restricted to small groups? Whether a discriminatory practice is classifiable as a private or public discrimination is not always easy to decide, as American experience (e.g., in the field of political parties or restrictive property covenants) shows. Everything that happens happens under the protection of the laws. And the State which permits, licenses, or enforces the results of individual discrimination is in some degree involved in the practice. But both inside and outside the law we still need a clear rationale for the extension of antidiscrimination measures from State operations and services in the most obvious sense into the field of communal and domestic activity. Proceeding from the certain to the less certain, we might, perhaps, set out in descending order of conviction the fields in which we believe prohibition of discriminatory practices—based on race, sex, or religion—to be justified:

1. state and governmental services;
2. services offered to the public generally;
3. a service financed or subsidized from public funds;
4. important professions or occupations regulated or licensed by statute;
5. services or occupations in which large numbers are employed;
6. services provided by individuals which are economically important or of which the supply is scarce.

What stopping points are there along this line? Obviously a principle of free choice and a policy of protecting it enters at some point. But the right to free disposal of economic resources has already suffered a serious loss of esteem. Where it now stands

[23] The Monckton Report on the Constitution of Rhodesia and Nyasaland 1960 (Cmnd. 1148 at p. 78).

in most people's moral estimates is uncertain. May we properly
and freely use our resources to endow scholarships for white men,
or Christians, or red-haired men, or Jews? May we decline to offer
employment to Irishmen, or to leave our property to women? For
the most part we don't exactly know.

EQUALITY AND LIBERTY:
LAW AND MORALS

The area in which the claims to enforcement of plausibly
justifiable equality affect the claims of plausibly justifiable
liberty is one where legal policy may be confused because
individual morality is equally so. The consideration of equality
and liberty in legal contexts ought, perhaps, to assist moral
argument. In the case of some other concepts, this might not
be so because of the development of technical senses of the
relevant words. A study of the deployment of such terms as, say,
"intention" or "malice" inside the law would not necessarily
assist thought about them in a non-legal context. Equality and
freedom, however, when inserted in constitutional statutes, have
at least been intended to be used in their ordinary senses. Their
legal application should be relevant to their moral uses for this
reason and also because the legal process provides a ready-made
stock of limiting cases and crucial examples that might not otherwise readily turn up for inspection.

On the other hand, however, paying too much attention to the
way in which judges have applied the notions of equality and
freedom may distort what, outside the law, one might be inclined
to say about equality, freedom, and justice. Guarantees of equality in law may be treated and may have been intended to be
treated as if they were simultaneous guarantees of both equality
and justice. Thus, an arrangement that placed two identifiable
classes of people in a situation that was for *both* classes equally
unpleasant, evil, or unjust might find itself condemned under an
equal treatment guarantee, through a reluctance to say what, outside the law, might have been more accurate, namely that the
situation in question was one in which the parties were treated
equally but evilly. If one can imagine physically similar, but
segregated, educational or transport facilities for black and white
citizens in a society where the numbers of both were roughly

equal and there were not for other reasons differences of esteem between the races, "separate but equal" might be a morally acceptable description. The Supreme Court's latter-day formula that separate educational facilities are "inherently unequal" is justifiable not because inequality inheres like treacle and can be seen doing it but because of notorious contingent features of American society. If these were not present, it might be a mistake to disguise a situation that deprives both parties of freedom to integrate as one that deprives them of equality.

The judicial situation is also one in which the temptation to do justice at the expense of mildly stretching or abusing concepts has not always been resisted. Outside the law we are perfectly at liberty to approve of exceptions to principles; to prefer efficiency to equality or security to liberty. But a judge, when presented as a datum with a constitutional guarantee of "equality" or "liberty" and charged with enforcing it, may be reluctant openly to create or state exceptions to the principle. He may be reluctant to say, because of the pressures of a particular case: Liberty or equality are all very well, but not here or not now. There may be constraints upon him to produce what in practice is a similar result by announcing as applications of the principles what linguistically or morally would be better treated as exceptions to them or treated as a surrender of those principles to other overriding principles. Outside the context of legal guarantees, one may be freer to choose when to treat principles in this way and when not to.

The difference between qualifying, modifying or filling out a principle and allowing it to be overridden by another principle[24] perhaps needs more exploration in relation to equality and liberty. Can it be argued that justifiable legislation passed in the interests of welfare, morals, or security ought to be thought of as overriding or clashing with liberty, but that departures from "sameness" or "mathematical symmetry," when justified, help to define and constitute the principle of equality? In a recent discussion[25] Professor von Leyden has argued that "Just as liberty is not license, so is equality not sameness." This is to treat

[24] Cf. R. M. Hare, *Freedom and Reason* (1963), p. 168.
[25] W. von Leyden, "On Justifying Inequality," *Political Studies* (1963), p. 62.

equality and liberty in a parallel fashion. To contest this parallelism would be to say that justifiable differences do not stand to equality in the same relationship as justifiable restraints stand to liberty. Equality is defined by the first but liberty confined by the second.

If this is so, some morals may follow for philosophical constitution-makers. The trouble about equality seems to be that constituting and filling in the general principle, and thus properly applying it, requires a conspicuously legislative and creative act. With liberty the more typical predicament is that it is easier to see when the principle is impugned or overridden than to resist the temptation to impugn and override it. The characteristic virtues and vices of legislative and adjudicative functions may be matched with these differences. Hence a possible maxim for political science: Keep the delineation of equality away from judges and the protection of liberty out of the hands of legislators.

16

EQUALITY, DEMOCRACY, AND
INTERNATIONAL LAW

D. D. RAPHAEL

I

The distinctive features of democratic government are chiefly intended to ensure a maximum of liberty for citizens. Government with its rules of law restricts our liberty to do as we please. Democrats recognize the necessity of this, but they feel that, so far as possible, the rules should be self-imposed or at least should be in accordance with the will or consent of the citizens. If a man imposes a rule on himself, or agrees to its imposition by another, he is not being compelled but is acting voluntarily. Democracy is a doctrine of "Do it yourself," and, as someone has remarked, "Do it yourself" often means "Rue it yourself." The democrat is prepared to make his own mistakes rather than to be directed by someone else who may have superior wisdom. The idea at the back of all this is that self-direction, choosing for yourself, is far preferable to having decisions made for you, and imposed upon you, by another. This is why liberty is valued.

For the democrat, the idea of liberty goes along with that of equality. He believes that everybody, or at least every adult, is capable of exercising the power of self-direction and should be given the opportunity to do so. The democrat holds that all men have an equal right to liberty and self-direction.

Liberty and equality are what distinguish the democratic ideal from other political ideals. A notion of equality of some sort must figure in any concept of justice, but it figures most prominently in the democratic concept of justice. Liberty and equality are the distinctive aims of democracy. That this has always been so may be seen from the criticisms of democracy made by Plato in Book VIII of the *Republic*. Plato there sums up the ends of democracy as liberty, equality, and variety (*Republic*, 557-8), and it is because these are the leading features of democracy that he attacks it. Liberty, in the sense of doing what you like, is attractive, Plato says, but it cannot last; and it is furthermore less desirable than doing the right thing, even though most people, not being wise enough to know and to choose for themselves what is right, have to be directed by others. Equality, in his opinion, is wrong because it goes against nature; men are unequal in their capacities and should be given different functions in accordance with their different capacities. (Variety he considers objectionable because it runs counter to an integrated society.)

I have been speaking of democratic aims or ideals, and we often do use the words "democracy" and "democratic" to refer to these ideals, or even to one of them alone, especially equality. The latter tendency is particularly common in a country like New Zealand which is strongly imbued with egalitarian sentiments. When I was in New Zealand some twenty years ago, I found people there ready to call the British Civil Service "undemocratic" because it has a direct entry of University graduates to its policy-making grade, the Administrative Class. Or again, a good many New Zealanders were inclined to say that the British system of University education was "undemocratic" because it was more selective than their own in its qualifications for entry. By "undemocratic" they meant inegalitarian. But they are not alone in this usage. When I first read Professor George H. Sabine's *History of Political Theory*, I was puzzled by his statement, in the chapter on Liberalism, that John Stuart Mill's essay *On Liberty* "was in a sense a defense of liberty against democracy."[1] This struck me as virtually self-contradictory until I recalled that, for de Tocqueville at least, Democracy in America meant the cult of equality more than of liberty.

There is, then, one usage of the words "democracy" and "democratic" which connotes social ideals and perhaps especially egalitarianism. As contrasted with this usage, however, there is another, in which "democracy" means a set of political institutions. People who do not agree with the so-called "democratic ideal," and especially with the ideal of equality, sometimes protest sharply against the use of the words "democracy" and "democratic" to describe general social aims; democracy, they insist, is a form of government. Etymologically the word "democracy" undoubtedly began as the name for a form of rule, "rule by the people," as contrasted with "aristocracy" or "oligarchy" (rule by the best men, or by a few), and with "monarchy" (rule by one man). My reference to Plato, however, shows that, almost from the start, the word "democracy" was associated with a set of ideals as well as with a form of government. This is intelligible enough, for democratic forms of government will have been adopted only because it was thought that all citizens equally had a claim to self-direction, i.e., because of a belief in a right to equality and liberty. The word "aristocracy" is similarly used to mean a social ideal as well as a form of government. The "aristocratic" ideal values culture (the pursuit of knowledge and beauty) more than an egalitarian conception of justice. An expression of aristocratic values may be found in Clive Bell's book *Civilization* (and, of course, in Plato's *Republic*), but there have been plenty of other people who share this outlook, although it is not often boldly acknowledged in opposition to egalitarian justice.

---

[1] 1st ed. (1937, New York and London), p. 667; apparently omitted in the revised edition.

II

The ideas and the procedures of democracy do not apply only to the organization of the State. They apply also to associations within a State and to the relations between States. Equality (and likewise liberty) is a social, not just a political, principle. We may think that there should be equality of opportunity in education, without meaning necessarily that the whole of the educational system should be run by the State. We may think there should be equality between the sexes, not only in political matters like having the vote or in legal rights to property, but also in regard to opportunity for careers or to equal pay for equal work or to the position of husbands and wives (or sons and daughters) in the family. Democratic notions appear again in some aspects, and especially the legal aspects, of relations between States themselves in international society. "Democratic ideals" in the relations between States owe something to the analogy of democracy within the State itself and something to analogy from non-political associations, notably the family.

The idea of an international society of States is at times described by the phrase "the family of nations" (where "nations" means States). As in the language of religion, which speaks of the "fatherhood" of God and the "brotherhood" of man, a metaphor drawn from the most close-knit form of human community is felt to be best fitted to express the notion of a universal society. To a large extent, of course, this metaphor depicts an aspiration or ideal of the friendly relations that ought to exist, not an account of the actual relations that do exist. Apart from the question of ideals, however, the notion of a family does imply something about facts, namely a common outlook and common traditions. Earlier international societies have not been world societies but they could often be called a family of States in this sense. The Greek city-states, for example, despite frequent wars, formed an international society with a common language, common traditions, and some common religious practices such as a respect for the Delphic oracle and participation in the Olympic Games. Although they never formed any stable federation, they distinguished themselves as Greeks from "barbarians" (which meant, in the first instance, people who spoke a foreign language). In some degree this affected their behavior. For example, they were prepared to make slaves of conquered barbarians but not, usually, of conquered Greeks. Similarly the world of medieval Christendom was an international society with a common religion and a common legal system (derived from Roman Law). Modern international society has developed from the medieval one, with the tradition of Natural Law providing a foundation for International Law. This means that modern international society follows the traditions and structure of *European* society. Now the countries of Europe can be called a "family" of nations or States precisely because they share a common tradition, primarily that of International Law. Other States which have entered this international system have had to accept the European tradition. Often this has meant no hardship, for the former colonies of European countries have legal systems which are themselves founded on the legal systems of the colonizing States. Thus the United States of America and all the countries of the Commonwealth have legal systems based on English law, while former French colonies have systems based on French law, and so on. In some instances, however, States have had to adapt themselves to the European tradition. China and Japan, for example, are not in any sense members of the original European family.

This explains why the international society of States includes certain democratic procedures, and why these procedures are accepted by non-democratic countries. One example of democratic procedure arises from the doctrine of the sovereign equality of States. All States are treated as equal in International Law, regardless of size or power. Following from this, each member State of the United Nations Organization has one vote in the General Assembly, and the view of a majority of States in any vote taken in the Assembly is held to be the view of the Assembly as a whole. In some ways this is a misleading practice, but it is accepted by all States as being "democratic" and as built into the structure of international society.

I have said that International Law arose from the medieval European tradition of Natural Law. There is a difference, however, between the medieval international society and the modern one. The world of Roman Christendom in the Middle Ages was not a single State, but neither was it a collection of States in the modern sense of the term. Up to the time of the Reformation, the secular ruler of a European country did not possess sovereign (i.e., supreme) authority; he was subject to the superior authority of the international Church. When the national State arose as a sovereign autonomous unit, it was recognized that there still was and must be some form of loose association between States, and this was represented by their common acceptance of International Law.

In the thought of political theorists of the seventeenth century, like Hobbes and Locke, the notion of Natural Law, or a Law of Nature, was connected with the notion of a "state of nature" that preceded civil society and the positive law of civil society. Consequently Vattel, an international jurist of the eighteenth century, put forward the idea that States, whose relations with each other are regulated by something like Natural Law and not by an imposed and enforceable positive law, are in a state of nature. And because the earlier theorists had spoken of individuals in a state of nature as being free (or independent) and equal, Vattel thought the same must be true of States. States are independent, and must be regarded as equal.

The transfer of the concepts of liberty and equality to International Law from individualistic political theory indicates that the international society of States is conceived as analogous to a society of individuals. States are considered, in a sense, as persons. This doctrine has advantages, though it also has dangers. The dangers are familiar to students of political theory, but I think that in legal theory they are slight. Some political theorists who have thought of the State in organic terms have reached the conclusion that the State is an end to which its individual members are means; and so they have regarded the State as a real super-person. But when one says that States are considered in International Law as (legal) persons, this emphatically does not mean that they are considered to be real persons. States are purely legal entities; one can even say they are fictions. Lawyers know how to get along with convenient fictions, and are not misled by them. A corporation, for example, can be regarded in law as a person, i.e., as a subject of rights and duties; but no lawyer is thereby misled into thinking of a corporation as a real super-person, existing alongside the natural persons who act as the officers of the corporation. Similarly the notion of a State as a person in International Law simply means that the State is the subject of rights and obligations—the State, as contrasted with the nation, or with the individual who is the Head of the State, though of course certain individuals, such as the Secretary of State for foreign affairs, act in the name of the State when exercising the rights or fulfilling the obligations.

The advantages of the concept of States as persons are that this concept helps to ensure stability. Governments come and go, but if the State, and not a particular government or a particular Head of State, is regarded as the subject of rights and obligations, then successive governments inherit the position of their predecessors. It is less easy for a new government to repudiate obligations undertaken by its predecessor; and likewise it is not legitimate for a foreign government to say "We made a treaty with your predecessor, not with you, and so you have no rights under it."

III

The sovereign equality of States is a legal concept, a concept of International Law. In the political institutions of the United Nations Organization, it is accepted for membership of, and voting in, the General Assembly, but not for the Security Council. The latter tries to make proper allowance for the special position of the Great Powers, or at any rate for those States that were leading powers at the time when U.N.O. was set up. Political realities do not often correspond to legal formalities, and there is a common opinion among political scientists that the concept of legal sovereignty, with its doctrine of the equality of States, is pretty useless. In place of it, they speak of a concept of political sovereignty.

I myself think that the concept of political sovereignty is a confusion. Sovereignty means supremacy, and the sovereignty of a State is a form of supremacy in the sense that, while a State has inferiors subject to its will, it has no superiors to whose will it is subject. As a method of describing *legal authority*, the concept makes sense and has application to all recognized States. As a method of describing *political power*, it can make sense but has little application.

I remember hearing a discussion some years ago between Professor Hans J. Morgenthau and Professor Raymond Aron at a

Congress of the International Political Science Association. Professor Morgenthau had argued that the only "viable" States in the present-day world were the U.S.A. and the U.S.S.R. Britain and France had once been viable States, but they were not now, because their freedom of action was limited by the policies of America and Russia, as could be seen in the halting of the Suez operation of 1956. Professor Aron replied that Morgenthau was simply using the phrase "viable State" to mean "Great Power." It was of course true that Britain and France used to be Great Powers and were no longer such, but this did not mean that they were no longer viable States. According to Morgenthau's argument, he went on, the United Nations consisted of two viable States and a hundred or so non-viable States, yet the fact was that all these allegedly "non-viable" States managed to get along as States.

The argument was conducted in terms of what was a "viable" State, but it could equally well be applied to the notion of a "sovereign" State. The concept of political sovereignty, as distinguished from legal sovereignty, must mean sovereignty in terms of political power as distinguished from legal authority. Now political power is the ability to carry out one's will and to get others to carry out one's will. Such power can be limited by the power of others. In these terms, some States have great power, while most have little power. One could therefore imagine a holder of the notion of political sovereignty saying that Britain and France used to be sovereign powers but are no longer so. But he would have to go farther still. Sovereignty means supremacy, so that a sovereign power would be one whose freedom of action was not limited by other powers. If so, not only Britain and France but also the United States and the Soviet Union would fail to qualify as sovereign powers, for the freedom of action possessed by the United States, while not as limited as that of Britain or France, is limited by the power of the Soviet Union, and *vice versa*. This is what is meant by "the balance of power." A sovereign *power,* strictly speaking, exists only if the State so described is in control of a world empire or something approaching a world empire. There have been such powers at times, but there is none today, and it will follow therefore that no modern State is a sovereign State.

Nevertheless the idea of State sovereignty fulfills a role, and the context in which it does so is that of law. Sovereignty is a matter of legal authority, not of political power. And despite the inequalities of States in political power, in area, in size of population, and in resources, their sovereignty is held, in International Law, to be equal.

IV

This is not to say that the sovereign equality of States is a suitable concept for political international institutions. According to Oppenheim,[2] four practical consequences follow from the doctrine of the equality of States. They are: (1) In any question that falls to be settled by consent, each State has a right to one vote and only one vote. (2) The vote of the weakest State is to count for as much as the vote of the strongest. (3) No State can claim jurisdiction over another State. (4) The internal jurisdiction of any State is not usually questioned by the courts of another State. The third and fourth of these principles in fact relate more to the independence of States, i.e., to sovereignty itself, than to their presumed equality. The first and second, however, are implications of equality and are direct analogues of democratic voting procedures: "One State, one vote," (like "One man, one vote") and "One vote, one value."

In the United Nations Organization, these democratic principles are followed in the General Assembly but not in the Security Council, where the leading powers have an ascendancy. The constitution of the Security Council gives expression to the real political facts, namely that leading powers have always had, and are bound to have, more of a say in the conduct of international affairs than smaller powers have. Consequently the rules for voting in the Assembly are misleading in hiding the inevitable facts about decision-making, and are liable to bring international organization into disrepute. Because of the facts of international affairs, and of the voluntary character of International Law, a majority vote in the U.N. Assembly does not bind those who are outvoted, as does a majority vote in a national parliament. The resolutions of the U.N. Assembly constitute

---

[2] *International Law*, 8th ed. (1955, London), vol. i, § 115, cited from J. L. Brierly, *The Law of Nations*, 6th ed. (1963, Oxford), p. 131.

recommendations only. Nevertheless it would not be true to say that the democratic procedures of the Assembly are simply a sham, concealing the realities of power. Although the vote results only in a recommendation, a heavy vote in the U.N. Assembly against a powerful State (as in 1956 against the Soviet Union's intervention in Hungary, and against the action of Britain and France in the Suez operation) does on occasion have *some* influence on the policy of that State. To this extent, majority opinion can act as a check against the reliance on power alone.

Still, the presumed equality of States is not a very satisfactory way of gauging world opinion. A State with 100 million inhabitants has one vote, and a State with 10 million inhabitants has one vote. If ten States, each having a population of 10 million, outvote a single State having a population of 100 million, the vote is 10 to 1 but the populations represented on the two sides are equal.

It is not easy, however, to find a more satisfactory alternative to the principle of "one State, one vote." I have spoken as if world opinion would be best gauged in terms of world population. At first sight this seems sensible, because the voting principle of "one State, one vote," is formed on the analogy of the democratic principle of "one man, one vote." Now if we were to drop the analogy between a man and a State, and instead to carry the original principle of "one man, one vote," into international affairs, we should have to give States voting strength in proportion to their populations. Suppose we were to allot one vote for every group of 10 million people. Then Britain, with 50 million inhabitants, would have five votes; the United States, with 180 million people, would have 18 votes; the Soviet Union, with 270 million, would have 27 votes; India, with 440 million, would have 44 votes; and China (assuming she were a member of the United Nations) , with 650 million people, would have 65 votes.[3] Would we be prepared to stomach this? If not, why not? Not simply because we dislike the policies of China. We should be uneasy also about granting 44 votes to India, even though we preferred the policies of India to those of China. We should be

[3] My (rough) figures of populations are taken from U.N. estimates, 1962. The figure for China relates to 1957-8 and is certainly too low for the present-day population of China.

uneasy because we should feel that most of the 650 million Chinese or the 440 million Indians are not in a position to express an opinion on world issues, while on the other hand quite a large number of the 50 million Britons or the 180 million Americans *are* in such a position. World *opinion* cannot be gauged in terms of world *population*.

If we accept this line of argument, we are presupposing the idea, commonly thought to have been abandoned by modern democrats, that a man is entitled to a vote only if he has a reasonable measure of knowledge and education. In other words, our idea of democracy in the international sphere is one of a limited or qualified democracy. Perhaps this is a sound view in the national sphere also. I imagine that British democrats would not be so ready to give a vote to all adult British citizens if Britain had not had a reasonable system of universal education in force for some time. This prompts the reflection that we should not expect a country like China to practice democracy until the Chinese have had a reasonable system of universal education in operation for some time.

At any rate we can see that the transfer of democratic institutions to the international society of States is not a simple matter. The concept of "one State, one vote," while manifestly unreal and illogical, fills a gap in the meantime, but one cannot expect it to command much respect. So far as *voting* goes, the supposedly democratic procedure of the U.N. Assembly is a bit of a sham. But not so far as *discussion* goes. Democratic procedure means not only decision by majority vote but also decision after discussion. In the U.N. Assembly, as in a national parliament, sensible opinion and criticism can make themselves felt, irrespective of the numbers of votes that they can command. Democracy is a matter of liberty as well as equality, and liberty includes the freedom to express one's opinions and one's criticisms of those who have the whip-hand.

17

EQUALITY OF STATES WITHIN THE UNITED NATIONS

ROBERT W. GREGG

The doctrine of equality of states in international organizations has come under increasing fire since the package deal on membership applications in 1955 opened the doors of the United Nations to quantitative and qualitative membership changes of such proportions as to shift the UN's center of gravity from the relatively stable Western world to the revolutionary world of Africa and Asia. Two events on the eve of the United Nations' twentieth anniversary served to call attention once more to this already controversial doctrine. The first of these was the 1964 United Nations Conference on Trade and Development (UNCTAD), which seemed to institutionalize the division of the world into developed and developing states; the second was the protracted dispute over assessments for peace-keeping forces, which culminated in 1964 in the almost complete paralysis of the

Nineteenth General Assembly. In each case a fundamental question was raised: Should a coalition of states, each with a vote equal in weight to that of every other state, attempt to override the opposition, on a matter of vital interest, of a state or group of states whose continued support is essential to the survival and growth of the organization? Fortunately, the dénouement in each of the two cases has not been the disaster for the UN that some observers were predicting. However, UNCTAD and the "financial crisis" suggest that it may be appropriate to reexamine the doctrine of political equality of states in international organizations in order to determine whether it is functional or dysfunctional and how it may be adapted to the demands that a changing international system place upon the UN.

Two coequal elements comprise the doctrine of political equality. One of these, derived from traditional international law, is the rule that every state shall have an equal voice in the decision-making process of the organization, i.e., "one state, one vote." The other is the principle of majority rule, borrowed from the theory and practice of democratic institutions. Equalitarianism and majoritarianism may, of course, be viewed as competitive, rather than complementary, principles.[1] However, equality without capacity to reach a decision is no more satisfactory to UN members than a capacity to reach decisions without equality; inasmuch as a primary function of equalitarianism is to give to all states an opportunity to play a significant role in the decision-making process of the organization, majoritarianism has emerged as an important corollary of equalitarianism in international organizations. It can be, and has been argued that the equalitarian doctrine is a fiction and that it has been smuggled into the theory and practice of international organizations through spurious analogical reasoning.

> Everybody knows that all sovereign states are not equal. The differences between them in population, in territory, in wealth, in armed strength, in their habits of thought, in their conceptions of law and right—in all that goes to

[1] See Edwin D. Dickinson, *The Equality of States in International Law*, Cambridge: Harvard University Press, 1920, pp. 280ff.; Inis L. Claude, Jr., *Swords Into Plowshares*, 3rd ed., Rev., New York: Random House, 1964, pp. 111–131.

make up civilization—are amongst the most obvious and insistent of facts. . . . The simplest common sense is enough to teach us that Powers like Great Britain, France, Germany, Japan, Russia, and the United States will not, and cannot, in any circumstances, allow Haiti, Salvador, Turkey, and Persia to have an equal right with themselves in laying down the law by which their fleets, their armies, their diplomatists, and their jurists are to be guided on matters of the supremest moment. The suggestion that they should submit to such a doctrine is simply fatuous.[2]

This sharply worded editorial appeared not in the course of some recent UN debate but in *The London Times,* in 1907 after the conclusion of the Second Hague Conference. Similar sentiments were still being voiced in many editorial columns more than half a century later, with such new entities as Barbados, Lesotho, and the Maldive Islands now contemptuously labeled "mini-states." But if equality of states is a myth, it is not one that can be banished by calling attention to the unwisdom of extending the cloak of equality to cover the bare facts of inequality. Although the doctrine is not all pervasive and yields to other arrangements in most international organizations some of the time and in some international organizations most of the time, the concept of political equality has by now become so tightly woven into the fabric of the United Nations that it almost certainly cannot be removed without doing violence to the organization itself.

EVOLUTION OF THE DOCTRINE OF EQUALITY WITHIN THE UNITED NATIONS

The basic facts have been recited countless times. The Charter reflects both an equalitarian and a power orientation; the former is most conspicuous in the General Assembly, the latter in the Security Council. It was in the Council that principal responsibility was originally vested for handling the security problems whose existence was the major raison d'être for the creation of the UN. But events and some of the membership conspired to downgrade the importance of the Council and to

[2] Quoted in Dickinson, p. 286.

shift to the Assembly primary political responsibility within the United Nations. The explanation for this institutional revolution is to be found (a) in the disposition on the part of the Cold War antagonists to use the UN as an instrument of their foreign policies, (b) in the dramatic increase in membership, and (c) in the shifting emphasis among UN tasks which resulted from the changing size and nature of the membership and from the changing character of the Cold War. Ascendancy of the General Assembly meant more equalitarianism in UN decision-making, a consideration that had, of course, strongly influenced the many advocates of the change. To many of those who had agreed with Sir Carl Berendsen of New Zealand that the marriage of veto to Charter was a shot-gun wedding,[3] the new role of the General Assembly must indeed have seemed a vindication of views so strongly urged at San Francisco by the smaller states.

Equalitarianism has served different functions in the different phases of the United Nations' existence. The first of these more or less discrete phases began with the early realization that there was to be no post-war honeymoon between the Soviet Union and her wartime allies and ended with disenchantment over the UN's role in the Korean War. This was a period of Western dominance, during which the UN was used to support the policy objectives of the non-Communist group in an acutely bipolarized world; it was the period in which the Soviet Union took refuge in the veto and the United States mobilized support for a policy of circumventing the veto. The Uniting for Peace Resolution, adopted during the Korean War, was the coup de grace to the veto, the signal that the equalitarian doctrine had triumphed over the privileged position of sheer power. But the sweet taste of triumph soured quickly. A conviction grew that equalitarianism and its corollary, majoritarianism, would have to serve some purpose other than ratification of the policies of one of the principal contenders in the Cold War.

In subsequent years the system changed with the admission of dozens of Asian and African states whose commitments to the termination of colonialism and to their own economic development transcended their interest in the Cold War. The opportu-

---

[3] See General Assembly, *Official Records,* First Session, Second Part, 39th Plenary Meeting, p. 790.

nities afforded by the General Assembly for the realization of these goals served to modify the function of equalitarianism; it came to be used more for purposes of bargaining. To a modest extent, the actors began to see the UN's political process as a non-zero-sum exercise.

As the United Nations' membership roster and agenda of functional interests lengthened, the application of the equalitarian doctrine became increasingly problematic. The doctrine sanctions equal participation by *all* states in the consideration and disposition of *all* issues, but in practice it has been difficult to make such an arrangement workable. The dilemma has been "solved" by pragmatic adaptation of the doctrine. On the one hand, the General Assembly, both in plenary and in its seven main committees, considers virtually all issues, including many that have already been dealt with at great length by the limited-member bodies. The unwieldiness of the Assembly has been somewhat mitigated by the aggregation of interests in a crude party system. On the other hand, the General Assembly has sought to ease its burden and expedite the handling of critical issues by creating representative bodies that are microcosmic replicas of the Assembly[4] and by promoting modification in the size and composition of the limited-member Councils so that they, too, will resemble the more equalitarian Assembly.[5] An important result of these institutional developments has been a practical substitution of the equality of groups for the equality of states.

In practice, the member states of the UN have exercised their political equality in two ways: first, in the act of voting on resolutions in the General Assembly and its main committees, and second, in the act of creating limited-member bodies and selecting states to serve on them and on the limited-member Councils established by the Charter.

[4] See Catherine S. Manno, "Problems and Trends in the Composition of Nonplenary UN Organs," *International Organization,* Vol. XIX, No. 1 (Winter 1965).

[5] See Eric Stein, *Some Implications of Expanding United Nations Membership,* New York: Carnegie Endowment for International Peace, 1956; Norman Padelford, "Politics and Change in the Security Council," *International Organization,* Vol. XIV, No. 3 (Summer, 1960); Norman Padelford, "Politics and the Future of ECOSOC," *International Organization,* Vol. XV, No. 4 (Autumn, 1961); Robert W. Gregg, "The Economic and Social Council: Politics of Membership," *Western Political Quarterly,* Vol. XVI, No. 1 (March 1963).

Those who denigrate the equalitarian doctrine have a recurring nightmare in which an important resolution is adopted over Major-Power opposition by a majority composed of states paying a minute fraction of the UN's budget or of states lacking either will or capacity, perhaps both, for assuming responsibility. Hypothetical combinations of states may be adduced to prove that this is possible; in fact, there is evidence that it has happened. But although the equalitarian doctrine has encouraged voting, it has also, by helping to develop more numerous and more varied functions for the UN, encouraged bargaining. And bargaining dulls the abrasive, cutting edge of many votes. Consequently, if we think of states as falling into three groups—those which positively approve a resolution, those which will tolerate it (they may vote yes, no, or abstain), and those which positively disapprove—we should have to note that there has been a tendency for the bargaining process to soften controversial resolutions sufficiently to convert important segments of disapproval into tolerance, even if the tolerant states vote negatively.

Concerning the use of the equalitarian doctrine to create and fill limited-member bodies, the UN membership has opted to use its voting power to replicate the General Assembly but not to treat all states as equally entitled to play a representational role. Replication of the General Assembly in various elected bodies has been guaranteed either by resolutions specifying formulae for geographical-ideological distribution or by ad hoc negotiations. Charter stipulations and gentlemen's agreements suggesting a privileged position for certain states or certain categories of states have been bypassed wherever possible in favor of the single criterion of geographical distribution. This has led to a crude approximation of equality among groups of states, or, more precisely, to a form of proportional representation. A policy of systematic rotation of states within the several groups could have extended the equalitarian doctrine into elective and appointive bodies. However, the states with less power in terms of gross national product, nuclear weapons, and permanent seats on the Security Council have been anxious to achieve the substance, not the shadow, of equality within the UN. This can best be achieved by a consciously adopted policy of countervailing power, e.g., by tapping Brazil more often than Ecuador,

India more often than Afghanistan, Nigeria more often than Upper Volta, and the United Arab Republic more often than Jordan, to serve on the UN's Councils and its key committees. To insist upon perfect equality might only serve to widen the gap between the elephants and the mice.

FUNCTIONAL AND DYSFUNCTIONAL ATTRIBUTES OF THE DOCTRINE OF EQUALITY

Whether the presence of equalitarianism in the United Nations is functional or dysfunctional depends upon the tasks of the organization. The fundamental minimal function of the UN, the function about which there appears to be nearly complete consensus, is that of a permanent conference machinery. In a recent essay, Chadwick Alger identified some of the important attributes of this seemingly basic role: It affords continual access of the officials of more nations to each other; it affords access of more kinds of officials of each nation to officials from other nations; it diminishes restraints upon day-to-day intergovernmental contact; it constitutes a learning experience for the participants; it creates new roles with concern for the total system; and it facilitates extended contact between intergovernmental social systems and the outside world.[6]

These are some of the non-resolution consequences of the United Nations. States also seek to use the UN to achieve foreign-policy objectives that are not shared by other states and that may in fact conflict with the objectives of other states. Then the UN becomes a forum for non-violent conflict, important to the international system even when conflict is not resolved. Agreement on the functions of the UN begins to break down, however, as it becomes an arena for conflict rather than for mere contact. It breaks down further as the UN undertakes to play a legislative, coercive role with respect to conflict. Ernst Haas suggests that "the historical purpose of the UN is to encourage the evolution of a world community beyond the minimal level of cooperation represented by a permanent conference of governments; to reach

[6] Chadwick Alger, "Intergovernmental Relations in Organizations and Their Significance for International Conflict," in Elton B. McNeil (ed.), *The Nature of Human Conflict,* Englewood Cliffs, N.J.: Prentice-Hall, 1965.

a stage at which the organization can act autonomously for constructive and universal ends . . . ."[7] As the UN becomes more ambitious, as emphasis shifts from the minimal conference to the maximal supranational agency, and as it moves along a spectrum of activity from discussion to decision, from exhortation to demand, from voluntarism to compulsion, from technical assistance to capital development, and from observer groups to military forces—the less agreement, then, there is, not only on the particular issue but also on the legitimacy of the UN's role.

The equalitarian doctrine with its majoritarian corollary is today functional roughly in inverse proportion to the ambitiousness of the UN's undertaking. It is more acceptable, albeit less interesting, when the UN is playing a modest, hortatory, noncoercive role. There is a certain irony in this. A maximal UN, a UN acting "autonomously for constructive and universal ends," would obviously reflect a more highly integrated international system; it would presumably be characterized by sufficient value consensus to permit decision-making according to equalitarian-majoritarian principles. However, present efforts to use the United Nations for more than minimal functions reveal some of the dysfunctional qualities of equalitarianism.

It will perhaps be argued by some that to employ the "one state, one vote" principle at the lower end of the spectrum of international organizational tasks is harmless but not functional. I do not agree; I believe it is functional. The significant point today is not that member states of the United Nations are not comparable either to persons within a democratic society or to states within a federal system (although the UN is in fact based upon a kind of Connecticut Compromise between the claims of power and of parity). Rather, the important point is that the equalitarian doctrine is an integral part of the UN idea, and that idea performs the valuable function of promoting commitment among many states to the organization and its purposes. The doctrine serves as an incentive because it grants status, because it is a source of prestige. It is instrumental in overcoming that condition which Gustavo Lagos terms *atimia,* or the status

[7] Ernst B. Haas, *Beyond the Nation-State,* Stanford: Stanford University Press, 1964, p. 124.

gap.[8] It permits participation of the non-powers in an apparently meaningful way, and it may serve to moderate somewhat the behavior of the powers, thereby contributing to the ultrastability[9] of the international system. Insofar, therefore, as states are induced to use the UN's multilateral and bilateral diplomatic opportunities and to channel their penchant for conflict through the UN mill, however slowly and coarsely it may grind, the equalitarian incentive may be said to be functional.

But the danger does exist, as the critics have alleged, that the equalitarian doctrine may hinder the achievement of some of the UN's purposes. There is almost certainly a feedback from equalitarian voting which reinforces the conviction of each state that, no matter how modest its credentials, it shall play a role in the UN's political process on a par with the role played by every other state. Thus equalitarianism, harmless enough in a minimal UN, may create patterns of behavior and expectation which are positively dysfunctional when transferred to more difficult issues or other levels of action. If the doctrine promotes an artificial sense of capacity and power, it may lead to a kind of specious decision-making by sheer weight of numbers which cannot be translated into influence on realities. Whether this is the consequence of major-power initiative, as it frequently was in the first phase of the UN's existence, or of small-state initiative, as was more often the case in the second phase, twin dangers lurk in the shadows cast by these votes. The first is that the members will be deluded into thinking that they have accomplished something when in fact they have not; the second is that they will become disenchanted when they realize that their decisions are ineffective. Furthermore, voting according to equalitarian-majoritarian principles has alienated virtually all of the major powers at one time or another, and their commitment to international organization is, after all, as important as that of the less powerful states.

[8] Gustavo Lagos, *International Stratification and Underdeveloped Countries,* Chapel Hill: The University of North Carolina Press, 1963, pp. ix, 24–25.

[9] An ultrastable international system is one which may be, and probably is, characterized by instability, but which tends to reject the more extreme manifestations of instability that jeopardize the system itself. See Morton A. Kaplan, *System and Process in International Politics,* New York: John Wiley & Sons, 1957, pp. 6–8.

THE PRINCIPLE OF CONCURRENT MAJORITY

We are, therefore, faced recurrently with the necessity of distinguishing between an insistence upon equalitarianism, which is functional because it contributes to a sense of status and encourages commitment, and an insistence upon it, which is dysfunctional because it fosters disillusionment or disdain among elements within the organization whose support is vital. If equalitarianism is to be functional, there must be tacit acceptance of the thesis that decisions shall be reached by a concurrent majority of the essential actors. Essentiality is relative to the issue and to the level of commitment requested. But on any given question it should be possible to ascertain whose support is necessary for the preservation of the minimal UN and for some progress toward that day when, to repeat Ernst Haas' words [see note 7], "the organization can act autonomously for constructive and universal ends." Although it is not possible to identify essential actors without reference to specific issues, it should be noted that they may include both individual states and groups of states. Thus the concept of the concurrent majority, already implicit in the requirement of extraordinary (two-thirds) majorities on some questions in the General Assembly, draws upon both the principle of Big-Power unanimity in the Security Council and the now dormant Soviet proposal for a troika in the Secretariat. Unlike the two-thirds majority, concurrence is qualitative rather than quantitative. Unlike Big-Power unanimity and the troika, concurrence is a tacit rather than an explicit requirement, more flexible and less invidious in the designation of privileged parties.

Concurrent majorities may, and probably will, include a number of states that tolerate rather than actively support the proposed course of action. Such actors may even vote against a resolution that embodies the dominant opinion within the UN. What is imperative, however, is that no decision fundamental in nature be taken over opposition by an essential actor. Such opposition should be reduced to the level of toleration by bargaining or by lowering the level of commitment required by the resolution. Concurrent majorities constructed in this fashion are not, of course, new to the United Nations. They are frequently the product of an effort to produce a two-thirds majority.

However, a two-thirds majority is not necessarily *prima facie* evidence that concurrence of the essential actors has been achieved. It is the quality and intensity of the opposition that is crucial.

In effect, decision-making by concurrent majority modifies the equalitarian doctrine by reintroducing a species of veto into the process. But it is a veto shared by more states (acting independently or as members of a group or bloc of states) and rendered less capricious, and hence less oppressive, by the rule of essentiality. In fact, the principle of concurrent majority does not confer a veto so much as it forces consideration of intensity and centrality of interests. It does not negate equalitarianism so much as transform it from a sterile exercise in head-counting into a functional mode of decision-making.

RECAPITULATION: A PRESCRIPTION

The preceding observations, systematically arranged, constitute a prescription for the use of the equalitarian doctrine in the United Nations.

1. The functions of the UN, in order of priority, are (a) to provide a permanent forum for maximizing intergovernmental contacts and for waging non-violent conflict (minimal functions); and (b) to facilitate conflict resolution and to enlarge upon the value consensus, thereby serving an integrative function (maximal functions).

2. If the UN is to perform these functions effectively, member states must regard the existence of the organization and participation in it as important, and their commitment must be active, not passive.

3. On the one hand, the principle of the political equality of states may contribute to the strengthening of commitment to the UN (a) from states that rank relatively low in power, by giving them a larger role and more status, and (b) from those more powerful states in a position to command or support a UN majority. On the other hand, the principle may weaken the commitment (a) from states that rank at or near the top in power, by depriving them of the role and status that are presumably functions of power, and (b) from states that consistently find themselves in a minority on crucial issues. The principle may, therefore, be both functional and dysfunctional.

4. Because the principle is functional, and too deeply rooted in the practice of the UN to be easily eradicated, it must be frequently employed in reaching decisions within the organization. Because the principle may be dysfunctional, it must be employed with discretion and restraint.

5. The risk that the equalitarian principle may become dysfunctional grows in direct proportion to the magnitude of the demands made upon the states and/or groups of states whose support is essential for achieving both minimal and maximal UN goals. Consequently, decisions should be reached within the UN in accordance with the principle of equality of states, qualified by a prudential insistence upon a concurrent majority of actors whose support is essential, not so much for the realization of some immediate objective as for the achievement of the UN's broader purposes of both a minimal and a maximal variety.

6. The principle of the concurrent majority must not be formalized in a body of rules. Were this to happen, divisive, dysfunctional voting might be eliminated, but at the price of brittleness.

SOME OBSERVATIONS ON THE EQUALITY OF STATES IN A CHANGING UNITED NATIONS

Twice, once within each of the first two phases of its existence, the United Nations tackled a major crisis that proved to be, upon reflection, the end of an era for it. In each case it found itself engaged in task expansion that carried it beyond the most elastic limits of the principle of the concurrent majority; however, it returned, in each case, to a more modest assessment of its tasks. The crises were those in Korea and in the Congo. In Korea, the UN endorsement of a new goal (reunification) and denunciation of a new aggressor (the People's Republic of China) transformed a collective-security operation into a coalition war, a state of affairs that was quite unacceptable, not only to the Soviet bloc but also to an increasing number of other member-states. Subsequently the UN developed peace-keeping forces under the rubric of preventive diplomacy. The most ambitious of these, ONUC, the United Nations Operation in the Congo, became involved in a range of functions too diffuse to permit satisfaction of all essential actors; in the end, the operation precipitated a financial crisis and the debacle of the Nineteenth General Assembly.

Just as the UN retrenched after Korea, eschewing attempts to improve upon the Charter's limited-use model of collective security, so has the UN since the Congo crisis trimmed its preventive diplomacy model to the United Nations Emergency Force (UNEF) prototype, minus obligatory financing. Now the United Nations is in a new and as yet not clearly defined phase, reflecting a changing international system. The new system is characterized by symmetry of nuclear weaponry and space capability between the major polar actors, the USA and USSR, which preserve their duopoly over such indices of power. However, the convergent interests of the superpowers in avoiding war contribute to more freedom of action both for their clients and for non-aligned states.[10] The result is the reality of a modified bipolar system and the illusion of a heterosymmetrical multipolar system.[11] Some of the attributes of the latter model are present in nascent form, but real heterosymmetry would introduce bargaining opportunities that simply do not now exist. The major difference between the second phase of the UN's existence and the present one is that whereas the second was characterized by uncertainty about the stability of the bipolar system and a conviction that other actors could use other issues to effect cross-cutting voting patterns and genuine bargaining, the present phase is marked by greater confidence in systemic stability, but, paradoxically, by a decline in bargaining within the UN.

Although the non-aligned states may seek to keep the Cold War out of the United Nations, East-West issues continue to dominate debate and voting.[12] North-South issues, which were once expected to introduce a significant cross-cutting dimension into UN politics, have failed to do so. The substitution of political for military goals on the part of the superpowers tends

[10] See Herbert S. Dinerstein, "The Transformation of Alliance Systems," *The American Political Science Review*, Vol. LIX, No. 3 (September 1965), pp. 589–601.

[11] For a discussion of a heterosymmetrical system, see Haas, p. 484, and Wolfram Hanrieder, "The International System: Bipolar or Multibloc?" *The Journal of Conflict Resolution*, Vol. IX, No. 3 (September 1965).

[12] See Hayward R. Alker, Jr. and Bruce M. Russett, *World Politics in the General Assembly*, New Haven, Conn.: Yale University Press, 1965, for quantitative analysis of politics in the UN which supports this thesis.

to perpetuate the bipolar character of UN voting. The non-aligned states, on the whole, tend to vote with the Soviet bloc on East-West issues, intensifying bipolarity. The Soviet bloc votes with the non-aligned states on colonial questions, converting this issue into an East-West issue, which also reinforces bipolarity. At the same time, while the superpowers are unable to control allies and influence neutrals as effectively as they had previously, they are themselves impervious to influence. They have determined to reserve to themselves the management of the more serious levels of conflict in a thermonuclear age; moreover, they are unwilling to revise their trade and aid policies to satisfy the underdeveloped countries. On few, if any, questions before the UN do the non-aligned, developing states enjoy real bargaining power. As Herbert Dinerstein has observed in a penetrating analysis of the contemporary international system,[13] these states have nothing to give or withhold in exchange for significant concessions from either East or West.

What we have, in sum, is an organization faced with the prospect of less flexibility and more frustration. Midway through the Development Decade the gap between have and have-not states is actually widening. Six years after the adoption of the Declaration on the Granting of Independence to Colonial Countries and Peoples, the colonial redoubt in Africa's southern quadrant is as strong as ever. The most serious war since Korea rages on, with the UN's much publicized fire brigade unable to find a means whereby that organization or any other can put out the blaze. The People's Republic of China stands poised either to enter the UN and further embitter the dialogue there or to reject the proffered invitation, thereby dashing the hopes of those who see Chinese participation in the councils of the world as the only way to meliorate the Cold War and promote meaningful talks on arms control. The encapsulation of central war[14] may have served to legitimize and to remove some of the element of

---

[13] Dinerstein, pp. 597–98.

[14] Encapsulation is a term employed by Amitai Etzioni to denote a situation in which certain forms or levels of conflict are, by mutual agreement among prospective enemies, determined to be unacceptable and hence "out of bounds." The rules defining the boundaries between acceptable and unacceptable conflict constitute the capsule. See Amitai Etzioni, "On Self-Encapsulating Conflicts," *The Journal of Conflict Resolution*, Vol. VIII, No. 3 (September 1964), pp. 242–255.

risk from other forms and levels of conflict; in that event, the UN's peace-keeping role may seem somewhat less urgent.

This is not the picture of a dynamic organization. For the immediately foreseeable future the tasks that the UN can reasonably be expected to perform (and that it ought to essay) are all much closer to the minimal than to the maximal end of the spectrum of possible tasks. This does not mean that the United Nations is irrelevant. The UN's role as the preeminent setting for multilateral diplomacy of both a public and private variety remains vitally important. It can canalize tentative and tacit agreement among essential actors in areas where their interests converge, as they did in the Indo-Pakistan War of 1965. It can continue to experiment in functional areas, generating modest programs that complement those of a bilateral nature and that may suggest alternative ways of thinking about economic problems and post-independence stability. These are not inconsiderable assignments. It is submitted that they are critically important, that they keep open institutional options, maximize communications among a wide range of actors, afford a surrogate for more violent conflict, and contribute to the socialization of participants.

But all are in jeopardy if the members of the United Nations insist upon carrying the equalitarian doctrine to the point of decision by voting on issues beyond the compass of the organization. Paradoxically, the equalitarian doctrine has reached its apogee in the UN at the very time when the international system is undergoing changes that make the application of that doctrine increasingly dysfunctional. Present attitudes and expectations of UN members have been shaped in no small part by the belief that membership confers equality and that majorities composed of such equal states shall control the pace and direction of UN activity. Until recently this may not have been an unreasonable belief. In virtually all fields the United Nations was demonstrating a capacity for innovation and creative involvement in problems that have plagued the international system; a certain momentum was generated in the fields of peace-keeping, self-determination, and economic development.[15] A growing UN

---

[15] See UNEF and ONUC, the admission of thirty-odd African states and establishment of the Committee of 24 on Colonialism, the UN Special Fund and UNCTAD—all significant benchmarks.

membership could vote its will and leave its mark on many issues.

Now the dysfunctional character of such a doctrine, always latent, is becoming apparent. The smaller states that had most to gain by its acceptance are finding that the will of the majority, recorded in numerous resolutions, cannot be translated into satisfaction of interests in any one of these fields. The larger powers are finding that they cannot reliably manipulate majorities, and that their own interests are frequently discounted, often quite rudely, by a majority of states exercising voting equality. These are not, of course, new phenomena. What gives them special significance in the present phase of the UN's life is that systemic conditions do not appear to be conducive to early changes in the capacity of the UN to take decisive action in any field. Instead of a situation where some states are intermittently disenchanted with the United Nations, virtually all states may be expected to experience some degree of disaffection over a protracted period. This disaffection will be the more acute for the expectations developed during its more creative second phase. The result could well be a slow erosion of commitment to the United Nations.

It would be gratifying to be able to report that the achievements of the UN are cumulative, that the crises resolved, the programs launched, the institutions established, and the practices pioneered in earlier phases of the UN's existence—all have become building blocks for the construction of a more highly integrated international system. Unfortunately, yesterday's precedents and practices often prove useless as the conditions that made them possible undergo change. In these circumstances, the more modest functions of the UN must constantly be cultivated, not taken for granted. Without the survival of the minimal UN, the more ambitious purposes of the organization will recede even further into a remote future. It is, of course, desirable that as many UN decisions as possible upgrade the interests of the participants. A continuous effort should be made to probe the frontiers of consensus and to enlarge the area in which the UN's writ may run. But the possible should never be sacrificed on the altar of perfection, especially when the less spectacular functions of the United Nations are themselves so important to the maintenance of ultrastability in a revolutionary world. If the UN is to remain a meaningful component of the international system, decision-making according to the principle of one state, one vote, with respect to several highly divisive issues will have to be eschewed in favor of other modes of involvement. These will necessarily include both more reliance on the Security Council, a practice already in evidence, and less formal and less conspicuous pursuit of the concurrent majority outside of Council and Assembly chambers. The members of the UN will need to display self-restraint at a time when stalemated issues and frustrated expectations invite either the angry vote that commands and censures, or, conversely, the tacit withdrawal of active interest in the UN. This is no easy mandate.

At the beginning of this essay it was suggested that UNCTAD and the financial crisis had helped to focus attention upon the problem of equality of states within the United Nations. It may be useful to return briefly to these two events, whose unfolding may be symptomatic of the UN's dilemma. In the case of UNCTAD, the developing states, 75 strong, coalesced into a remarkably cohesive bloc that commanded a working two-thirds majority; the result was a situation in which the doctrine of equality, mechanically applied, provided the developing states with a number of automatic "victories" over the developed states, and more particularly over the United States. In the case of the financial crisis, the United States sought to mobilize a majority of the membership for the purpose of penalizing states that refused to pay assessments for UNEF and ONUC, and in particular the USSR. The financial crisis was the more serious of the two events because a majority did have it within its power to invoke Article 19, whereas no combination of states at Geneva could have compelled the United States, for example, to modify its trade policies. But in both cases a strong disposition existed to override the opposition of states whose support for the UN must be deemed essential. Neither the 75 at Geneva nor the USA in the Nineteenth General Assembly seemed particularly interested in the principle of the concurrent majority. The United States was ultimately deterred from its determination to burn down the barn to roast the pig by the fact that it could not muster the requisite quantitative majority, much less a qualitative or concurrent majority. Subsequently the United States retreated from its untenable position, sacrificing in the process a more ambitious but as yet unattainable UN in order to recover a more modest but nonetheless functional organization. Similarly, prospectively important conciliation procedures were devised in sober afterthought by a special committee following conclusion of the Conference on Trade and Development.[16] Those procedures, which countenance the temporary suspension of voting and the consideration of the issues by a representative conciliation group, reflect a realization that victories such as those registered at Geneva are only Pyrrhic unless the support of the major industrial and trading states can be secured.

It would appear that the UN has retreated twice from the brink of an unrealistic and imprudent application of the doctrine of equality. It remains to be seen whether the more realistic UN of painstaking, piecemeal progress through UNCTAD and of voluntary payment for peace forces and non-application of Article 19 will be sufficiently attractive to command the continuous, active support of essential actors who had demanded more of the organization. The maturity of the United Nations may perhaps best be measured by the extent to which its members, having imbibed the heady wine of equalitarianism and effective influence, still recognize the fundamental importance of the less spectacular, minimal UN and the need for prudential pursuit of concurrent majorities whenever the organization essays more ambitious tasks.

It is neither possible nor desirable to eliminate conflict in the United Nations. There will be, and should be, sharp debate and divisive votes. These, too, are functional, especially in an age when more violent forms of conflict do not recommend themselves to rational statesmen, but when interstate tensions remain acute and intrastate tensions may demand release in interstate conflict. It is to be hoped, however, that the equalitarian doctrine will be tempered by pragmatic realization that it becomes dysfunctional when adhered to at the wrong time on the wrong issue. Respect for the need to secure concurrent majorities will not destroy equality of states, but it will facilitate the preservation of that minimal UN, which is so necessary a foundation for progress toward a more highly integrated world where equalitarianism would be a natural, not an artificial, phenomenon.

[16] See Report of the Special Committee, United Nations Document A/5749; see also General Assembly Resolution 1995 (XIX), December 30, 1964, establishing UNCTAD as an organ of the General Assembly.

18

EQUALITY AND INEQUALITY OF STATES IN THE UNITED NATIONS

THOMAS M. FRANCK

For all these many years since the United Nations was founded, a small, lonely band of scholars, including Professors Louis Sohn and Leland Goodrich, have toiled in the stony field of weighted voting by the General Assembly.[1] For almost all of those years, their efforts were dismissed with that ultimate weapon of verbal disapprobation: "academic." They must feel as bewildered by, and suspicious of, their sudden popularity as a rebellious avant-garde artist whose works suddenly become the favorite of the Establishment.

The ostensible reason for this sudden popularity of work so

[1] Cf. Grenville Clark and Louis B. Sohn, *World Peace Through World Law*, 2nd ed., Cambridge: Harvard University Press, 1960.

long unrecognized is the current widespread feeling that the balance of power in the United Nations, in recent years, has become distorted through the admission of some fifty "new nations" that enjoy exactly the same vote in the General Assembly as the United States or Russia but that are, for the most part, small, poor and unstable.

In the abstract, a good case can be made for a weighted voting system in the General Assembly—one that more closely accords with the power of member states to give economic and military effect to U.N. decisions and recommendations. It is certainly unhealthy that, currently, a very high percentage—perhaps 75 per cent—of the General Assembly resolutions calling for action by members are never carried out. And it is a credible hypothesis that this is so at least partly because the big political majorities that steam-roller these resolutions do not have the economic and military equivalence necessary to secure implementation.

However, if we are to have a weighted voting system in the General Assembly, it must be built upon a sound analysis of the facts. The most important mistake of fact we tend to make is to think the imbalance between small states and others a recent development. If it were indeed a new factor, it would, of course, justify a new remedy and we would be doing no more than our duty to urge it upon the international organization.

But it does not happen to be true that there has recently been a radical shift in the composition of the General Assembly toward small states in such a way as to dilute the voting strength of the major powers. If we take 10 million as the population dividing-line between smaller states and the "respectable" middle and large powers, then in 1965 the proportion of states with populations over 10 million to those with populations under 10 million was approximately 2 to 3. This is exactly the proportion these two categories of states bore to one another in 1946. If we took some smaller figure, such as 5 million or even 1 million, as the point of division for the ratio, the results would again be about the same for 1946 and 1965. A ratio based not on population but on economic development or military power would show a somewhat greater disparity, but the nations that have joined the U.N. since 1946 are a mixture of poor and rich, of weak and powerful, not so very different from the mixture compounded at San Francisco in 1945.

When we are told, therefore, that the reason the General Assembly's voting system must be changed is that the United Nations has been swamped by new, small states with disproportionate voting power, we are really being told *not* that the ratio of small states to total membership has increased but that the small nations admitted since 1957, unlike the small nations admitted at the beginning, are not *our* small nations. They are an independent third force that adheres neither to the United States nor to the Soviet Union, and this situation, of course, raises the possibility that the small states, with the voting majority they have always had in the General Assembly, may now actually use that power to enact resolutions and pursue policies—in the name of the United Nations—of which the Great Powers do not approve. This, and only this, is new. Previously, small states tended to follow the leadership of the great: The Soviet Union had its satellites, the United States its Latin American "good neighbors," Britain its Commonwealth. Today, not only the new among the small nations but even some of the old small nations are beginning to pursue independent policies and produce their own leadership.

If I am right in asserting that current proposals for voting reform in the General Assembly are really motivated by a concern for the growing independence of, rather than the growing number of, small states, then it seems to me to follow that an attempt by the United States or the Soviet Union to curtail this power, which the smaller states have always had but have only recently begun to exercise, would not only fail but would further alienate the very group of states whose alienation is the real cause of our concern.

The new nations of Africa and Asia would certainly consider any initiative on the part of the United States at this time to alter a voting system that it did not challenge for 18 years as nothing less than an attempt to reduce them to second-class citizenship in the United Nations. It should be remembered that many of these Afro-Asian nations were only recently colonies in which the colonial powers, small white minorities, used various systems of weighted voting to retain political control. These attempts were known as "fancy franchises." In Kenya and Southern Rhodesia, various schemes have been put forward to give a citizen additional votes for having a high income, owning property, being a member of the clergy or a veteran, and all that sort of nonsense. It would be a foolish country that now proposed a world fancy franchise to these small Afro-Asian states.

I cannot believe that we have not traveled a long way since 1920 when a distinguished professor of international law at Harvard wrote:

> Most of the modern publicists recognize that equality can be the rule only among states having common standards of civilization. Fiore has stated the prevailing opinion effectively: "The very necessity of things requires, therefore, that certain states should not be called to enjoy international rights in an integral fashion and with perfect equality. So it is reasonable that the states of Europe should not admit perfect equality of right with Turkey and its dependencies; with the states of Africa, with the exception of Liberia and the English and French colonies; with the states of Asia, with the exception of Siberia and Hindostan. In fact, certain limitations are made necessary by the exceptional situations in which these countries are placed. . . ." Inequalities of legal capacity arising out of differences in civilization are manifested in several important rules of the positive law of nations. Those imposed in the form of extra territorial jurisdiction, in the application of the right of diplomatic protection of citizens abroad, in the exclusion of aliens, and in the practice of granting asylum in legations and consulates and on public vessels.[2]

We have learned from our own experience that legal equality is the essential prerequisite to equal development. As with the underprivileged minorities of the United States, so with the underprivileged nations of the world. The demand that underprivileged persons or nations bootstrap themselves socially and economically before receiving the *imprimatur* of full rights, that they first learn to drink tea with the accepted curl of the fingers, or that they practice "civilized" standards of conduct towards foreigners and their investments, is, consciously or otherwise, a way of withholding indefinitely both equal rights *and* equal development. The bad manners of the mob and the

---

[2] Edwin DeWitt Dickinson, *The Equality of States in International Law*, Cambridge: Harvard University Press, 1920, pp. 223–224.

"uncivilized" or "irresponsible" conduct of small states is not, after all, merely an annoying habit, like nail-biting, of which they must cure themselves. It is a reaction against their poverty, a manifestation of the despair and anger they feel toward a social, political and economic system they believe to be rigged against them. Only when these conditions of despair and anger abate, can the "manners" reasonably be expected to improve. And history has shown that of the three citadels of privilege—political power, economic power, and social power—the first to fall is political power. Dr. Nkrumah was, of course, quite correct in giving the underprivileged of the world the same advice Dr. Martin Luther King gives the underprivileged of the United States: Seek first full equality before the law—"the political kingdom"—and only then will all else be open.

Closely related to this is the factor of nationalism. The insistence of new nations on "one state, one vote" is not only a way of seizing a measure of political power from the powerful nations of the West. It is also an expression of the history of anti-colonialism, which took the form of campaigns for *national* liberation. The *national* emphasis of these campaigns was dictated not by any ideological commitment to the philosophies of nineteenth-century Europe but by a realistic response to the facts of colonialism. The European colonial powers had scooped Africa into artificial political-administrative entities, many of them small and unviable, and it was for control of these entities that the liberation struggle occurred. It could not, of course, succeed without developing a national ethos in each little unit. Consequently, the basic unit in international affairs is, today perhaps more than at any time in our history, the state. We may wish that it were not so. Africa and Asia are a reprise of Europe in the age of nationalism, the age of dissolution of empire and birth of new states. And the reprise is louder and more strident than the original tune. We in the U.S. must learn to live with it. For as long as the state remains the basic unit in the international community, it is unthinkable to me that a nation devoted to the egalitarian philosophy of John Locke would become the advocate of inequality.

This does not mean that we should cease experimenting with functional inroads into this doctrine. We know, for example, that in practice power is a many-faceted thing. It has, in the international community, financial, military, and other aspects. Even in the General Assembly with its egalitarian system of voting, it is common knowledge that the richest states, the states with the best military forces, as well as the states whose conduct has given special weight to their moral suasion, have more influence than the other members. This influence makes itself felt in votes on resolutions, but even more so in the implementation or non-implementation of these resolutions.

In certain of the specialized agencies and peripheral institutions of the United Nations, ad hoc arrangements for voting have also been made which, because of the specialized nature of the institution, recognize the power-preponderance of certain of the members. The International Bank for Reconstruction and Development and the International Monetary Fund have institutionalized voting by the shareholders in accordance with the number of shares held. UNTAD has devised a conciliation procedure, which, under certain circumstances, can prevent votes that would only alienate the states whose cooperation for economic development is most urgently needed. It may be that some such system of non-voting or postponed voting would also be useful in certain highly controversial matters before the General Assembly. In its own way, the nineteenth session of the General Assembly did establish that a certain amount of business can be transacted without voting at all. Perhaps certain resolutions are best not passed if they do not have the active support of those nations most necessary to give them effect. Increasingly, the Big Powers are voting for resolutions just to "go along" with the numerical majority but without any intention of implementing them. This is bad for the General Assembly's prestige and the small nations, which for the most part are responsible for these resolutions, are beginning to know it.

However, even when we focus our attention on military, financial and other integers of power, a note of caution is necessary. Perhaps this inequality is not really as great as we might think. For example, where military force is concerned, the United Nations troops in the Middle East, the Congo, and Cyprus have been drawn almost entirely from the smaller and often even the poorer states. Therefore, that element of military potential which is of most direct relevance to the United Nations—the ability to place military contingents at the disposal of an impartial international peace-keeping operation with an international point of view—is disproportionately concentrated in smaller and poorer states. When we raise the issue of U.N. military intervention in Southern Rhodesia or South Africa it is such littler armies as those of Tanzania, Ceylon, Nigeria, Venezuela, the Sudan, and Sweden that would primarily be charged with its execution and not the juggernauts of the U.S.A. or Russia. If a weighted system of voting were to be introduced, these states would, of course, rightly insist that this be taken into account.

As if this were not a sufficient complication, there are even more subtle military integers to frustrate a simple weighted system of voting based on military power. A rather substantial proportion of the members of the United Nations are now, or soon could be, in a position to build nuclear weapons and achieve the capacity to deliver them at least by conventional means and by short-range missiles. They have *not* done so because of the expense involved, because of an enlightened self-interest in non-proliferation, and because their territorial integrity has been guaranteed by other nuclear states. Even at that, the balance of interest between producing and not producing nuclear weapons is for most of these states a very even one. If, however, the voting power of a nation in the assembly of states were to depend upon its producing nuclear weapons, that might well be enough to tip the scales. It is true that tiny Israel *with* nuclear weapons and a delivery system would be militarily the equal of very much larger powers. But to enshrine that hypothesis in the voting system of the General Assembly would be to encourage the very scramble for arms that it has hitherto been the urgent policy of the United Nations to discourage.

What conclusions can we draw? There may well have been a time, a decade ago, when the nations of the Northern Hemisphere, by an imaginative initiative, could have introduced a system of weighted voting into the United Nations of the sort long advocated by Professor Sohn. Perhaps, had the new nations of Africa and Asia been born to such a system, they would have accepted it. "It might have been"—sad words! But to devise a new system now, more or less specifically to curb the independent exercise of voting power by these new nations, is quite unacceptable both to the new nations and to persons in the United States who are concerned that relations between it and the new nations should not worsen but improve.

By starting with peripheral experimental use of functional weighted voting in certain specialized subsidiary organizations of the United Nations, we still can be usefully engaged until the flood of nationalism begins to recede and makes possible the transformation of the General Assembly from a body representing states to one representing persons. Meanwhile, the best prospect for the General Assembly is not weighted voting but, perhaps, less voting.